Marguerite Duras

Marguerite Duras: Apocalyptic Desires is the first fully detailed, complete account in English of the fiction and films of France's best-known and most controversial contemporary woman writer. It considers all aspects of the author's work, ranging from her early novels of the 1950s to her radically innovative experimental films of the 1970s and her best-selling autobiographical text of the 1980s, *The Lover*. It also contains the most extensive listing yet available in any language of all Duras's work, including her journalism, interviews, and television and radio appearances. *Marguerite Duras: Apocalyptic Desires* throws new light on Duras's relationship to feminism, psychoanalysis, sexuality, literature, film, politics, and the media; it shows how desire for Duras is conceived throughout as a profoundly transgressive, catastrophic force that lays waste to the world in order to reach the sublime intensity of pure affirmation.

Marguerite Duras: Apocalyptic Desires will be of concern to all readers with an interest in contemporary writing, writing by women, feminism, recent European cinema, literary theory, and modern French literature.

Leslie Hill is Lecturer in French Studies at the University of Warwick.

Marguerite Duras
Apocalyptic Desires

Leslie Hill

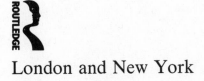

London and New York

First published 1993
by Routledge
11 New Fetter Lane, London EC4P 4EE

Simultaneously published in the USA and Canada
by Routledge, Inc.
29 West 35th Street, New York, NY 10001

© 1993 Leslie Hill

Phototypeset in 10/12pt Times by Intype, London
Printed in Great Britain by T.J. Press (Padstow) Ltd, Padstow, Cornwall

British Library Cataloguing in Publication Data
Hill, Leslie
  Marguerite Duras: Apocalyptic Desires
  I. Title
  843.912

Library of Congress Cataloging in Publication Data
Hill, Leslie
    Marguerite Duras : apocalyptic desires / Leslie Hill.
      p. cm.
    Includes bibliographical references.
    1. Duras, Marguerite–Criticism and interpretation.
  2. Apocalyptic literature–History and criticism. I. Title.
  PQ2607.U8245Z73 1993
  843'.912–dc20   92–34599

ISBN 0–415–05047–2 – ISBN 0–415–05048–0 (pbk)

Contents

Acknowledgements

In writing this book I have benefited from the encouragement of many students who have shared with me their own fascination with Duras's work. For them, therefore, this book was primarily written. I should like to thank Andrew Benjamin, Mig Kerr, Mark Treharne, and Chris Turner for their help and support in completing this project. I am also indebted to Marianne Alphant and Marin Karmitz for the generosity with which they made archive material available to me. I must also thank staff at the Cinémathèque française, the Institut national de l'Audiovisuel, the Cinémathèque Royale de Belgique, the Cinémathèque suisse, Editions Gallimard, Editions de Minuit, *Libération*, *Elle*, *Le Monde*, *Le Figaro*, *Le Nouvel Observateur*, TF1, *The Guardian*, as well as Peter Larkin and other members of staff in the University Library at the University of Warwick for their invaluable assistance. I am grateful to the University of Warwick for the granting of sabbatical leave and the provision of funds that enabled me to carry out the research on which this book is based. This book draws on material first published in *Modern Language Review* and *Paragraph* and I wish to thank the editors of these publications for permission to republish some of that material here. Finally, I should like to dedicate this book to the memory of my mother, and to Susanna, whose life began, so to speak, in the interval between chapters five and six.

Abbreviations

All references to Duras's work will be given in the text, using the abbreviations listed below. Titles of English translations, where they exist, are given in parentheses. Page numbers refer to the current French edition; where two figures are given, the second, wherever possible, refers to the available English translation. On occasion, these versions have been modified. Unless otherwise indicated, all other translations are my own. Full details concerning texts and translations used may be found in the list of works by Duras (pp. 178–96).

A	*L'Amant* (*The Lover*)
AA	*L'Amante anglaise* (*L'Amante anglaise*)
ACN	*L'Amant de la Chine du Nord*
AG	*Agatha*
AM	*L'Amour*
AMA	*L'Après-midi de Monsieur Andesmas* (*The Afternoon of Monsieur Andesmas*)
ASD	*Abahn, Sabana, David*
B	*Un barrage contre le Pacifique* (*The Sea-Wall*)
C	*Le Camion*
D	*La Douleur* (*La Douleur*, aka: *The War: A Memoir*)
DD	*Détruire, dit-elle* (*Destroy, She Said*)
DH	*Dix heures et demie du soir en été* (*Ten-Thirty on a Summer Night*)
E	*L'Eté 80*
EC	*L'Eden Cinéma* (*The Eden Cinema*)
EL	*Emily L.* (*Emily L.*)
H	*Hiroshima mon amour* (*Hiroshima Mon Amour*)
HA	*L'Homme atlantique*
HC1	'L'Homme assis dans le couloir', *L'Arc*, 20, October 1962, 70–6

HC2   *L'Homme assis dans le couloir*, 1980 revised version ('The Seated Man in the Passage')

IS   *India Song* (*India Song*)

J   *Des journées entières dans les arbres, suivi de: Le Boa; Madame Dodin; Les Chantiers* (*Whole Days in the Trees and Other Stories*)

L   *Les Lieux de Marguerite Duras* ('The Places of Marguerite Duras', *Enclitic*, 7, 1, 1984, 54–61 [=A]; and 7, 2, 1984, 55–62 [=B])

MC   *Moderato cantabile* (*Moderato Cantabile*)

MD   *Marguerite Duras*, edited by François Barat and Joël Farges, Paris, Editions Albatros (1975), revised edition 1979 (*Marguerite Duras*, translated by Edith Cohen and Peter Connor, San Francisco, City Lights Books, 1987)

MG   *Le Marin de Gibraltar* (*The Sailor from Gibraltar*)

MM   *La Maladie de la mort* (*The Malady of Death*)

N   *Le Navire Night, suivi de: Césarée; Les Mains négatives; Aurélia Steiner; Aurélia Steiner; Aurélia Steiner*

NG   *Nathalie Granger, suivie de: La Femme du Gange*

O   *Outside* (*Outside*)

P   *Les Parleuses* (*Woman to Woman*)

PC   *Les Petits Chevaux de Tarquinia* (*The Little Horses of Tarquinia*)

PCN   *La Pute de la côte normande*

PE   *La Pluie d'été* (*Summer Rain*)

R   *Le Ravissement de Lol V. Stein* (*The Ravishing of Lol Stein*)

S   *Le Square* (*The Square*)

SB   *Savannah Bay*

T1   *Théâtre I: Les Eaux et forêts; Le Square; La Musica* (*The Rivers and Forests; The Square; La Musica*)

VC   *Le Vice-consul* (*The Vice-Consul*)

VM   *La Vie matérielle* (*Practicalities*)

VT   *La Vie tranquille*

YA   *Yann Andréa Steiner*

YB   *Les Yeux bleus cheveux noirs* (*Blue Eyes, Black Hair*)

YV   'Les Yeux verts', *Les Cahiers du cinéma*, 312–3, June 1980 (*Green Eyes*)

Au fond, tu vois, la littérature, c'est une fatalité comme une autre, on n'en sort pas.

Les Petits Chevaux de Tarquinia

At bottom, don't you see, literature can't be avoided, just like everything else, there's no way around it.

1 Images of authorship

In a number of different texts, including a novel, a play, a semi-fictional autobiography, many interviews, and a variety of other autobiographical fragments as well as, more recently, a novelised film script, Marguerite Duras recalls some of the circumstances of her early life.[1] But though she dwells on her childhood and adolescence at some length, much of the information she provides is fragmentary and subject to question. Inconsistencies exist from one account to another and it is never easy to distinguish truth from fiction. Gaps and contradictions remain, and the effect is less of a set of verifiable facts than of a personal myth inseparable from each of its different manifestations. As many later interviews demonstrate, Duras is adept at suddenly disclosing fresh autobiographical information or denying what was thought to be firmly established; and it is clear from this that the uncertainties she thus introduces into the biographical record are the result of a calculated strategy designed to undermine any reductive attempt to use biography as a means of accounting for her writing. Let it be clear, then, from the outset, that, extensive though they are, Duras's many retellings of the story of her formative years do not add up to a reliable autobiographical narrative; rather, what they describe is a network of complex and ambivalent relationships most often dramatised in the form of a series of superimposed scenes which, like so many screen memories, have become detached from any linear or causal narrative sequence.[2]

Some facts, however, go unchallenged. Duras was born Marguerite Donnadieu, the youngest of three children, in April 1914, in the small town of Gia-Dinh, near Saigon, in what is now southern Vietnam, but at the time was part of the French colony of

Cochinchina, which since 1887, together with Tonkin, Annam (i.e. northern and eastern Vietnam), Laos and Cambodia, had been a member of the Union of French Indochina. Both parents were teachers, her father was from a modest background in the south-west of France, and her mother from a large but poor farming family in the Pas-de-Calais. They met in Indochina, but both had been married before, the mother to a school inspector by the name of Obscur (*A*, 113; 98), who, according to one account, fell in love with her during a visit to her classroom (she was teaching in a primary school in Dunkirk at the time). The date of their departure to the colonies is given as some time between 1900 and 1903. It is not clear when Duras's parents married, but in 1918 her father, just appointed to a post teaching mathematics at a school in Phnom Penh, was forced for health reasons to return to France, where he died of amoebic dysentery.[3]

This left Duras's mother, together with Marguerite herself, aged 4, and her two brothers, 9 and 7 at the time, having to survive in much reduced circumstances. Living first in Phnom Penh, then Vinh Long, and Hanoi, then near Kampot on the Cambodian coast, where the mother attempted – with catastrophic results – to cultivate that barren, regularly flooded plot of government land that figures so importantly in Duras's family mythology, and finally in Sa Dec, in the Mekong Delta, the family seems to have dwelt on the narrow borderline between white respectability and native indigence. As for Duras herself, in the years leading to her *certificat d'études* or first school certificate, which she took early, at the age of 11, she more often spoke Vietnamese than French, and enjoyed a large measure of physical freedom as a result of both the tropical climate and family circumstances (*L*, 59–60; A: 60–1).

At various stages (and probably for good in 1929, if one believes *L'Amant de la Chine du Nord* [*ACN*, 26]), Pierre, the elder of the two Donnadieu brothers, was repatriated to France, to the Lot-et-Garonne, with the result that the most memorable part of Duras's adolescence, as she depicts it in many fictional as well as autobiographical texts, was spent living alone alongside her mother and younger brother. In numerous interviews, Duras evokes the intensity of her experiences of those early years; they provide much of the material for a number of her later works, the best known of which is *L'Amant*, the author's greatest popular success, for which, in 1984, at the age of 70, she was awarded the Prix Goncourt.

At the age of 18 Marguerite Donnadieu left Indochina for mainland France, where she began studying for a degree in mathematics.

This she soon abandoned to concentrate on political sciences, and then law. Subsequently, for some seven years in all, she worked for the French Colonial Office as a researcher and archivist. In 1939, shortly before the outbreak of war, she married the writer, Robert Antelme. Two years later, she offered her first novel to the publisher Gallimard, who already, in 1940, had brought out the only work ever published by Marguerite Donnadieu under her own family name, a volume of didactic nationalist propaganda called *L'Empire français* (done in collaboration with Philippe Roques).[4] The novel was rejected, but the manuscript did attract the enthusiastic attention of Raymond Queneau, who encouraged the author to continue writing; and, in 1944, Gallimard did bring out her second novel, *La Vie tranquille*.[5] The first book, meanwhile, by now having been turned down by seven or more different publishers, eventually appeared in 1943, under the title *Les Impudents*, signed, not Marguerite Donnadieu, but with the name Marguerite Duras. The pseudonym was borrowed by the author from the name of the small town of Duras in the Lot-et-Garonne where her father died. The novel itself, loosely based on elements of the author's own family life, is set in the same area, where she spent two years as a child from about 1919 to 1921. Her father had originally kept a small house there, which was later sold by her mother to settle debts incurred by Pierre Donnadieu (*A*, 94; 81).[6]

Duras's choice of a pseudonym raises a number of issues. In 1974, in *Les Parleuses*, she was invited by Xavière Gauthier to reflect on her reasons for refusing her father's name, and she speaks with horror of the prospect of ever writing under that family name (*P*, 23–4; 10). Admittedly, the name Donnadieu does have a faintly ridiculous ring to it, but Duras attributes her repugnance rather to the fact that she barely knew her father, and says later, to her Italian interviewer, Leopoldina Pallotta della Torre, that she learnt very little about him from her mother.[7] Duras's adoption of a pseudonym was evidently, therefore, at least on one level, an attempt to achieve some independence from the powerful and unapproachable model of her father, the author of a mathematics textbook. Her mother evidently had wanted her to follow in his footsteps and study for the *agrégation* in mathematics. Duras finally refused to do this, though only after she had begun studying mathematics on her arrival in France.

But in 1943 she chose to relinquish not only her father's name, Donnadieu, but also her married name, Antelme. To this extent, the pseudonym was arguably more than a rejection of the father's

name: it amounted to a more general refusal of the law of patri-
linear descent which gives men's surnames to their daughters or
wives. It affirmed the independence not just of a writer but also of
a woman writer. It had the effect of delivering a rebuff to her
mother and her (by then) sole surviving brother, Pierre, the only
true remaining Donnadieu, who is charged, in *L'Amant*, with the
crime of his younger brother's death; but it also had a protective
– and self-protective – role in that it clothed the author in relative
anonymity and did not compromise the family name in the eyes of
her disapproving mother. And paradoxically, as the writer struggled
in this way to assert her independence, she did so by the use of a
term that, because of its geographical associations, clearly still did
recall the memory – if no longer the name – of the dead father;
and the writer herself in 1981, in Montreal, was still making the
connection between the name Duras and the event of her father's
death. The name Duras, then, is not an arbitrary signifier on the
covers of the author's books; it functions as a condensed shorthand
for all the competing motifs – independence, self-protection, desire,
anger, mourning – that go to make up the drama of authorship in
the case of Marguerite Donnadieu.

In December 1942, according to *L'Amant*, Paulo, the younger of
Duras's two brothers, to whom she was devoted, died in Indochina.
This followed seven months after the loss of her first child, a son,
who was stillborn. In 1943, together with her husband, Robert
Antelme, and Dionys Mascolo, whom she had met the previous
year, Duras became active in a resistance group led by François
Mitterrand. Mitterrand was to remain a personal friend, and Duras
campaigned for his election and re-election to the presidency in the
1980s. But in June 1944 Robert Antelme was arrested by the Ge-
stapo and taken to the concentration camp in Dachau, and it was
only by chance, and thanks to Mitterrand's intervention, that he
survived and returned.[8]

In 1946, as *La Douleur* describes, Duras and Antelme were
divorced, and Duras's liaison with Mascolo produced a son, Jean,
born in 1947. After the end of the war, Duras and Mascolo,
together with Antelme and a number of others, remained active
for a period in the French Communist Party (PCF), which Duras
herself was the first to join in the autumn of 1944. However, their
attempt to preserve within the PCF their libertarian commitment
to a revolutionary radicalism of the kind set out by Mascolo in his
philosophical essay, *Le Communisme*, in 1953, was, rather predict-
ably, a failure, and Duras had resigned from the Party – or been

expelled from it – by 1950 (though she claims in one interview to have remained a member till as late as 1956).[9]

Henceforth, political activity was restricted mainly to her work as a writer and journalist. In 1957 and 1958, she began publishing a series of journalistic pieces mainly in the left-wing weekly *France-Observateur* (the forerunner of *Le Nouvel Observateur*). These were chiefly in the form of interviews, character sketches, vignettes, anecdotes, book reviews or small news items. She recalls in the anthology *Outside* (*O*, 12; 9), which collects some of these articles, that her activities as a journalist were sometimes dictated mainly by material considerations. But this was only partly the case, and in 1988 Duras did admit, in the first of her interviews with Luce Perrot for *Au-delà des pages*, that she rather regretted not having pursued a career as a political journalist. But Duras was clearly reluctant to accept the usual constraints of routine journalistic analysis or commentary and, already in the late 1950s, as she was to continue doing during the 1980s, she was dealing with political issues by linking them to the problems of conveying in writing the specific texture of everyday individual experience.

In these journalistic texts of the late 1950s and early 1960s there are a number of recurrent preoccupations that echo some of the concerns explored by Dionys Mascolo in *Le Communisme*. One common centre of interest was the question of exclusion and marginality. As a journalist for *France-Observateur*, Duras undertook a series of brief investigations into the hidden world of groups or individuals who had little access to the press and the media, and thus never had a voice within French society at the time. The subjects Duras chose to write about were people on the fringes of society: an Algerian immigrant worker and illegal flower seller, a malajusted schoolchild, an illiterate woman worker, a Carmelite nun, a young tightrope-walker, an exceptionally gifted 7-year-old, a 71-year-old woman shoplifter, or a class of primary school-children. At least one of these pieces, her interview with the nun, under the title 'Dialogue avec une carmélite', published in January 1958, proved to be surprisingly controversial in its attempt to make public some of the unspoken realities of everyday convent life which were at odds with received assumptions about such places. It gave rise, over several weeks, to a lively – and not always friendly – correspondence in *France-Observateur*. As in many of her other articles for the magazine, what Duras was concerned with here was the need to give expression to experiences that were otherwise denied any legitimate voice by the norms and conventions of bourgeois society. The stories she uncovered also served to reveal the high price in human suffering or social injustice paid – usually in silence – by those whose lives did not necessarily fit those norms.

Another focus of Duras's articles was violent crime. In several pieces, as in many later fictional texts, she displays a fascination with the way in which otherwise drab and banal lives can suddenly give rise to extraordinary and inexplicable acts of violence, motivated only by the remorseless logic of an extreme and all-consuming passion. In an interview given in February 1963, in answer to a question about her play *Les Viaducs de la Seine-et-Oise*, which portrays one such apparently motiveless crime, she explained that for her, as she put it, 'dans tout meurtre il y a une nécessité impérieuse, inexplicable, et qui jamais ne s'exprime clairement: après qu'on a tué on se trouve en face d'un secret incommunicable' ('every murder contains an urgent, inexplicable necessity which is never properly expressed: after the killing one is left with an incommunicable secret').[10] And it was with a similar sense of the dramatic possibilities of an act which defied language – especially the language of legal inquiry and argument – that, in June 1957, and again in October 1958, she reported in *France-Observateur* on the story of Simone Deschamps, charged in court with murdering her lover in an attack of erotic frenzy (*O*, 119–25; 94–9); or, in January 1958, she described the case of Charles Clément, an unfaithful husband who hit on a pragmatic, if unfortunately homicidal solution to the expense of running two households (*O*, 70–3; 60–2).

More generally, in addition to these novelistic forays into the realm of the marginal and the unspoken, Duras was interested in using her newspaper articles to express opinions on specific issues. Her usual method was to do this by use of a telling anecdote or small news item. Thus, in 'Racisme à Paris' in March 1958 (*O*, 77–8; 66–7), she voices her condemnation of racism by telling the story of Marcelle B., a waitress, who becomes a victim of police harassment after travelling home late at night with an Algerian man; and similarly in ' "Poubelle" et "La Planche" vont mourir' (*O*, 114–18; 90–3), the same month, she declares her opposition to the death penalty. Elsewhere, too, there is a persistent concern with the fate of the dispossessed – children, criminals, foreigners, and workers – and the oppression of which, for Duras, they were often the victims.

It was no doubt this preoccupation with injustice, together with memories of her own childhood in Indochina, that made her a convinced critic of French colonialism (though she continued to display much sympathy for those who, like her parents, had gone to the colonies in naïve good faith). By the autumn of 1958, *France-Observateur* had been seized by the government censor three or four times in as many months for its critical reporting of the Algerian war. During the same period, Dionys Mascolo, who was still living in Duras's flat (though their personal relations seem to have ended in 1957), was increasingly active in the anti-war movement and in July 1958, with Jean Schuster, took the initiative of launching the journal, *Le 14 Juillet*, to channel protest at de Gaulle's return to power in May with the support of the pro-colonial French military in Algiers. The fear at the time, according to one manifesto, was that what de Gaulle represented was a French version of Fascism; and in the first issue of the journal Duras made much the same point in a piece that condemned de Gaulle in the same terms as it expressed its outrage at the execution of Imre Nagy, the leader of the 1956 Hungarian uprising suppressed by the Soviet army. Between Soviet tanks and French paratroopers, Duras implied, there was little to choose. 'On peut encore vomir, en France,' she conceded, adding merely: 'C'est là un acte positif' ('Vomiting is still allowed, in France. The act is a positive one', *O*, 90).

Three years later, in 1961, in much the same vein, Duras lent her name, together with other prominent intellectuals, to the 'Déclaration sur le droit à l'insoumission dans la guerre d'Algérie', otherwise known as the 'Manifeste des 121', after the original number of signatories.[11] The purpose of the statement was to defend the right of members of the French army – primarily conscripts – to refuse to take up arms against the Algerian resistance and called upon 'all free men' to support Algerian independence. Initially drafted by Mascolo and Schuster, the 'Déclaration' acquired its more incisive title from Maurice Blanchot. From this point on, Duras and Blanchot were to remain close in both political and other ways; their lives converged again during the events of May 1968.

Throughout the 1940s and 1950s Duras began to establish herself as a writer, and by the end of the 1950s she had published eight novels and had her first play produced, an adaptation of *Le Square*. A second play, *Les Viaducs de la Seine-et-Oise*, followed in 1960. But 1959 was a turning point. It was the year of Alain Resnais's *Hiroshima mon amour*, which was based on a script by Duras and one of the triumphs of the Cannes Film Festival. With the critical success of the novel *Moderato cantabile* the previous year, this was something of a watershed. Duras's reputation was now assured, both in France and internationally. In 1961, *Une aussi longue absence*, directed by Henri Colpi (who, with Jasmine Chesnay, had done the editing for *Hiroshima mon amour* and for Resnais's earlier Auschwitz documentary, *Nuit et brouillard*), shared the Golden Palm at the Cannes Film Festival with Buñuel's *Viridiana*. The film was from a script by Duras written in collaboration with Gérard Jarlot. The years that followed were for Duras a period of great productivity, and saw the publication of a number of important texts: *L'Après-midi de Monsieur Andesmas* (1962), *Le Ravissement de Lol V. Stein* (1964), *Le Vice-consul* (1966), *L'Amante anglaise* (1967), and *Détruire, dit-elle* (1969). In 1965 the first volume of Duras's collected plays appeared and in 1966 she co-directed her first film, *La Musica*, with Paul Seban.

Duras's last text of the decade, *Détruire, dit-elle*, was much influenced by the political events of May 1968. During May, together with Blanchot, Mascolo and others, Duras was a member of the 'Comité d'Action étudiants-écrivains', the joint committee of revolutionary students and writers that was formed on 20 May and continued to meet until the following spring. One of its aims was what it called a radical communism of thought. What this meant was the collective – and thus anonymous and non-proprietorial – elaboration both of ideas and texts; this echoed to some extent the process that had led up to the 'Manifeste des 121' seven years earlier (in which Blanchot, Mascolo, and Duras were already involved). The committee achieved very little in terms of a specific political agenda. It saw its role rather as challenging all received definitions of what constituted politics. According to one piece published anonymously in the committee's paper, *Comité*, later attributed to Blanchot, the need was for a new understanding of the political: 'le théorique,' Blanchot wrote, 'ne consiste évidemment pas à élaborer un programme, une plate-forme, mais au contraire, en dehors de tout projet programmatique et même de tout projet, à maintenir *un refus qui affirme*, à dégager ou maintenir une affirmation qui ne s'arrange pas, mais qui dérange ou se dérange, ayant rapport avec le désœuvrement ou le désarroi ou encore le non-structurable' ('the task of theory obviously does not consist in devising a programme or platform, but on the contrary, outside of any programmatic project or any project at all, in maintaining an *affirmative refusal*, in articulating or maintaining an affirmation which does not make compromises, but challenges and is challenged, and has to do with worklessness, confusion, or the

unstructurable'). On this account, May was a radical, apocalyptic
event that disabled any humanistic theory of identity, continuity,
or progress. And Blanchot ended this appeal to the imminent promise of international communism with the words: 'Le hiatus théorique
est absolu; la coupure de fait décisive. Entre le monde libéral-
capitaliste, notre monde, et le présent de l'exigence communiste
(présent sans présence), il n'y a que le trait d'union d'un désastre,
d'un changement d'astre' ('The theoretical hiatus is absolute; and
the historical break decisive. The liberal-capitalist world, our world,
and the present [without presence] of the demand of communism
are separated only by disaster, and a change in the heavens').[12]

Duras's own position in the 'Comité', as is shown by a text
published anonymously in June 1969 and reprinted ten years later,
was one of similarly uncompromising radicalism and absolute
refusal.[13] This meant not only a rejection of the nationalistic values
associated with the ten-year-old Gaullist regime, but also a repudiation of any alternative political party or institutional framework.
Some of the inspiration for this position seems to have come not
only from Blanchot but also from Georges Bataille (whom Duras
had interviewed in 1957).[14] Absolute refusal, Duras proposed, was
the only valid form of resistance, the only means of surviving the
repressive machinery of political representation and the inevitable
threat of recuperation or reassimilation within the dominant power
relations in modern society. This anti-authoritarian rejection of political solutions, coupled with a radical commitment to politics, was
accompanied by a virulent hatred of the bureaucratic inertia and
conservatism displayed by the French Communist Party in the wake
of May 1968; much of Duras's work throughout the following
decade was to be coloured by her opposition to the PCF, as the
film she made with Gérard Depardieu in 1977, *Le Camion*, perhaps
best exemplifies.

The events of May set in motion complex changes in Duras's
writing. *Détruire, dit-elle* is a work that is written seemingly without
distinction as a novel, play, or film-script, and can be read as any
one of these. It was the first of a number of such hybrid texts
written during the 1970s (notably *India Song*, with its catch-all
subtitle, 'texte théâtre film', or the *Aurélia Steiner* series), all of
which exist in an uncertain intermediary zone midway between
book and theatre, script and performance, page and cinema screen.
Since her work on *Hiroshima mon amour*, Duras herself had been
involved in other film projects as scriptwriter; and a number of her
own novels had themselves been adapted for the screen (including

Un barrage contre le Pacifique, *Moderato cantabile*, *Dix heures et demie du soir en été*, and *Le Marin de Gibraltar*). But in 1969, out of impatience with the fate her work had suffered at the hands of other directors (like, for instance, René Clément, who, in 1958, had made, in Duras's view – though she claimed initially to have liked the film – a falsely heroic, sentimental screen version of *Un barrage contre le Pacifique*), Duras turned to making films herself.[15] She had already shot *La Musica* jointly with the television director Paul Seban in 1966. But *Détruire, dit-elle* was the first film that Duras wrote and entirely directed on her own. Many more followed: *Jaune le soleil* (1971), *Nathalie Granger* (1972), *La Femme du Gange* (1972), *India Song* (1974), *Des journées entières dans les arbres* (1976), *Son nom de Venise dans Calcutta désert* (1976), *Baxter, Véra Baxter* (1976), *Le Camion* (1977), *Le Navire Night* (1979), the two screen versions of *Aurélia Steiner* (1979), *Agatha et les lectures illimitées* (1981), *L'Homme atlantique* (1981), *Dialogue de Rome* (1982), and, finally, in collaboration with Jean Mascolo and Jean-Marc Turine, *Les Enfants* (1985).

II

By the mid-1970s, partly as a result of her shift into film-making, Duras had acquired a devoted personal following. This made *India Song*, after it opened in 1975, a long-running attraction at the small cinema in the Latin Quarter where it eventually became an almost permanent fixture. But it is important to remember that Duras had long been a controversial figure. From the outset, her work had met with mixed reviews. By 1958, eight years after publication, *Un barrage contre le Pacifique*, though it had originally been a strong candidate for the Prix Goncourt, had, according to Duras, still sold only 3,070 copies; and both *Les Petits Chevaux de Tarquinia*, in 1953, and *Le Square*, in 1955, particularly when it was put on stage the following year, divided critics roughly into two groups: those who thought of Duras as a writer unduly influenced by Ernest Hemingway and with an insufficient grounding in French grammar, and those who, like Blanchot or Samuel Beckett, were conscious of a powerful new talent.[16]

Some of the more polemical critical reaction to Duras's work was probably due in part to her outspoken political opinions and her unconventional private life; but it stemmed, too, from the unusual mixture of obliqueness and sexual explicitness to be found in her work. Though her early fiction may seem unexceptionable to readers today, it is clear that, for instance, her denunciation of the corruption of French colonial rule in *Un barrage contre le Pacifique*, or her portraits of independent women cruising for male companions – both literally and figuratively – in *Le Marin de Gibraltar* and *Moderato cantabile* had the capacity to shock audiences in the 1950s. Her high profile as an avant-garde film-maker in the 1970s only added to this general notoriety, and by the time *India Song* was released, interest in Duras's work had become largely indistinguishable from fascination with the authorial persona she had come to embody.

The role of the media in creating this persona was crucial. But this was not an entirely recent phenomenon. Since even before her involvement in *Hiroshima mon amour*, Duras had been an object of press curiosity. One reason for this media interest was the increasingly public nature of her work, and many of the interviews she gave in the late 1950s or 1960s were connected with the release of a film or the opening of a stage play. But a second important reason was simply that Duras was a woman; for it is worth remembering, in the years prior to 1970, how few woman writers the French literary establishment was willing to accept as members of the artistic fraternity: perhaps only Colette (given a state funeral in 1954) and Simone de Beauvoir (awarded the Prix Goncourt for *Les Mandarins* the same year), together with Elsa Triolet and Marguerite Yourcenar, seem to have escaped some of the worst effects of the general rule of marginalisation or exclusion.

In the early 1970s, however, partly as a result of the social and political changes brought about by the events of May 1968, there was a general, if arguably short-lived resurgence of feminism in France and this made the climate quite a different one. The fact that Duras's own turn to the cinema, with the greater public visibility this entailed, together with the appearance of more radically experimental works like *Détruire, dit-elle* or *Abahn Sabana David*, coincided with a renewal of interest in women writers and film-makers in general made it certain that Duras's own texts and films would be the object of fresh critical debate. The prominence of themes like exclusion, marginality, desire, and madness in Duras's texts and films was an additional reason for the overlap between reception of her work and some of the concerns of the women's movement in France at the time. Indeed, despite a temporary withdrawal on Duras's part from the public eye during the period between 1969 and 1972, the list of topics touched on in most of the interviews she gave in the years following 1972 readily confirms this convergence, and much of the international interest in Duras's work throughout this period, especially in America, focused on the – thorny – issue of Duras's involvement with feminism and her relationship to the women's movement.

Throughout the 1970s and 1980s, Duras enjoyed an ever increasing amount of attention from the media and the effect of this exposure was considerable not only on her own work as a writer and film-maker but also on the audience's perception of her. Duras is one of the first major writers in France whose work has been radically affected by the growth in importance of the audio-visual media during the last few decades. In France, it is clear that by the end of the 1960s artistic production and intellectual debate were coming to be influenced increasingly by television, and were less and less reliant on institutions such as universities, or the more traditional monthly or quarterly journal (the prototype for which, in France, was the literary and critical journal, *La Nouvelle Revue française*, at its height in the 1920s and 1930s). By the mid-1970s these relatively sedate vehicles of intellectual activity began to give way to the technologically faster, more responsive, fashion-conscious audio-visual media. For some commentators, such as Régis Debray, the most significant changes date from 1968.[17] Since that time, the increase in the involvement of the media in the culture industry has been tremendous. As a result, as Debray puts it, where the writer of the 1950s and 1960s relied on the editorship of a monthly journal or a position within a publishing house to exercise intellectual influence, in the 1970s and 1980s authors had to give interviews, appear on television chat-shows, or have their work adapted for television or the cinema. In this respect, the shift in Duras's work from the written text to the film screen was not an isolated one; whatever the idiosyncrasies of her relationship to cinema, her interest in the relationship between the image and the written word was consistent with more deep-seated changes taking place in France in the 1970s.

It is worth distinguishing a number of different aspects to Duras's response to these changes. The first relates to her own active involvement in film-making, initially as scriptwriter and subsequently as director. In itself this was not necessarily new. In some respects, in her dual commitment to text and screen, as Jean-Luc Godard argues, Duras can be seen as belonging to a recognisable, if recently established tradition in France, that of the literary film-maker.[18] According to Godard, in her turn to the cinema Duras was following in the footsteps of earlier innovators (as Godard describes them) such as Marcel Pagnol, Sacha Guitry, and Jean Cocteau, all of whom brought to the cinema an expertise initially gained in the theatre. This was not the case with Duras, though it is no doubt significant in this respect that almost all of Duras's films have, at one time or another, also been adapted for theatrical performance (including of course *India Song*, *Véra Baxter*, *Le Navire Night* and *Aurélia Steiner*, even *Hiroshima mon amour*). In other ways, however, Duras is not very different from the forerunners Godard mentions. Like them, she writes for several media; but, with the sole exception of *Le Camion*, none of her texts, unlike, say, Godard's *Le Mépris*, or *Pierrot le fou*, is indissolubly linked, in both theme and treatment, to any one single medium.

However, in addition to working for the cinema, Duras in the 1970s also began to take on the mantle of a television personality. In the mid-1960s she was already appearing on television as an occasional interviewer for Daisy de Galard's influential documentary series *Dim dam dom*; but by the end of the 1980s she herself had been made the subject of a string of documentary films and television programmes. Notable amongst these were Michelle Porte's two sympathetic television films that in 1976 provided the text to the book, *Les Lieux de Marguerite Duras*. In 1984 Duras recorded four lengthy interviews with Dominique Noguez to accompany the release of eight of her films on videotape; and later in the same year, after the publication of *L'Amant*, she agreed to be interviewed by Bernard Pivot on the influential television literary chat-show, *Apostrophes*. Pivot's role as a shaper of public opinion in the literary sphere was unrivalled at the time, and Duras is generally thought to have received much favourable publicity as a result of the hour-long interview devoted solely to her and her work. In the programme, she does show herself able – no small feat in the circumstances – to dictate the pace of the discussion and thus take control of the interview. And in 1986 she could be seen on television as one of a group of intellectuals pledging their support for François Mitterrand. In December 1987 she appeared once more, this time in conversation with Jean-Luc Godard; and in June and July 1988, the main French commercial channel, TF1, showed four hours of Duras being interviewed by Luce Perrot.

As a result of these and other television appearances, as well as a similar number of radio interviews, by the mid-1980s Duras was a familiar – even overly familiar – media presence, instantly recognisable by both fans and detractors as 'Duras' (or 'la Duras', as though she were some world-famous *diva*). Here there was something more than a writer turning to making films based on her work; it was a case of the author herself being transformed into a visual icon and becoming increasingly inseparable from her own media representation. The process is unmistakable in many of the programmes devoted to Duras. In *Les Lieux de Marguerite Duras*, shot in Duras's house at Neauphle-le-Château and on the Normandy coast at Trouville, in over ninety minutes of film the audience never once sees the interviewer, Michelle Porte, and the impression is of Duras herself performing spontaneously for the camera and very much in control of her own performance. The same is true of the interviews for *Au-delà des pages*, where the questioner is glimpsed only once or twice, and where Duras, appearing in different-coloured clothes, permits herself from time to time, at least in the first interview, to amplify or rework some of her own earlier statements in the programme. And the fact that Duras's best-known television appearance, the interview with Pivot, centred on an autobiographical work like *L'Amant*, and showed the writer endorsing the accuracy of the text – though also modifying it – played a major role in establishing the apparent consubstantiality of Duras the author or narrator and her television image. The programme, which showed the author wearing a white polo-necked sweater and black waistcoat, with a straight skirt and calf-high boots, had the effect, according to Duras (*VM*, 75–6; 65–6), of getting one fashion house in 1985 to try introducing a 'Duras look' (or, in French, 'un look Duras')! And interestingly enough, when Duras appeared on TF1 in *Au-delà des pages*, in 1988, she made a point of wearing the same uniform, contenting herself merely with a change in colour, swapping the white sweater for a green or blue one.

As this last instance demonstrates, Duras was without doubt a willing participant in her transformation from writer into audiovisual icon. A number of interviews (like some of the discussions with Xavière Gauthier in 1974 [*P*, 160–1; 117]) show Duras very sensitive to critical reaction to her work, and one reason for granting so many interviews was obviously that she might exert some direct influence over her readership. On numerous occasions Duras was evidently at pains to maintain as much control as possible over her own media representation. When working with Luce Perrot, for instance, she took an active interest in editing the material.[19] The sessions themselves, like the interview with Godard, were filmed within the familiar surroundings of Duras's Paris flat in the rue Saint-Benoît (she had initially wanted the same arrangement for the *Apostrophes* programme).

Throughout the 1980s, Duras once more became a regular contributor to newspapers or magazines, notably *Libération* and *L'Autre Journal*. She gave extensive interviews to the daily and weekly press to mark the publication of a text, the release of a film, or the opening of a new play or adaptation. After 1975, few works by Duras appeared without an accompanying series of interviews to assist in the launch of the work and offer the audience some kind of semi-official authorial commentary. The process rapidly acquired the predictability of a ritual, one which reflected the insatiable demands of the media for biographical facts and ever more official authorial comment, but also had something to do with the marketing policy adopted by Duras's publishers given that, ever since *Hiroshima mon amour*, she had the reputation of being obscure or difficult.

But this promotion of Duras as a media figure also depended on the author's own readiness to answer questions about her life and work, and Duras goes some way towards explaining why she agreed to so many interviews when shortly after the publication of *L'Amant* she talked to Hervé Le Masson about the mixed emotions associated for her with authorship. Duras tells him:

> Quand on fait paraître un livre, c'est une période toujours difficile. Même quand la critique est bonne, cette période est mal vécue. Un peu comme un deuil. Elle met le livre dans une situation coupable. Et l'auteur dans la situation d'avoir à le défendre. D'en parler me fait aussi peur que lorsque j'avais à traverser une place vide après cette cure anti-alcool. Justifier qu'on écrit des livres un peu comme si c'était mal, c'est ça qui est intolérable.[20]

> (When you have a book coming out, it's always a difficult time. Even when you get good reviews, it's a painful moment. A bit like going into mourning. It puts the book into the position of being guilty, and means the author has to defend it. Talking about it frightens me as much as it did to cross an empty square after I was treated for alcoholism. The unbearable part is having to justify the fact that you write books almost as though there was something bad about it.)

As separation takes place between the author and her book, the key affects, as in mourning, are a sense of guilt and personal loss. Duras's response to this anxiety is twofold: to seek to defend the book, by multiple interviews or *ex cathedra* statements to the press, against a – perceived – external threat, and to compensate for her own sense of vulnerability by challenging the world's right to pass judgement on her. The scenario at work here seems largely a projective one, with Duras thematising as an external threat what is in fact an anxiety internal to the author; but Duras's attitude is also almost a parental one, with the author wanting the reader to greet her new work with the same fond certainty as she has that each text or film enjoys a special place in her affections. Behind the exacerbated assertiveness that is often characteristic of Duras's media persona lies not so much overweening egotistical arrogance, as some readers or viewers have been quick to assume, but rather an abiding sense of the author's own anxiety and the fragility of her relationship to her own writing. (The anxiety of dispossession associated with authorship is also no doubt a factor in Duras's continual rewriting of her own texts, the most spectacular case of which was, in 1991, the transmogrification of *L'Amant* into *L'Amant de la Chine du Nord*.)

But whatever its causes, the extent of Duras's exposure to the media had wide-reaching consequences. Some of these are visible in the work she did from the mid-1970s onwards. For after the filming of *Les Lieux de Marguerite Duras* in 1976, in which Duras volunteers much autobiographical material to gloss her work, and as the almost mythical media persona of 'Duras' began to take on an independent life, not only did the avowedly autobiographical content of Duras's writing increase, but also in interviews, as Aliette Armel suggests, the author's own recourse to autobiographical explanations or reinterpretations of her work became more frequent.[21] The result of this rehabilitation of the autobiographical mode, which Duras was minded to resist in the late 1950s or 1960s, was a shift in the status of Duras's writing that considerably blurred the distinction between fact and fiction, or reality and performance.

By the mid-1980s, then, Duras can be found writing without observing the rigid separation between the autobiographical and the imaginary; indeed the two cease almost to be perceived as contradictory. As early as 1977 Duras set the agenda for this merging of character, narrator, author, and media persona in the film, *Le Camion*, in which, beside the instantly recognisable icon of Gérard Depardieu, the main role is taken by Marguerite Duras herself, who acts on film the role of 'Duras' the author and narrator, and in the process embodies the central character of the film, the conjectural and invisible persona of the 'dame du camion' of the title, whose story the film is recounting in the hypothetical or conditional mode. Here, in Marguerite Duras herself, it seems no longer possible to draw with any certainty the distinction between the reality and the icon, the author and the actress, the person and the persona.

This blurring of the border between the real and the fictitious, the actual and the imaginary, extends beyond Duras's films or literary works. Writing 'outside', as Duras puts it, in public places like newspapers or for the media, is already at least halfway on the road towards invention and in this sense the division between fiction and non-fiction in Duras's later work is an increasingly precarious one. *L'Eté 80* began as a weekly column in *Libération*, but then turned into a book – and audio tape – that enabled Duras to rediscover literary narrative (after nearly ten years of plays and films), and in *La Vie matérielle* in 1987, with the help of Jérôme Beaujour, Duras was experimenting with a fluid mode of writing (or 'écriture flottante' [*VM*, 8; 2]) in which the distinction between the major and the minor, literature and journalism, becomes redundant. But as the preface to *La Vie matérielle* points out, though the conversations or texts in the book do represent reasonably faithfully what Duras thinks on various topics, the reader should not take them as necessarily authoritative or even final; rather what the book does is to record what she thinks 'certaines fois, certains jours, de certaines choses' ('sometimes, some days, about some things', *VM*, 7; 1).

This caveat is well worth remembering. It highlights a major difficulty with Duras's many statements or assertions made in interviews. For whatever the creative changes brought about in Duras's writing by her involvement with the media, one more problematic consequence is that much of what audiences read or see of Duras's work today is filtered through a kind of pre-emptive authorial self-commentary. Her work has become surrounded with a seemingly instantaneous, semi-official critical discourse largely of the author's own devising, though the role of the media in generating such an interpretative frame is of course far from negligible. And throughout the 1980s, as this discourse became more and more autobiographical in tenor, it was also increasingly supplemented by a patchwork of impromptu authorial opinions, some banal, some outrageously provocative, and some indeed both provocative and banal (take for instance her views on men, women, and male homosexuality in *La Vie matérielle* [*VM*, 38–47; 33–41]), but all with the potential to be elevated to the status of an all-encompassing world-view, with the result that access to Duras's texts or films has often been impeded rather than facilitated by this profusion of authorial commentary.

There is, of course, a strong temptation on the part of readers, including literary critics, to view Duras's published interviews, since they emanate from the author, as being somehow authoritative; and for this reason critics have tended to rely extensively on select-ive quotation from the author's published views. But this is unsatis-factory on a number of counts. First, it accords a degree of priority to declared intentions (if not secondary justifications) that is at odds with the evidence of Duras's writing. Secondly, as on the vexed issue of Duras's relationship to feminism, commentators have taken many of her statements out of context and referred to them in fragmentary or piecemeal fashion.

But critics have also neglected to consider the problematic status of remarks made in interviews. In many cases, as the preface from *La Vie matérielle* warns, it is far from self-evident how much truth value should be granted to the more assertive declarations that Duras is in the habit of making to her interviewers. There is an element of provocation inevitable in such encounters, and Duras's interviews need to be seen primarily as performances rather than occasions for imparting reliable truths. With Duras, it is difficult to maintain the usually secure distinction between a text and an author's paraphrase or commentary, between what is presented as fiction and what is claimed to be the origin of that fiction in the author's lived experience. At times self-consciously improvised, at others ambitiously speculative, Duras's interviews are more like theatrical exercises in fiction-making than truth-telling; it is as though the discourse of self-commentary has become an end in itself, an after-hours extension to the writing, prolonging the work of the text rather than clarifying it.

One illustration of the performative function of Duras's inter-views is provided at the start of the first programme in the *Au-delà des pages* series (and the same passage is repeated in the last programme). Here she describes herself and her work, in strongly self-dramatising, even declamatory vein, as a constant subject of scandal. After the brief preamble, which insists on the author's image of herself as a writer ('Elle écrit, M.D., elle fait ça et rien d'autre' ['She writes, M.D., that's what she does and nothing else']), this is how Duras begins:

> Il y a aussi le scandale que je suis. Et c'est ça qui m'échappe, pourquoi je suis, en permanence, un objet de scandale. Il y a le

côté politique, [. . .] et il y a le scandale qui est celui de la littérature. Je crois que la littérature est scandaleuse. Parce qu'elle est rare, qu'elle rend les gens fous. Ce scandale, est-ce qu'il est dépourvu de tout fondement? Est-ce que je ne suis pas scandaleuse, d'oser tout le temps, de me casser la gueule, d'oser encore? [. . .] J'ai l'impression que j'écris dehors, j'écris ouvertement, j'écris de façon indécente, je crois que le scandale est là. [. . .] C'est la sorte de littérature que j'écris qui fait ça.

(There's also the scandal I represent personally. That's what I can't understand, why I'm continually an object of scandal. There's the political side, [. . .] and there's also the scandal of literature. I believe that literature is scandalous, because it's out of the ordinary, and drives people mad. Is the scandal totally without foundation? Isn't it true that I'm scandalous, taking risks all the time, falling flat on my face, but still taking risks? [. . .] I feel as though I write outside, openly, indecently, and that's what's scandalous. [. . .] It all comes from the sort of literature I write.)

There is a strange rhetorical complexity to this attempt to disown – yet also lay claim to – the charge of being scandalous. The real power to scandalise, Duras says, belongs to literature, not the author or writer. But by denying or displacing the accusation, Duras repeats and re-enacts it, and thereby endorses the assertion that her writing constitutes a transgressive act. And by claiming the scandal for herself – as a writer – Duras offends against the usual standards of propriety or modesty, and transgresses again. Duras's affirmation performs its own meaning and becomes its own best demonstration. It is no longer possible to fail to be scandalised by Duras's claims or denials (though one may well be irritated by their circularity). The viewer or reader is placed within a curious double bind, by which one can either reject what Duras says about her own scandalousness and be scandalised by her apparent arrogance, or else accept what she asserts and be scandalised again by the transgressive power of her writing.

Such declarations are a frequent and conspicuous part of Duras's later interviews. It is important, however, to realise that they function not as elements towards a theory for reading Duras. They serve rather to sustain and protect – and thus partially legitimise – Duras's writing. The purpose behind many of Duras's statements to the media is not to analyse, but to provoke, disturb, seduce, justify, or admonish, and thereby incite the audience to read or watch Duras. But, by surrounding the writing with an authorised commentary, Duras also attempts to preserve her writing from the attritional effects of a critical reading. By laying down in advance how she expects her texts or films to be received, she in effect desires her audience to subscribe to the transcendent self-evidence of her work with no more than a gesture of silent complicity. Her image of herself as a woman of scandal is symptomatic; it reveals how much her relationship to her audience rests on a curious dialectic of exposure and concealment, vulnerability and defence.

In these circumstances, Duras's tactic is to issue the audience with a series of injunctions that most clearly resemble those commanding sacred texts (and it is worth remembering here that for Duras, as she tells Dominique Noguez in 1983, writing has to do with God: 'l'écrit a à voir avec Dieu'). What is at issue here is perhaps best encapsulated by the brief statement she posted in *Le Monde* for the Paris opening of the film, *L'Homme atlantique*. Duras writes:

> Il m'a semblé que si j'acceptais la sortie d'un tel film, même dans une seule salle, j'étais tenue de prévenir les gens de la nature de ce film, de conseiller aux uns d'éviter complètement de voir *L'Homme atlantique* et même de le fuir, et aux autres de le voir sans faute, de ne le manquer sous aucun prétexte, que la vie est courte, rapide comme un éclair et qu'il va être montré peut-être seulement pendant quinze jours.[22]

> (It seemed to me that if I agreed to the release of this film, even in just one cinema, I was duty bound to warn people what sort of film it was, to tell some members of the public to avoid seeing *L'Homme atlantique* completely and even to run in the opposite direction, and tell others to see it without fail, not to miss it under any pretext whatsoever, that life is short, swift as a lightning flash and that it will perhaps be showing only for a fortnight.)

The warning enacts a peculiar hermeneutic paradox. There is no viewer of Duras, it seems, who is not already a viewer of Duras; no outsider who has not already been intimidated by the film. Access to Duras's work has always already taken place. The effect is to divide the audience from itself according to an invisible line of demarcation. The audience for *L'Homme atlantique* is no longer homogeneous, but split according to the undecidable dual address of Duras's statement: whoever has eyes will see; whoever is blind will see nothing.

But Duras seems not to envisage the possibility of a viewer passing from one side of the divide to the other. To this extent the circularity of Duras's formulation with regard to *L'Homme atlantique* is self-defeating: if the spectator to whom Duras's remarks are addressed is already a spectator of Duras's work, her comments only serve to congratulate the viewer on that allegiance; they do nothing to persuade the hesitant outsider. Finally, it appears, the author has little to say except to reiterate the injunction to watch or read. But if this is true, all authorial commentary becomes redundant and the seemingly endless glossing of her own work that Duras provides in her interviews turns into so much anxious and unnecessary chatter. And it is, interestingly, her own writing that deprives her of the authority conferred upon her by her authorial position.

III

Though the authorial discourse that accompanies the diffusion and reception of Duras's work has a performative rather than analytical function, it does nevertheless have a history, and it is that history that I want to retrace briefly here. This will make it possible to sketch in some of the background to Duras's work and look more closely at the ways in which the act of writing is framed, articulated, and thus sustained by Duras in her interviews and journalism. This in turn will provide some clue to the reasons for the more controversial aspects of her work.

From the outset, in her first interviews as an author, dating from the mid-1950s and 1960s, Duras can be found returning regularly to a number of specific issues or preoccupations: her colonial childhood and her relationship with her mother, who already in 1959 (as in *L'Amant*, a quarter of a century later) is described as being touched with madness; her political involvement and painful break with the Communist Party in the early 1950s; the close links between writing, silence, oppression, and injustice; her fascination with fear, violent crime, madness, and other extreme psychological states; and her long-term abuse of alcohol, which gave her cirrhosis of the liver at the age of 50 and necessitated a series of admissions to hospital.[23]

At times in these interviews Duras appears content to supply the biographical or other information her questioners require; but at other moments she takes care to stress the radical and exploratory impetus which alone, she argues, gives writing its value. Thus, in conversation with Madeleine Chapsal, in 1960, she defends her commitment to authors like Leiris, Blanchot, Bataille, Queneau, or des Forêts, with the remark that these writers 'ont tous une passion irrésistible de la recherche romanesque. Chez les autres romanciers' she adds, 'je la vois toujours, cette recherche-là, plus ou moins truquée, plus ou moins plagiaire' ('all have an irresistible passion for fictional innovation. I find with other novelists that there is always something fake or second-hand about their experiments').[24] Seven years later, the idea and the assertive tone are much the same: writing in the true sense of the term, says Duras, is a radically transgressive activity beyond morality, prescription, or theory. This is why, to the extent that it attempts to moralise literature and subordinate writing to the pursuit and defence of freedom, Sartrian *engagement*, for instance, is fatally flawed. (This rejection of Sartre as a writer – though not always as a political activist – is a recurrent and symptomatic feature of Duras's interviews, as of Mascolo's *Le Communisme*, and is evoked again at some length on the 1984 *Apostrophes* programme.) For Duras, on the other hand, as for Georges Bataille, there is radical incompatibility between writing and commitment to a determinate set of political objectives. As Duras puts it to an interviewer in 1963, writing is a journey into the unknown: 'l'acte d'écrire est un voyage dans l'inconnu'; 'écrire,' she tells Hubert Nyssen in 1967, 'c'est se laisser faire par l'écriture. C'est savoir et ne pas savoir ce que l'on va écrire. Ne pas croire qu'on le sait. Avoir peur' ('writing is a case of letting writing do what it wants. It's knowing and not knowing what you're going to write, not believing that you know the answer, and being afraid').[25]

This belief in what she describes in this last interview as the transgressive, magical function of writing is reflected in an impatience with the psychological novel as traditionally conceived. In the 1960s Duras is already a writer concerned with exploring states of extreme intensity – such as love, desire, criminality, or madness – in which character motivation becomes impossible to reconstruct. She recalled in *Combat* in 1963 that what interested her in writing *Les Viaducs de la Seine-et-Oise* was the peculiar void and innocence that somehow preceded the violence of both word and deed that characterises Claire, the play's protagonist. 'L'amour,' Duras told Yvonne Baby in March 1967, 'est un devenir constant comme la révolution' ('love is constant process like the revolution'), and later the same month she makes a similar point to Jacqueline Piatier about madness: 'Dans le monde de la folie, il n'y a plus rien, ni bêtise, ni intelligence. C'est la fin du mani-chéisme, de la responsabilité, de la culpabilité' ('In the world of madness, nothing is left, neither stupidity nor intelligence. Mani-chaeism, responsibility, culpability are finished').[26]

By the end of the 1960s, the emphasis in Duras's interviews was beginning to fall more and more on political issues. It is true that political concerns had been crucial for her from the start: her meeting with Chapsal in 1960, for instance, concludes with Duras declaring that she herself was politicised for life and that those who failed to take sides in the Algerian war were little short of criminals ('des criminels').[27] At the same time, as the decade wore on, Duras's relationship to specific political causes was increasingly mediated by broader, even metaphysical concerns, and, unlike Jean-Luc Godard and other left-wing intellectuals at the time, Duras seems to have taken little opportunity to voice in public her opposition to the Vietnam war, despite her own personal connection with the former French colony (which she never revisited after her departure in 1932). Nevertheless, it is clear that Duras's relationship to politics was always more visceral than theoretical. After the events of May 1968, this was even more plainly evident in both the tone and content of Duras's remarks. The fullest exposition of her political views in the wake of May came in a lengthy interview with Jacques Rivette and Jean Narboni published, significantly for Duras, in *Les Cahiers du cinéma* for November 1969. The interview coincided with the release of Duras's film *Détruire, dit-elle*, and it is as though the turn to the cinema, on the basis of such a hybrid text as this – a text, Duras says, 'qui pouvait être à la fois soit lu, soit joué, soit filmé, [. . .] soit jeté' ('which might be read, acted, filmed, [. . .] or thrown away, all at the same time')[28] – was in itself already a political act fully consistent with the apocalyptic radicalism associated by Duras with the events of May.

In the course of the interview, Duras quotes from the trailer to her film. In it she enumerates several figures which she sees as forces of radical opposition. Chief amongst these vehicles of revolutionary dissidence are the madman and the Jew. For Duras, both madness and Judaism are profoundly subversive of Western rationality. They point to the possibility of a world in which individuals are released from the burden of self-identity, and where each of the earth's inhabitants, leaving reason behind as though it were a piece of unnecessary and irksome property, is left to roam the world as a foreigner, in a state of perpetual exile, restored to innocence and freedom, ecstatically open to otherness, subject to a process of constant revolutionary transformation. Here, the Jew and the madman combine to prefigure the messianic communism to which many of Duras's other statements in the interview are dedicated. Part of the trailer, which is in the form of a dialogue, runs as follows:

> – Je suis pour qu'on ferme les écoles et les facultés. Pour l'igno-rance. Pour qu'on s'aligne sur le dernier coolie, et qu'on recom-mence.
> – Pour qu'on s'aligne sur la folie?
> – Peut-être. Un fou est un être dont le préjugé essentiel est détruit: les limites du moi.
> – Est-ce qu'ils sont fous?
> – Dans la vieillerie de la classification actuelle, on peut le penser. L'homme communiste de l'an 2069, qui disposera complètement de sa . . . de sa liberté, de sa générosité, serait actuellement considéré comme un fou. Il serait interné.
> – Pourquoi juif allemand?
> – Il faut entendre: nous sommes tous des juifs allemands, nous sommes tous des étrangers. C'est un mot d'ordre de Mai. Nous sommes tous des étrangers à votre Etat, à votre société, à vos combines.[29]

('I'm in favour of closing down schools and universities. And of ignorance. Of aligning ourselves with the lowliest coolie, and starting over from scratch.'
'In favour of aligning ourselves with madness?'
'Perhaps. A madman is someone in whom the essential prejudice has been destroyed: the limits of the self.'
'Are they mad?'
'According to the present antiquated taxonomy, this may be. Communist man of the year 2069, who will have complete control over his own . . . freedom, and generosity, would in the present climate be considered mad. He would be locked away.'
'Why a German Jew?'
'This means: we are all German Jews, we are all aliens. It's a slogan from May. We are all aliens as far as your state, your society, your corrupt deals are concerned.')

There is, of course, much one might want to criticise about this vision of the future. As Duras admits to her interviewers, it posits, as a necessary point of departure, the creation of an impossible *tabula rasa*, an apocalyptic void that would efface the past and reveal the future in its primeval innocence and gaiety. But to do this Duras's blueprint adopts a largely romantic view of madness, albeit one that, owing to the efforts of the anti-psychiatry movement, did have some currency in the 1960s; it relies, too, in covert fashion, on well-worn mythical figures like that of the wandering Jew; it displays a fondness for simple binary inversion that repeats rather than changes the system it opposes; and as a political project it owes more to messianic predication than to any understanding of practical political realities. Taken together, these drawbacks were reason enough why Jean Narboni, in the original interview in *Les Cahiers du cinéma*, was perhaps not alone in feeling uneasy.

Nevertheless, here was a position that sustained Duras in much of her work over the following years. In the early 1970s, however, to complement the Jew and the madman, a new group was added to the cast of subversives: that of women. This was no doubt due in part to the widespread re-emergence of feminist thinking in France at the time, although Duras had already voiced her enthusiasm for Michelet's witches – the *sorcières* – as early as 1965 (and largely repeats what she said then in the passage about witches in *Les Lieux de Marguerite Duras* in 1976 [*L*, 12–14; A: 55]).[30] The convergence was important, though, and as a result much of what Duras had to say about her work as both writer and film-maker was articulated – and read, particularly outside France – against the backdrop of the debates taking place in the early 1970s about the position of women with regard to language and writing in general.

Some of this discussion is perhaps worth recalling briefly here. One important focus of attention was an argument about writing by women. Like numbers of others, Hélène Cixous, for example, argued that persistently, for centuries, women had been diminished, objectified, and excluded by the male-centred metaphysical tradition. The place of women with regard to male language and culture was that of an outsider or exile. On one level this meant that current representations of women were more than likely to repress and disfigure women's thoughts, lives, and bodies. But, if one accepted this account, Cixous continued, more controversially, it also followed that male-centred culture already contained within it its own homeopathic remedy or counter-poison. The very exclusion of women from male culture, by strategic reversal, could act as an Archimedean lever and give women the possibility of radically challenging androcentric models of writing and speaking.

Women, as the repressed other of male-centred culture, thus had the means to challenge and undermine that culture.

In this way, Cixous suggested, the repressed and deformed image of women given by the male tradition could be revised to reveal a radical alternative. The hierarchy of male over female could be challenged and displaced, and the repressed characteristics of women rediscovered: the alleged passivity of women could be re-articulated as a principle of generosity and giving; female emotionalism could be rewritten as a refusal of the universalising rationality of male-dominated metaphysics, as *pathos* against *logos*; and so-called 'hysterical' female bodies could be reinterpreted as transgressive of male-centred reason because sexual difference was precisely what logocentric discourse failed to acknowledge, and repressed. In the course of the argument, terms like male and female became divorced from gender in the strict sense and began to refer more to modes of thought rather than biological facts; and in the end, Cixous suggested, they were words which were probably not worth preserving, for they encapsulated a metaphysical view of the world which denied the fundamental bisexuality of all bodies. In the meantime, however, writing remained a crucial arena, for it was through reinventing women's language that some of these transvaluations might be achieved: 'Aujourd'hui,' Cixous concluded, 'l'écriture est aux femmes' ('Today, writing belongs to women'). Less prone to sublimation than men, she said, women had more bodily intensity at their disposal. There was, she concluded, more writing in their texts; the claim produced a powerful but notorious slogan: 'plus corps, donc plus écriture' ('More body, therefore more writing').[31]

The argument, conducted as it was in a metaphorically charged and polemical language, turned out to be hugely controversial. The claim that women's writing, or *écriture féminine* as it quickly became known, was different in principle from that of men, as well as being more transgressive, more multiplicitous, and more closely based on bodily experience, was seen by some readers as offering an important new platform for writing by women. But it was clear that for others, despite Cixous's qualification that the reference to *féminin* was to an economy or mode of thinking and not to a restrictive criterion based on pairs of chromosomes, the whole contention seemed to rely on a refusal to accept that gender was a social construct. From this standpoint, the whole affair smacked less of radical change and more of obscurantism, elitism, and biological essentialism.

The debate reached a high point in 1974. This was the year of Luce Irigaray's *Speculum: de l'autre femme*, which undertook a philosophical critique of Freud and Plato in the endeavour to arrive at an understanding of the otherness of women, and of Annie Leclerc's *Parole de femme*, an impassioned work which, despite its vagueness and fondness for hasty generalisations, sold enormously well and became a key reference point for all advocates of *écriture féminine*. In 1974, too, the publishing house *Des femmes* was founded and began issuing a number of experimental literary texts by women. And the same year saw the publication of Duras's conversations with Xavière Gauthier, *Les Parleuses*, in which Gauthier attempted to claim Duras for feminism and for the *écriture féminine* cause. Shortly after, in a famous footnote to her article, 'Le Rire de la Méduse', Cixous named Duras, alongside Colette and Jean Genet, as one of only three modern French authors writing in the *féminin* mode.[32]

The debate was in full swing as Duras began to be read more widely on the international stage. As a result, especially in English-speaking countries, Duras has often been seen – mistakenly – as an exponent of *écriture féminine*. This in turn has led to accusations of biological essentialism.[33] Admittedly, though Duras never aligned herself explicitly with the position of, say, Hélène Cixous, it is true that in many interviews of the early 1970s (though markedly less so in her fiction or films, with the exception of *Nathalie Granger*, made in 1972), Duras does offer a polemical and starkly polarised view of relations between the sexes. Men are given the role of the hierarchically inferior 'bad other', and women are seen as the radical reverse of men. One example of this tactic of rhetorical inversion will probably suffice. It comes from an interview in 1973 with Suzanne Horer and Jeanne Soquet, in which Duras, still full of enthusiasm for the May *événements*, contrasts women's silence with men's talk:

> Il faut que l'homme apprenne à se taire. Ça doit être là quelque chose de très douloureux pour lui. Faire taire en lui la voix théorique, la pratique de l'interprétation théorique. *Il faut qu'il se soigne*. On n'a pas le temps de vivre un événement aussi considérable que Mai 1968, que déjà l'homme parle, passe à l'épilogue théorique et casse le silence. [. . .] Immédiatement il a fait taire les femmes, les fous, il a embrayé sur le langage ancien, il a racolé la pratique *théorique ancienne* pour dire, raconter, expliquer ce fait *neuf*: Mai 1968. [. . .]

Non, il a fallu que l'homme casse tout, et *arrête le cours du silence.*

Un grand découragement s'empare de moi quand je pense à ce crime. Car ça a été un crime, et *un crime masculin.* C'est l'homme qui m'a donné la nausée à l'idée de tout militantisme après 1968. Ce n'est pas par hasard que le mouvement de libération des femmes est venu tout de suite après 1968.)[34]

(Men must learn to be silent. It must be very painful for them, to silence in themselves the voice of theory, the practice of theoretical interpretation. *They have just got to get treatment.* We've hardly had the time to finish living through an event as huge as May '68 before men are already talking about it, holding forth with their theories and breaking the silence. [. . .] Without stopping, men have silenced women, and the insane, and slotted back into using yesterday's language, and gone touting for *yesterday's theories* to put into words and into narrative this wholly *new* event: May '68, and explain it all away. [. . .]

No, men had to ruin everything and *stop the flow of silence.*

I become very despondent when I think of this crime. Because that's what it was, *a crime committed by men.* It was men who made me sick at the idea of political activism after '68. It was no accident that the women's movement came straight after '68.)

Here, by joining in the call for women to develop their own language and their own specific forms of political organisation, Duras makes her own the demands of many feminists in the early 1970s. But as she takes up this agenda, Duras dramatises it with a rhetoric that is as emphatic as it is Manichaean. Male and female are hypostatised and turned into warring principles that are more imaginary than real. No attempt is made to address the historical or political shortcomings of May 1968, and what Duras offers her reader is not an analysis but a polemical discourse whose prime purpose is to exhort or provoke. The result is less a coherent political programme than a harangue founded in apocalyptic myth. By using myth, Duras's main aim is to identify, as a means to an end, a repressed historical agent that might serve as a vehicle for radical, subversive transgression. Symptomatic in this respect is the fact that in the interview women, as a group, are ranged alongside the insane ('les fous'), Jews, and the proletariat as the privileged vehicles of an unnamed yet sublime, contestatory energy, the impact of which, according to Duras, is to overwhelm all established modes

of theoretical discourse as well as all constituted forms of political
– and literary – representation.

Around this time, Duras recorded a number of interviews with
American critics or academics, the best known of which is a conversation with Susan Husserl-Kapit that appeared in the journal *Signs*
in 1975. The discussion seems to show Duras readily endorsing an
essentialist version of women's writing. These, at any rate, are
Duras's opening remarks (in Husserl-Kapit's translation):

> I think 'feminine literature' is an organic, translated writing . . .
> translated from blackness, from darkness. Women have been in
> darkness for centuries. They don't know themselves. Or only
> poorly. And when women write, they translate this darkness.
> [. . .] Men don't translate. They begin from a theoretical plat-
> form that is already in place, already elaborated. The writing of
> women is really translated from the unknown, like a new way
> of communicating rather than an already formed language. But
> to achieve that, we have to turn away from plagiarism.[35]

Here, as before, there is a strong attack on the poverty of theoretical discourse and an emphasis on the radical newness of women's
writing. In this regard Duras's position is unchanged from two
years earlier. However, the reference to 'organic' writing may be
misleading. For when Duras uses these words, this should not be
taken – as it often is – to imply a kind of writing that derives, as
though in transparent and unmediated fashion, from the body
viewed as an essential and unchanging self rooted – gender and all
– in biology and nature. (It is worth remarking that when Duras
uses the word again, in the same context, in *Les Parleuses* [*P*, 123;
88], a note is added to the effect that she no longer likes the term.)

The truth of the matter is almost exactly the reverse. Generally
in the early 1970s in France, the body is a figure for what escapes
consciousness and identity. As a result, it is a site of material
struggle and change; it is a force profoundly inimical to biological
purity, determinism, or stability. In the 1970s, this account of the
body owed much to the writings of Roland Barthes (for whom
Duras elsewhere professes a strong dislike [*VM*, 42; 36–7; *YA*, 21]),
whose book, *Le Plaisir du texte*, published in 1973, was explicitly
dedicated to reintroducing the body – whether as pleasure, enjoyment, flesh, or history – into the theoretical sphere. The body, for
Barthes, was not a concept or even a thing; it was more a textual
or theoretical operator. What it did was to reaffirm the materiality
and heterogeneity of textual production. From this standpoint, for

Duras as for Barthes, the body is not a mode of self-identity but a metaphor for whatever is excluded from identity: the body is a figure of madness, not self-possession. It is not an essence or nature, but the reverse of an essence or nature; it is a name for that which provokes crisis in the realm of representation by producing irreducible difference. And what it denotes most of all, in Duras as in Barthes, is desire. The reference to the body, then, is a reference to all that is transgressive in human behaviour. The seemingly dogmatic assertion in Duras that there are constitutive differences between men and women is not so much an essentialism, therefore, as a provocative tactical move – in the form of an appeal to myth – intent on undermining the notion of a transparently available and static human nature. Such a move is of course a risky one, since exploding rationalism by recourse to myth is inevitably to begin to treat male and female as pre-given extrahistorical entities rather than principles of sexual differentiation.

Nevertheless, when Duras describes childbirth, or erotic activity, or revolutionary change as miraculous, organic experiences ('des expériences organiques'),[36] it is not to lapse naively – as some critics have believed – into an endorsement of female nature as opposed to nurture, but to draw attention to what in nature actually exceeds and escapes nature and makes women's identity less than stable or constant; for all these upheavals are figures of excess, of forces that cannot be represented or contained within norms. In describing them as 'organic' Duras is not linking writing to a reductive idea of biological destiny, but rather using the body – or organism – as a metaphor for something that cannot be represented or defined and which has the power to transgress norms, limits, reason, and rationality.

It is evident here that in her description of women's writing, as in the account of madness or Judaism in the interview with Rivette and Narboni, the question that Duras is addressing is not the issue of the position of women, or Jews, or the mentally ill, in modern society. Rather, Duras is seeking to identify an agent, hitherto excluded from symbolic activity, that might serve as a vehicle for a transgressive force that challenges representation and the social order; to this extent little has altered in the structure of Duras's ideas since the late 1950s (even the mention of plagiarism in 1975 echoes a point made to Chapsal in 1960). What has changed since the *Cahiers du cinéma* interview, however, is that the list of subversives has become much more extensive; it now incorporates not only writers, madmen, and Jews, but also women, the proletariat, and the body. And this is not the only time that Duras can be found trying to expand her list of candidates. For in 1976, in conversation with Michelle Porte in *Les Lieux de Marguerite Duras*, Duras adds more names, citing Michelet's witches, music (notably Bach), children, and the painting of Goya, while in 1980, in an interview in the French gay monthly, *Gai Pied*, she included gays and lesbians, too.

What these figures have in common is not a latent essence (though Duras often behaves as though there were some deep complicity between them) but a trait that closely resembles what in aesthetics is known as the sublime. The sublime, in this expanded sense, refers to whatever, within a particular system of relations – gender, reason, language, even society itself – denotes an internal limit, a border zone where the system itself ceases to function smoothly and begins to break down. At this limit, excluded or repressed forces are released into the system and threaten to throw it into disarray. The process is one that Duras identifies at one point with her dissolute elder brother. She claims that his quasi-legendary status in her work derives from the fact that he embodies a destructive, subversive energy that is indistinguishable from the principle of family life itself. She explains that 'il y a toujours, dans les familles, un défaut par où la famille fout le camp, sort d'elle-même' ('there's always, in every family, some defect, through which the family falls apart and takes leave of itself').[37] What is true here of Duras's brother with regard to the family is true elsewhere, in more radical ways, of Judaism, madness, women, music, writing, and much else besides. For what is at stake in all these cases is the knowledge that within any given structure there is always a moment when the rules break down, often violently, and reveal the latency of some kind of primeval, mythic confusion.

The diverse agents of subversion that Duras assembles in this way share the same transgressive potential. But in themselves, beyond this capacity for apocalyptic destruction, they have no firm or stable definition: they are like so many moments of passage, border zones where identity gives way to heterogeneity and instability. Rather like the events that take place in *Hiroshima mon amour* – love and the nuclear holocaust, Japan and France, remembering and forgetting – all the agents of subversion Duras enumerates exist in a relationship of reciprocal equivalence. This might be summed up in a formula of the type: madmen are like Jews are like women are like the proletariat are like the body are like Bach's Goldberg variations are like. . . . In this open-ended list the law of non-contradiction is flouted; attributes are shifted at will from one item to another. The rule is one of metonymic contagion or contamination (and there are similarities here with the theme of leprosy that haunts *Le Vice-consul* or *India Song*). So, if Duras could tell Germaine Brée in 1972 that 'the Jew is a madman of the revolution', or that 'Judaism is the phenomenon of unconditional refusal', it followed, necessarily, as Duras remarked to Alain Vircondelet the same year (and later to Michelle Porte [*C*, 124–5]), that only the insane write completely: 'seuls, les fous écrivent complètement'; this last privilege is in turn transferable in principle both to the Jews and to women (as is verified by Duras's exchange with Xavière Gauthier about the phrase in *Les Parleuses* [*P*, 49–51; 30–1]); and in *Les Lieux de Marguerite Duras*, the same logic of general equivalence serves to link Bach, *The Art of the Fugue*, music in general, Goya, and the proletariat (*L*, 29–30; A:58), while in 1981 in Montreal, in a further twist to the spiral, Duras was proposing to Suzanne Lamy her view that children were mad: 'les enfants sont des fous.'[38]

The privilege ascribed to women in some interviews, therefore, is not specific to women by virtue of any principle of gender difference or biology; it is more a function of a particular state of exclusion from language and representation. What interests Duras in women is not women in themselves, but a possibility of language which may be found in women and speaks differently of the body – and of a different body – and thus challenges established norms of sense and identity. But although the silence of women points to a possibility of difference, this does not mean there is a specifically female language. In 1977, apropos of *Le Camion*, Duras sides with the view that there is no such thing as *un langage féminin*, or women's language: 'En fait,' she says, 'je crois qu'il n'y en a pas: il n'y a qu'un langage libre' ('In reality, there's no such thing, there's only language that is free').[39] This subordination of women's issues to broader – if rather indeterminate – ethical or literary questions explains how, despite her concern for the state of exclusion of women, Duras was never tempted to describe herself as a feminist.[40] At any event, like other French women writers or film-makers of her generation, she was not prepared to accept moral tutelage from the women's movement, and though she continued to speak publicly as a woman she slowly withdrew her – at best rhetorical – support for the militant feminism of the 1970s, which, she implied, did little more than to remind her of the dogmatic moralising she had experienced when once a member of the Communist Party. (But it is worth pointing out that as late as 1988, on the evidence of *Au-delà des pages*, Duras was still ready to affirm that she was 'against men', declaring on behalf of women in general that 'c'est terrible la sujétion dans laquelle nous sommes, dans laquelle ils veulent nous mettre. C'est épouvantable' ['it's awful, the subjection that we suffer, which men want to put us under, it's terrible'].)

But if by the late 1970s Duras was registering a gradual state of divorce between herself and the women's movement, the case was much the same regarding her relationship with politics in general. Duras was not alone in voicing growing scepticism towards political solutions: the collapse of belief in the historically progressive role of the left was an important feature of intellectual life in France in the late 1970s. So in an interview published in May 1977 to coincide with the release of *Le Camion*, it was not surprising to find Duras denouncing Marxism in loosely feminist terms as a continuation of male privilege by other means ('une phallocracie déplacée', she calls it), while at the same time, in another interview, she maintained: 'Je suis communiste. Je vis un communisme bafoué, égorgé' ('I am a communist. But the communism that is mine has been ridiculed and gutted').[41]

Le Camion itself voices a similar rejection of traditional working-class politics and a nostalgia for radical change reminiscent of May 1968; and what the film expresses most vividly is the bankruptcy of all ideologies when faced with a radical other such as the 'dame du camion' herself (in whom the motifs of Judaism, madness, being a woman, and exile are all combined). From the evidence of the film, the only valid response to this impasse looked like being an aesthetic one. But in 1981 Duras's professed political pessimism did not prevent her from giving her support to the election campaign of her former Resistance comrade François Mitterrand, in order to reject the aggressive neo-liberalism of the French right: 'Mais en cas de danger, il faut savoir prendre parti,' she told an interviewer. 'C'est comme si en 1940, on avait laissé les nazis s'installer en France' ('But in an emergency, you have to take sides. It's as if we'd let the Nazis settle in France in 1940'). And after Mitterrand's victory she wrote: 'Le miracle est là: c'est en inventant une gauche complètement libérée de la gauche fasciste issue du stalinisme que l'électorat français a porté le coup le plus décisif au stalinisme' ('The miracle is plain to see: by inventing a party of the left completely free of the Fascist left that came out of Stalinism the

French electorate has landed the most decisive blow yet against Stalinism').[42]

The 1980s for Duras, marked by the success of *L'Amant* in 1984, were largely years of consecration, but after the Goncourt she began once more to publish in the press. One particular piece was the source of much acrimony and polemic and in the long term proved to be relatively damaging to Duras's credibility. The article concerned was a three-page spread in *Libération* in July 1985 on what became known as the Christine Villemin affair. Villemin's son, the 8-year-old Grégory, had been found murdered the previous October. After months of speculation, during which time Grégory's uncle, arrested then released by the authorities, was himself shot dead by the boy's father, it was Christine Villemin's turn, at the beginning of July, to be charged with infanticide. Inquiries were still being made when Duras published her imaginary reconstruction of the killing. The article dramatised the possibility of Villemin's guilt and turned her into something of a latter-day female martyr. Duras concluded: 'Ce qui aurait fait criminelle Christine V. c'est un secret de toutes les femmes, commun' ('What allegedly made Christine V. into a criminal is a common secret, shared by all women').[43] With words like these, Duras transformed Villemin into a mythical character more like a figure from one of her own books. There were immediate protests at this merging of fact and speculation. The following week, the magazine *L'Evénement du jeudi* interviewed a group of other women writers, including Simone Signoret, Benoîte Groult, Françoise Sagan, Michèle Perrein and others, and asked for their reaction: they were virtually unanimous in condemning Duras for abusing her position as a writer by intervening irresponsibly – as they saw it – in a case that was still *sub judice*.[44]

As the Villemin article already shows, Duras in the mid-1980s did much to provoke the media and promote herself as a privileged witness of contemporary events. Three major concerns seem to have mobilised her attention. First was her intense admiration for the person of François Mitterrand. To give the President some intellectual support, much needed at the time, she published in *L'Autre Journal* a series of interviews with him to coincide with the 1986 legislative elections. The discussion began by evoking the common Resistance past of Duras and Mitterrand, and it is clear that, at the time, though for different reasons, each was seeking to profit from the reflected glory of the other. For her part, Duras used the opportunity to develop her view that Mitterrand was the perfect embodiment of an independent and pragmatic – and thus necessarily pessimistic – mode of socialism, the only one she believed to be genuinely post-Stalinist.

Next amongst Duras's main political concerns was a strong and often violent revulsion for the racism and anti-Semitism of the French extreme right, particularly the figure of Jean-Marie Le Pen, the leader of the *Front national*. Admittedly, the 1980s in France witnessed an unprecedented rise in the electoral fortunes of the party as well as much manoeuvring by mainstream right-wing parties to attract Le Pen's supporters into their ranks. Duras's verdict on this was given in *Le Monde* for 17 March 1985, under the title 'La Droite la mort': whether Chirac or Le Pen, she wrote, it was all the same; what the political right had on offer was merely the prospect of death. But Duras also went further and in 1988, in the first of the *Au-delà des pages* interviews, with clear provocative intent, she retold a particularly violent dream she claimed to have had, in which Le Pen is murdered and thrown from the Toulouse train by three North African conscripts. (The episode is an almost exact reprise and inversion of a notorious incident from November 1983, which Duras mentions in her second interview with Mitterrand, involving the killing of a young Algerian by a group of three would-be recruits to the parachute regiment of the French foreign legion.)

The third strand in Duras's political journalism of the 1980s was represented by her virulent hatred of Moscow and the French Communist Party. Duras had long been hostile to the PCF, ever since her expulsion in 1950. But in the 1980s, though by then the Party was in irreversible decline, her criticism became more strident. Her hatred of Soviet communism led her, like other ex-communists, to espouse views largely reminiscent of the rhetoric of the Cold War. In *L'Eté 80*, written against the background of the growth of Solidarity in Poland and the Soviet invasion of Afghanistan (which the PCF had at first warmly welcomed), she expressed her impatience with the emerging anti-nuclear and peace movements in the West by claiming that the major threat to world peace was not the nuclear bomb but the dangers of Soviet expansionism. It was this view that prompted her to support publicly the sinking of the Greenpeace ship, *Rainbow Warrior*, by the French Secret Service in July 1985 on the – at best speculative – grounds that, by trying to halt French nuclear tests in the Pacific, Greenpeace was jeopardising French independence and playing into the hands of the Soviets. And the same Manichaean view of international politics was no doubt also at the centre of Duras's decision to dissociate herself from the editorial position of *L'Autre Journal* in April 1986 in order to applaud President Reagan's bombing of Libya.[45]

If on the political front in the 1980s Duras's views became more outspoken, the same was also true of her remarks about literature. Indeed, together with politics, writing is the other main topic to which Duras constantly returns in the mid-1980s. Though the tone is more emphatic and there is a greater propensity for *ex cathedra* statements, there is little of substance that is new. Duras still holds to the view of literature as a fundamentally transgressive activity. Writing, she repeats, breaks with established authority and exceeds mastery; its role is to challenge and subvert the status quo, to undermine all established discourses and ideologies. To write therefore is not to represent the world by telling stories, it is to push narrative and human experience to that limit at which meaning falters and yields to an ecstatic otherness that no longer fits the bounds of ordinary language. At this point of sublime extremity, writing fuses with its own opposite, giving way to a moment of intense communicative excess: 'Écrire,' Duras puts it, 'ce n'est pas raconter des histoires. C'est le contraire de raconter des histoires. C'est raconter tout à la fois. C'est raconter une histoire et l'absence de cette histoire. C'est raconter une histoire qui en passe par son absence' ('Writing isn't just telling stories. It's exactly the opposite. It's telling everything at once. It's the telling of a story, and the absence of the story. It's telling a story through its absence', *VM*, 31–2; 27). And she adds a few pages later: 'J'ai beaucoup parlé de l'écrit. Je ne sais pas ce que c'est' ('I've talked a lot about writing. But I don't know what it is', *VM*, 37; 32).

Literature, then, for Duras, is a journey into uncharted territory, an exploration of extraordinary states – love, desire, madness – that no longer fall subject to meaning or rational decision and cannot be formulated except in terms of an ecstatic experience at the margin of words and speech. Writing, here, is heightened disclosure; and what it discloses is fundamental and irredeemable catastrophe. But this relationship between writing and disaster is not stable; subject and object are mutually contagious, and writing does not just speak of disaster but is its most radical and transgressive enactment. Literature, here, for Duras, as we shall discover throughout this book, declares its allegiance to the apocalyptic mode: it reveals by destroying, and destroys by revealing. Writing is both illumination and catastrophe, the one in the guise of the other, and the one because of the other; and literature becomes the name for a process of perpetual transformation, inversion, and paradox, in the course of which apparent obscurity is continually converted into messianic clarity, and all available borders and frontiers, divisions and distinctions are overwhelmed and destroyed.

The appeal of the figure of apocalypse is, for Duras, powerful and irresistible, and it is perhaps no exaggeration to say that it dominates each and every aspect of Duras's thematic concerns and aesthetic methods. What it embodies is a desire to treat the written text as somehow sacred, but then to value it not so much for itself, but with regard to the sublime, unrepresentable force that is buried deep inside it; to that extent, what gives the work its revelatory value is itself necessarily always obscured by the work, and it is as though Duras as a writer is haunted by the conviction that only a further, additional, purer or clarified version of the work will ever turn the promise of apocalyptic revelation into reality. Writing in itself, then, is never enough; and this is at least one reason why Duras is a compulsive rewriter of her own texts, and why literature for Duras must always aim to transgress itself in the quest for an elusive goal outside itself where the promise of radical apocalyptic change might ultimately be grasped.

The result of this process of continual transgression, however, is not definitive truth, but endless re-enactment, as Duras recycles tirelessly and necessarily throughout her work many of the same stories, motifs, and names. In the process, by a strange but characteristic inversion, while the figure of apocalypse seems to commit Duras to a belief in revelation, it also announces that the only true object of revelation is apocalypse itself and the crisis in understanding and temporality it effects. As a result, beyond the ecstatic moment which apocalypse embodies, it turns out that there is nothing further to be communicated; all that survives is a catastrophe affecting the structure of meaning itself, together with the certainty that the idea that there may be some truth to be revealed at the end has itself been severely compromised if not, indeed, obliterated. Apocalypse here, as Blanchot puts it, disappoints; it is a figure that destroys itself and thereby destroys truth, and one understands better perhaps why apocalyptic destruction, for Duras, is another name for the affirmation of desire, freedom, and hope.

By insisting on the fragility and precariousness of all borderlines, the figure of apocalypse promises a return to innocence; it holds out the hope of a new beginning arising out of the ashes and destruction of the past. In this way, by presenting destruction as a rediscovery of primordial simplicity, the apocalypse provides Duras with a means of reconciling her radical historical pessimism with a messianic belief in the value of love, desire, radical political change, or writing. Indeed, during the 1960s and 1970s, as we have seen, she put forward a variety of possible apocalyptic agents – madmen, Jews, women, children, music, the proletariat, much else besides – to whom this task of radical destruction or transformation might be entrusted, but from the perspective of the 1980s all these vehicles of sublime contestation turn out to have been incomplete metaphors for the act of writing itself. Literature generalises the functions previously delegated to one or other of these more specific apocalyptic agents; and, in the end, Duras suggests, perhaps writing alone can testify adequately – catastrophically – to the disasters that exceed the bounds of language and threaten the stability of human experience: desire, love, exile, suffering, silence, madness, or sexual difference.

But while, in this way, apocalyptic thinking provides Duras with a means of reconciling contradictory forces without reducing them to mere aspects of a prior totalising unity, the recourse to the theme of apocalypse is not without its difficulties. Indeed, the apocalyptic model necessarily relies on the availability of some extrahistorical vantage point, an ecstatic moment outside of time that somehow marks off the end of progressive history and embodies the possibility that the innocence and gaiety at the origin of time may be experienced anew. As a result, the theme of apocalypse is inseparable from a refusal of progressive history and thus an appeal to myth; and in many texts or interviews from the 1980s Duras can be found mythifing – if not, indeed, mystifying – the act of writing, just as she had done in earlier texts with madness, Judaism, women, and music. But by turning to myth in this way it is inevitable that Duras should end by privileging archetype over history, affect over argument, and personal fantasy over objective reality. And it is for those very things that Duras has on occasion been most bitterly attacked, as reaction to the Villemin article most clearly shows.

The polemic relating to the article illustrates the risks that are involved in the recourse to myth as a mode of argument and it comes as no surprise, perhaps, that Duras has been frequently attacked, particularly by feminists, for her Manichaeism, essentialism, and self-serving rhetoric. To some degree, as this chapter has shown, there is a necessary and evident logic to such criticisms. But to object to Duras on the grounds of her lack of theoretical rectitude is also to misunderstand the genre of Duras's remarks and mistakenly treat them as somehow aspiring to the status of a theoretically coherent discourse. Duras's authorial self-commentary does not provide a logical defence of her work as writer or film-maker but rather an affective or visceral one. Its aim is not to persuade by rational argument but to affirm the author's conviction of the value of writing as apocalyptic revelation; and to do this it adopts the peremptory – even fantasmatic – strategy that is itself characteristic of the apocalyptic mode both in literature and outside it. This should remind us that Duras's critical and political remarks need to be read not as constituting a theoretical discourse existing apart from her creative writing, but, more modestly, and perhaps more interestingly, as a wayward yet integral part of that writing.

2 Transferential loves

In Duras's texts of the 1940s and 1950s, the main motive force driving both character and plot is sexual desire.[1] Desire comes in a number of characteristic forms. In Duras's first novels, *Les Impudents*, *La Vie tranquille*, and *Un barrage contre le Pacifique*, all of which are fictionalised versions of the same – largely autobiographical – family melodrama, it functions as a kind of revolving door that separates the domestic world of the family from the social world of other adults, while also necessarily connecting them. To an extent, sexual desire is what allows the protagonist, a woman, to move beyond the authority of her mother or brothers and enjoy a measure of emancipation and independence; but it is clear too that desire remains largely held within the family, charged in the case of brother and sister with transposed, but nonetheless unmistakable incestuous overtones. The division between inside and outside remains permeable; to leave the family in Duras is also to rediscover, in displaced or transformed ways, the powerful but ambivalent bond of desire that has its origin in the promiscuity of family relations.

Thus Maud, at the end of *Les Impudents*, leaves her family, principally her mother and reckless spendthrift brother, Jacques, in order – somewhat implausibly – to marry Georges, who had earlier been a close friend of her brother. Marriage here resolves the rivalry between Maud and Jacques for Georges's friendship and allows Duras's heroine to extricate herself provisionally from her ambivalent identification with the elder brother, whom she evidently loves and hates in equal measure. In *La Vie tranquille*, similarly, the narrator, Françou, stricken with grief at the loss of her younger brother Nicolas (who has killed himself out of remorse at causing the death of his mother's brother, Jérôme), sleeps finally with Tiène, Nicolas's enigmatic friend, who has joined the family as though he too were another brother. In an odd but characteristic turn, the death of the one is mirrored in the awakening of desire for the other. But Françou admits her lover has done no more than replace her brother (*VT*, 171); and the book ends with the prospect of their wedding.

Un barrage contre le Pacifique, by comparison, shows a greater degree of fidelity to autobiographical fact. But it, too, reworks a similarly displaced or indirect scenario: the protagonist Suzanne, after her chaste affair with M. Jo (a textual precursor of the lover of *L'Amant*), decides to lose her virginity to a local philanderer by the name of Jean Agosti. It is striking how each of these names (*Jo*, A*g*osti) silently echoes that of Suzanne's brother, *Jo*seph, as though to announce that both lovers, at best, are no more than delegates for the brother who cannot take their place. As M. Jo in the novel astutely remarks, full of hesitation and embarrassment, to Suzanne: 'Ce que vous aimez c'est les types du genre [. . .] d'Agosti et de . . . Joseph' ('The kind of man you like [. . .] is a man like Agosti . . . and like Joseph', *B*, 77; 60). Finally, with their mother's death, Suzanne and Joseph give notice of their decision to quit the colony for good; in this case, at any rate, any proposal of marriage for Suzanne is ruled out.

If these early texts show a woman moving beyond the family to begin sexual relationships with other men, Duras's novels of the 1950s portray women and men contending with some of the pressures and constraints of living as a couple. *Le Marin de Gibraltar*, for instance, deals with the quest for the – imaginary – sailor of the title who becomes, for the narrator and his companion, Anna, who is busily combing the world for the man, the emblem of an indestructible love that can never be satisfied or contained, only approximated by the more transient relationship between Anna and the book's narrator. In its ironic contrasting and fusing of Anna's two lovers – the sailor and the narrator – what the novel seems to dramatise is the search for an impossible equilibrium between the absolute demands of desire and the limits imposed by membership of a couple.

Desire in Duras, as *Le Marin de Gibraltar* shows, is by nature errant; its course continually takes it beyond the closed arena of the couple. The reasons for this are related to the implicit theme of brother-sister incest that colours much of Duras's early fiction. Incest posits at the origin of desire both fusion and difference. It offers the powerful fantasy of a radical merging of identities with a sibling of the opposite sex in whom everything is familiar (and familial), except the fact of difference itself; yet it also acknowledges the sexual prohibition that renders sister and brother inaccessible to each other and, in the end, untouchable. But fusion and difference, though counterposed, are, as Georges Bataille points out, necessarily complementary. Prohibition is what reinforces desire; and, from the outset, desire itself is dependent on the separation the taboo effects.[2] The more unattainable the object of love, then, for Duras, the more powerful the desire to merge with it.

Conversely, if desire tends towards the ecstatic fusion of self with other, it may achieve that goal only by virtue of the difference in which it has its origin. A series of paradoxes flow from this. For Duras, any ultimate satisfaction of desire would also imply an exhaustion of desire; to survive its own demise, desire must perpetually defer the end which constitutes its only goal. Thus, in Duras's early fiction, allusions to incest are always covert or disguised. Desire avoids the shortest path to its object, preferring the more circuitous route; it promises less an immediate coalescing of bodies than a lengthy series of hesitations, detours, displacements, and transpositions. Incest, in Duras, is a singular and transgressive event but it partakes of a general economy. What it reveals is that desire achieves its goal only at the cost of its own abolition; and that love therefore cannot achieve satisfaction and necessarily always falls short of itself. As Duras herself puts it, in *Les Petits Chevaux de Tarquinia*: 'Tout amour vécu est une dégradation de l'amour' ('Any actual love is a debasement of love', *PC*, 88; 79); or, more famously, from the same novel: 'Aucun amour au monde ne peut tenir lieu de l'amour' ('No love in the world can take the place of love', *PC*, 168; 161).

Desire, in Duras's early novels, combines a powerful fascination with the possibilities of fusion with a realisation that the paradoxical condition of such a merging of identities or bodies is sexual difference itself. Fusion between bodies is a precarious state. To yield to it other than exceptionally is in fact to forfeit love; to preserve the possibility of desire it is necessary to reiterate difference. Suzanne in *Un barrage contre le Pacifique* is clear on this point. Though after intercourse with Agosti she vows to herself: 'Que dans l'amour les différences puissent s'annuler à ce point, elle ne l'oublierait plus' ('That love could abolish physical differences to such an extent she would never forget', *B*, 343; 270), she confesses to him there was never any thought in her mind of marriage (*B*, 354; 278). To remain apart from Agosti is the price Suzanne willingly pays for the new understanding, the 'intelligence nouvelle' (*B*, 356; 280) of sexual desire she has acquired as a result of this first experience.

In their disdain for socially legitimised relationships, Duras's characters are disturbingly anti-essentialist in questions of love or desire. Duras shows more interest in infidelity or flirtatiousness than in love as a process of enduring idealisation or sublimation. Desire is always already founded on a recognition of the prohibition that makes the object of desire remote and unattainable. As a result, it often turns out in Duras (as, for instance, in a novel like *Le Vice-consul*) that it is not satisfaction which is the culmination of desire but rather the realisation of the necessary impossibility of satisfaction. Desire, accordingly, is transmuted into a form of radical disbelief, and what Duras's early novels dramatise is how, repetitive and indestructible though desire is, love relations are also necessarily finite. The intensity of desire is matched only by the provisional quality of its realisation. Object choices in Duras are never fixed; a constant process of substitution or displacement is always affecting the object of desire. Love, here, is perpetual motion, and it is perhaps only at the end of *Les Petits Chevaux de Tarquinia* that Duras calls a temporary halt to this desirous sexual wandering, when she imposes on her protagonist Sara, after her brief adventure with a man named Jean (to the sound of *Blue Moon* [*PC*, 112; 107], as if in anticipation of *India Song* or *La Femme du Gange* twenty years later), an ill-advised, conventional marital reconciliation.

As desire begins to wander in this way in Duras, it generates its own peculiar logic of repetition and substitution. This is particularly evident in Duras's two best-known novels from the 1950s, *Le Square* and *Moderato cantabile*. The first of these, later adapted for the stage, is almost entirely in the form of an impromptu dialogue between an itinerant pedlar and a domestic servant, accompanied by the small child in her charge, who meet one afternoon in a Paris municipal garden and exchange experiences and hopes for the future.[3] They are a humble pair, amongst the socially lowest of the low, 'les derniers des derniers' (*S*, 65; 46), and the fate they share, like many of the people that figure in Duras's journalism of the later 1950s, is their exclusion from any established community. They live isolated and unskilled lives, without partners or children of their own, and have no special qualities other than the modesty of their needs or desires.

But despite their shared lack of status, Duras offers her characters no immediate mutual solidarity. She eschews facile or patronising sentimentality to emphasise the considerable differences that exist between the two, reflected in age, gender, and occupation. Their common condition is thus more a negative state than a positive one. While the pedlar, for instance, struggles to make the best of his meagre life without envisaging any significant new initiative, the maid, for her part, believes any temporary amelioration will only deflect her from decisive action. If his life makes him despair of the possibility of change, she, by contrast, is so desperate that radical change seems the only possibility worth envisaging. But this simple opposition is complicated later by the realisation that the woman, in her commitment to radical change, retains an attitude of relative passivity, while the man, settling complacently for his modest lot, adopts a more openly pragmatic approach to his existence. The differences between the protagonists are not static, and the positions of the two interlocutors shift and change as the dialogue between them develops.

Le Square, famously, consists almost entirely of such dialogue. But while casting the novel in this theatrical manner, Duras also uses a non-naturalistic, stylised mode of language that runs counter to realist expectations about the manner of conversation of the poor and the uneducated. As Blanchot points out, the excessive linguistic formality that *Le Square* displays works to rather paradoxical effect.[4] At first, the hesitant courtesy with which the two address each other suggests aloofness or distance. But this in turn implies not so much verbal facility as awkwardness and a lack of familiarity with conversational idiom. These function more as a sign of vulnerability than strength. Duras's two interlocutors do not inhabit their language with any confidence or security; rather, what is voiced in the language of *Le Square* is the sheer difficulty associated for them with intimate conversation. The excess of words is indicative therefore not of linguistic ease but of a painful state of divorce from language. It is as though within the very words of *Le Square* there is something like an absence from words; and this itself is a function of the state of exclusion from community that makes communication both problematic and hazardous for the pair.

However, like any prohibition, this state of exclusion works as a powerful stimulant, and in the lack of common speech demonstrated by the speakers in *Le Square* there is arguably more striving for mutual understanding than if communication had been taken for granted. Paradoxically, it is the failure of language to achieve self-evident communication that makes real dialogue possible, and this realisation in Duras is a first step towards a more creative use of language. Dialogue painfully articulated in *Le Square* becomes a basis for the sharing of intense emotion. Accordingly, as each of the two protagonists describes for the other their hopes and wishes for the future, each projects or transfers onto the other an image corresponding to what she or he desires the other to be. And it is that image which the other slowly comes to embody like a theatrical understudy or a double.

So, as the maid voices her need to be chosen by another – a man, for instance, who might marry her (*S*, 70; 50) – it is evident that in the dialogue of *Le Square*, though in unexpected fashion, she has already found that other by whom she might be, as she puts it, 'prise au sérieux positivement pour une fois dans ma vie' ('taken seriously just once in my life', *S*, 83; 58). And the pedlar, too, in a similar way, has arguably already found in dialogue with her that possibility of communication that is also a possibility of love. Dialogue in *Le Square*, by its very existence, tempers the state of exclusion to which both partners are confined while also underscoring the differences between them that make the dialogue both necessary and painful. It connects what was hitherto unconnected while respecting singularity and separation; it represents the possibility of a mode of desire that is both a striving for fusion and an affirmation of difference.

This possibility for desire has as its emblem the image of the setting sun. There is probably no more common or more recurrent motif in the whole of Duras's work, where it functions as a sign of climactic revelation, an allegorical fable of merging opposites and imminent separation. As in other texts, so too in *Le Square*, when towards the middle of the book the pedlar recounts how three years before, in another city, while looking for a restaurant, he had wandered by chance into the zoological gardens. What followed was an unexpected moment of intense happiness as a sense of his own singular fate mingled with a powerful feeling of communion with others:

> Dès que je suis entré dans ce jardin, je suis devenu un homme comblé par la vie. [. . .] Eh bien, j'ai été tout à coup aussi à l'aise dans ce jardin que s'il avait été fait pour moi autant que pour les autres. Comme si, je ne saurais vous dire mieux, j'avais grandi brusquement et que je devenais enfin à la hauteur des événements de ma propre vie. [. . .] La brise s'était donc levée, la lumière est devenue jaune de miel, et les lions eux-mêmes, qui flambaient de tout leur poil, bâillaient du plaisir d'être là.

L'air sentait à la fois le feu et les lions et je le respirais comme l'odeur même d'une fraternité qui enfin me concernait. Tous les passants étaient attentifs les uns aux autres et se délassaient dans cette lumière de miel. Je me souviens, je trouvais qu'ils ressemblaient aux lions. J'ai été heureux brusquement.

(The moment I entered those gardens, I was someone whose life was fulfilled. [. . .] Suddenly in that park I was so completely at home that it might have been made for me just as much as for everybody else. I don't know how to put it any better, except to say that it was as if I had suddenly grown up and become, for the first time, equal to my life. [. . .] The wind had got up, the light turned the colour of honey and even the lions, with their manes glowing in the setting sun, were yawning with the pleasure of being there. The air smelt of fire and the lions and I breathed it in as though it were the very fragrance of a community of which I was, at last, a part. All the passers-by were mindful of one another and basked in the evening light. I remember thinking they were like the lions. And suddenly I was happy.)

(*S*, 54–5; 38–9)

Poised between day and night, ending and beginning, communion and isolation, obscurity and conflagration (the pedlar's word for the honey-coloured glow of the sun is 'l'incendie' [*S*, 61; 43]), what this experience signifies for Duras's pedlar is the possibility of hope, hope detached from any specific object, just hope, in other words, what Duras calls the hope of hope: 'l'espoir de l'espoir' (*S*, 55; 40). The setting sun encapsulates extremes of light and dark; its power of illumination seems to be at its most intense when nightfall is at its most threatening. Sunset, in Duras's writing, is an image of violence as well as metamorphosis. As such, it functions most clearly as an apocalyptic emblem: it designates that moment when extremes meet and illumination comes forth from catastrophe. So at his moment of starkest penury the pedlar has a glimpse of something other that will allow him – momentarily – to rediscover hope, and entirely supplant his need for food or drink.

The pedlar's epiphany has two functions in *Le Square*. First, it acts as a partial prefiguring of the encounter in the municipal garden. As the pedlar tells his story to the maid, the two gardens merge, and there is some indication that the pedlar will re-enact his earlier experience at the zoo in his meeting with the maid. It is significant in this respect that *Le Square* itself begins in late afternoon, at 4.30 p.m., and concludes with the two protagonists lingering in the garden against the backdrop of a golden (*S*, 137; 95), then reddish (*S*, 146; 101) sunset. The novel also ends on the possibility that the pair will go dancing together at the weekend at the nearby 'bal de la Croix-Nivert' (*S*, 141; 98); dancing here, as in many other texts by Duras, is a metaphor for the deferred promise of sexual pleasure. But this prospect of a happy end is left unconfirmed. After all, the pedlar's story of revelation was only a story, perhaps designed merely to impress, and it is clear from *Le Square*, as from earlier novels, that the possibility of love does not erase the fact of difference; there is no guarantee in Duras that love will ever give rise to a love story. It seems unlikely that the encounter will have a sequel. Nonetheless, at the very end, the 1955 version of the novel suggested that the pedlar (and reader) might take some encouragement as to the possibility of a happy resolution; but in 1989 the author was more sceptical, preferring silently to excise this closing sentence.[5]

The pedlar's tale of epiphany has a second function in *Le Square*. It demonstrates the extent to which desire in Duras is inseparable from repetition. In *Le Square*, identities become like theatrical roles: the pedlar acts out the role of the man who may choose the maid; she plays for him the part of the woman he wishes to protect and care for. Each of these roles is a re-enactment of a past founded less in reality than in fantasy and need. Like the pedlar recalling his experience in the zoo, both protagonists imagine their future as the double of a past that is lost or unavailable, perhaps even non-existent, and survives only – as for the pedlar – as an apocalyptic memory or – as with the maid – a dream of apocalyptic transformation.

To desire, Duras's novel suggests, is to repeat or re-enact the past in anticipation of the future, but repetition here is a dynamic process that does not respect identity. Rather it constantly remodels and transforms the present in the light of the past. Repetition is like a rhythm marking out the insistent but ever-changing temporality of desire. It drives Duras's characters towards the future, and in so doing gives *Le Square* the texture of an impromptu or inadvertent play, one which follows a pattern of rehearsal, re-enactment, and speculation, in which the other is always playing the part of a double in a mise-en-scène scripted by the person opposite. The result is to transform the municipal garden in which the dialogue is set into a theatrical stage upon which positions of desire are articulated and acted out.

In 1974, in *Les Parleuses*, Duras commented to Xavière Gauthier that the real purpose of *Le Square* was not to write a love story but to explore the theory of needs, 'la théorie des besoins' (*P*, 67; 44). The remark is a reference to Dionys Mascolo's book, *Le Communisme*, published in 1953, two years before Duras's novel.[6] The aim of the work was to develop an approach to communism based not on socio-political or economic arguments but on ethical ones. To do this, Mascolo's first move was to appeal to a much expanded concept of material needs. He argued that it was inadequate to recognise merely material necessity – the need for food, drink, and shelter – as the basic threshold which had to be crossed before human life could be sustained and acknowledged as fully human. A theory of needs, Mascolo proposed, had to go much further and develop an understanding of the intersubjective dimension of human life. This meant attaching importance to the need for self-expression and acknowledgement by others, for language and community. This list of needs became a list of fundamental human exigencies; it was the basis for an ethics and, thus, a radical politics. Need, in all its forms, Mascolo maintained, had to be seen in materialist terms; by creating inequalities and maintaining oppression, social and historical conditions were what hindered the legitimate satisfaction of human needs. It was the task of politics to devise ways of satisfying all human needs in a just and equal way; communism, he suggested, was nothing more than 'le mouvement de la satisfaction des besoins matériels' ('the movement towards the alleviation of material needs').[7]

The theory of needs does not refer human experience to already constituted external values, which for Mascolo were likely to be prescriptive and repressive. It starts rather from the view that what humans have in common is what they lack. Drawing for instance on the 1844 Manuscripts of the early Marx, Mascolo commented that

> l'universalité du besoin est négative: elle est l'universalité du manque. C'est le point où le besoin est *le besoin d'être un homme*, qui s'identifie à son tour avec le pur et simple besoin de communication.[8]

> (the universality of need is a negative entity; it is the universality of lack, and the point at which need is *the need to be human*, which in turn is nothing other than the need for communication pure and simple.)

As these words show, it was important for Mascolo in the last resort to identify material need with the need for communication. This enabled him to put forward a version of communism based on the pluralist idea of a community of difference, and not the cynically bureaucratic exercise of authority (as was the case with the PCF, from which Mascolo, like Duras, had already been expelled). The concept of need, for Mascolo, functioned as a kind of radical origin prior to determinate desires or political objectives; it provided – he hoped – the foundation for an ethics of communication or community that would be valid for aesthetics as well as politics.

Such an ethics would not be prescriptive. For Mascolo, communication meant nothing if it was not the communication of difference; and it would be an empty word if it failed to challenge established values in the name of everything – including both individuals and their experiences – that was reduced to silence or deprived of legitimate expression by society. Particularly crucial for Mascolo's political project, then, were all those that society chose to exclude from representation: the very poor, immigrants, the indigenous peoples of the colonies, the disenfranchised workers of Eastern Europe. These were the ones whose lives illustrated most vividly the nature of fundamental material needs and who lived closest to the limit between what was and was not recognisable as human. And it was Mascolo's belief, which he put to the test by campaigning on behalf of the Algerian Resistance and the pre-Solidarity Polish workers' movement, that the experience of the dispossessed was the only legitimate touchstone for a type of communism that remained ethically open to difference as well as politically committed to solidarity and community.

Duras's characters in *Le Square* are not only subjects of desire, then, but also, in Mascolo's sense, subjects of need. Their desires are not directed towards a distinct object, but address a prior, more fundamental question: the need to be acknowledged by another as a desiring human subject. The maid's yearning for a man, or for possessions – such as a refrigerator or gas-stove (*S*, 36–8; 25–7) – is not one simple passion amongst others, it voices a need for recognition. Desire here rests on the need for communication, and it is only when that need is satisfied that the maid will be able to affirm her desires as her own. In this regard, the regular references to hunger and thirst with which the child punctuates the adults' dialogue are programmatic; they suggest that in their search for love the pedlar and the maid are engaged in a process as basic as the child's craving for food and drink: 'Seule, tenez,' the maid reminds the pedlar, in a moment of despondency, 'sans amour aucun, je crois que je me laisserais mourir de faim' ('Alone, without love, I think I should just die of hunger', *S*, 104; 73). As these words imply, desire in Duras always exceeds its object; it is not just a promiscuous state of body or mind, but has radical ethical and political implications, too. Desire for Duras is an affirmation of fundamental values; it is what divides humanity from inhumanity, or life from death, while itself having a foot in both camps. Correspondingly, it is also what communicates, often to disturbing effect, with the problematic margins of human experience: violence, loss of identity, human destruction, and death.

If *Le Square* dramatises desire as a category of fundamental need, *Moderato cantabile*, Duras's next novel, published in 1958, goes further in staging desire as a violently transgressive experience.[9] The plot of the novel is melodramatic, even lurid. The book opens with the murder of an unnamed woman by her male lover in a café, and traces the effects of the crime on two chance and incomplete witnesses, Anne Desbaresdes, the mother of a small boy taking music lessons in a flat overlooking the scene, and Chauvin, the man she meets in the café the following day, with whom she explores and finally acts out, metaphorically, the killing she has witnessed. Like other texts by Duras, the novel is circular in structure; it begins explosively, with a climactic event, only to linger on the deferred effects of this beginning.

As a result, reading *Moderato cantabile*, like *Le Square*, is mainly a matter of making sense of textual repetition. Repetition operates on two levels. The first of these is plot, with the repeated meetings between Anne and Chauvin being staged in such a way that Duras's two protagonists re-enact the – imagined – events that led up to the murder. The novel concludes with a scene that clearly invokes the earlier killing. Secondly, repetition has an important function on the level of narrative discourse. Distributed throughout the text is a wealth of recurrent motifs or images that organise meaning by a process of metonymic association or juxtaposition; they include for instance numerous allusions to the sunset and the sea, repeated references to music, magnolia flowers, and childbirth, as well as the insistent recourse to the theme of looking, or the use of colour symbolism to link, say, the blood of the murder victim with the wine that Anne drinks to excess in her encounters with Chauvin.

However, despite the frequency of these repetitive effects, they fall short of establishing any firm pattern of narrative causality. The actions in the book are not explained by reference to established social or psychological norms, with the result that by the end of the novel the exact nature of the relation between the murder scene and the meetings of Anne and Chauvin is still to be elucidated. There are of course a number of ways in which it is possible to construe that relation: one can for instance read the murder as prefiguring – in positive manner – the violent intensity of Anne's encounter with Chauvin; or the murder can be understood as indicating a risk of further violence and as a warning which Anne rightly heeds when, on the very last page, she finally walks away from Chauvin; alternatively, the murder may be viewed not as a real event, but more as a sado-masochistic fantasy that Anne endeavours to act out by allowing herself a taste of dockland lowlife; but perhaps, in that case, the murder scene ought to be seen less as an act of violence than as a dream of intense passion that reveals the dispiriting banality of Anne's everyday married life.

From the outset, however, *Moderato cantabile* resists the imposition of any single frame of interpretation that would allow these dilemmas to be resolved. Various possibilities of reading co-exist in the text without any one version being privileged to the detriment of the others. Ambiguity and ambivalence are endemic; and like many of Duras's novels, the book is set in a world of blurred margins and uncertain border zones. The town in the novel is by the sea, as often in Duras, and the action unfolds in the morally (and sexually) dubious environment of the harbour. Similarly, when the novel opens, the time of day, as in *Le Square*, is mid-afternoon, and the sky is poised, in apocalyptic manner, between luminosity and obscurity, the intensity of the sun matched by the inevitability of its progressive decline. And when the murder does happen, Anne hesitates, not knowing whether what has taken place is something or nothing (*MC*, 10; 5); the reader may well ask the same, uncertain whether the killing, taking place as it does at the very start of the novel, should be taken as a rehearsal or a performance, a real event or a quotation from some pulp melodrama, an actual occurrence or a figment of the imagination.

The murder scene enjoys a peculiar status in the novel. First, it is a dramatic, even melodramatic scene, which takes on the compulsive fascination of a visual fantasy. Anne, when she goes to view the immediate aftermath of the crime, is in the position of a theatrical spectator; rooted to the spot yet distanced from the scene, she looks on with all the intensity associated with an absolute activity (the word here is: 'voir', used intransitively). And what she sees is a kind of darkened theatrical stage:

Au fond du café, dans la pénombre de l'arrière-salle, une femme était étendue par terre, inerte. Un homme, couché sur elle, agrippé à ses épaules, l'appelait calmement.
– Mon amour. Mon amour.

(At the far end of the café, in the semi-darkness of the back room, a woman was lying motionless on the floor. A man was lying on her, clutching her by the shoulders, and calling out in a calm voice:
'My love. My love.')

(*MC*, 14; 19)

Dramatised in this way, with the murderer echoing Anne's own words to her son (*MC*, 11; 16), and the text linking desire and pain by suggesting some similarity between the victim's cry and Anne's own experience of childbirth (*MC*, 30; 43), the scene has all the qualities of an unconscious fantasy, with Anne more an active participant in the scene than just an external spectator.

This is confirmed by the second important role the murder plays in *Moderato cantabile*. For as well as being a powerful inaugural event, the scene also functions as a latent subtext implicit in the ensuing dialogue. The murder provides Anne and Chauvin with their sole topic of conversation, and thus, in the theatrical sense of the term, with their text; and at times it is evident that the personal pronouns used to refer to the murderer and his victim have begun to apply more convincingly to Anne and Chauvin themselves (*MC*, 40; 57). Like the protagonists of *Le Square*, they become caught up in the transferential re-actualisation of an earlier episode. As a result, the line of demarcation between the main plot and the frame narrative is erased; it can no longer be said which of the two takes logical precedence. The two sets of events reflect each other like an infinite series of mirror images, and it is impossible to decide which story events are repeating or rehearsing which others, or which chain of actions is a metaphorical transposition of the other. As a result, any point of origin is lost and the distinction between literal and figurative, proper and improper, real and imagined seems no longer applicable.

To an extent, this crisis of understanding is already implicit in the murder scene itself. It provides a disturbing image of desire and violence mingling as one. This, for instance, is what Anne sees when a photographer's flashbulb momentarily illuminates the scene:

Dans la lueur du magnésium, on put voir que la femme était

jeune encore et qu'il y avait du sang qui coulait de sa bouche
en minces filets épars et qu'il y en avait aussi sur le visage de
l'homme qui l'avait embrassée. [. . .]

Il resta là, dans une résolution apparemment tranquille,
agrippé de nouveau à elle de ses deux bras, le visage collé au
sien, dans le sang de sa bouche.

(By the glare of the flashbulb the crowd could see that the
woman was still young, and that blood was coming from her
mouth in thin trickles, and that there was blood on the man's
face where he had kissed her. [. .]

He lay there, seemingly resolute and calm, holding her tightly
in his arms, his face pressed to hers, in the blood flowing from
her mouth.)

(*MC*, 15; 20–1)

Here, the symbolism of blood has a dual function. The mingling of
blood in the murderer's mouth is a powerful sign of intense erotic
fusion between the two bodies; but it also underlines the finality of
death and the unbridgeable divide it enacts. Desire here is in the
mode of oral eroticism: the aim is to merge with the object of
desire by incorporating it; in the process, however, the object itself
is destroyed and can no longer be perceived as different and therefore desirable. The culmination of desire is finally an abolition of
desire. As a result, the distinction between desire and aggression,
fusion and difference is lost; and the situation raises some of the
same issues as does Bataille when he describes eroticism, famously,
as the affirmation of life beyond death, 'l'approbation de la vie
jusque dans la mort'.[10] At some stage in *Moderato cantabile*, the
border between life and death has become confused. Similarly, the
difference between symbolic and literal is suspended, yielding to a
crime passionnel whose distinguishing trait is that it is not so much
mitigated by overwhelming passion as committed as the logical
dénouement of that passion.

Reader reactions to the scene of desire and murder in Duras's
novel are bound to be mixed. The novel itself already acknowledges
as much by allocating a range of contradictory reponses to the
bystanders who witness the crime. These include curiosity, pity,
repugnance, annoyance, shock, condemnation, fascination, even
admiration. But by mentioning each of these virtual interpretations
of the murder in turn, the novel endeavours to illustrate their
inadequacy. None of these single reactions measures up to the
ambivalence contained in the scene. Each one fails to formulate

the dynamic of desire at work in the murder; as a result, desire remains an enigma that exceeds meaning. It is mobilised by Duras as a sublime and transgressive force that overwhelms any single effort at understanding. Demarcation lines are effaced, and it is difficult as a consequence even to know to what genre *Moderato cantabile* itself belongs, whether it should be read, for instance, as romantic melodrama or serious fiction, as high art or low sensationalism, and whether in fact the killing of a woman by her lover should be taken as an elaborate literary conceit or as an occasion for anger and indignation on the part of the novel's readers.

These difficulties are not gratuitous. Duras's refusal to subordinate desire to any prescriptive moral code is one of the main sources of disturbance and provocation in *Moderato cantabile*. But here, as in *Le Square*, ethical concerns outweigh moral ones; Duras's main interest is not in determining the morality and meaning of desire but in exploring the problematic aspects of experience that are silenced or repressed by normative discourse. In desire, as the murder scene in *Moderato cantabile* shows, one cannot tell what is literal or proper from what is figural or improper; and this loss of origin severely undermines the competence of any moral code to decide what is and is not legitimate or acceptable in the realm of desire. As the story of Anne and Chauvin shows, desire, like fantasy, is governed by a logic of deferred action such that the meaning of a scene like the one that opens *Moderato cantabile* cannot be determined in advance; meaning, if at all, can only be furnished belatedly, as it is by Anne and Chauvin, as the result of a transferential re-enactment or repetition of the scene by its interpreters. Such repetition, however, does not supply a stable meaning with any claim to universality. Desire exists singularly and in the future perfect tense: what Anne and Chauvin are at the outset is what they will have become by the end of their story.

In *Moderato cantabile*, past and future, violence and desire converge. Meaning encounters non-meaning and the scope of narrative becomes a problematic one. As extremes meet in this way, they do so against the backdrop of an apocalyptic sunset that works in the story like a kind of theatrical spotlight, projecting the shadows of the two protagonists against the rear wall of the café, as though they were just actors in some mythic ritual (*MC*, 33; 46). The effect is obscurity as well as illumination, metamorphosis as well as innocence. The murder, as reinvented in the conversations between Anne and Chauvin, is seen to enshrine some reciprocal bond of mutual desire. The word for this bond, as Duras's two characters formulate it, is surprising, but it is the same as in *Le Square*; the word is hope, 'l'espoir'. The following exchange makes clear what is at stake; Anne begins, referring to the murderer and his victim, but also to herself and Chauvin:

> – Du moment qu'il avait compris qu'elle désirait tant qu'il le fasse, je voudrais que vous me disiez pourquoi il ne l'a pas fait, par exemple, un peu plus tard ou . . . un peu plus tôt.
> – Vous savez, je sais très peu de choses. Mais je crois qu'il ne pouvait pas arriver à avoir une préférence, il ne devait pas en sortir, de la vouloir autant vivante que morte. Il a dû réussir très tard seulement à se la préférer morte. Je ne sais rien. [. . .]
> – Elle avait beaucoup d'espoir qu'il y arriverait.
> – Il me semble que son espoir à lui d'y arriver devait être égal au sien. Je ne sais rien.

> ('Once he had realised how much she wanted him to do it, I'd like you to tell me why he didn't do it, say, a little later or . . . a little sooner.'
> 'Really, I know very little about it. But I think that he couldn't make up his mind, couldn't decide whether he wanted her alive or dead. He must have decided very late that he preferred her dead. But that's pure conjecture.' [. . .]
> 'She hoped very much that he would manage to do it.'
> 'It seems to me that he must have hoped so just as much as she did. I don't know really.')

(*MC*, 62; 89–90)

Oscillating between life and death, ending and beginning, love here becomes an apocalyptic event, one that destroys as it reveals, and reveals as it destroys.

In *Moderato cantabile*, Duras takes as her theme the enigmatic, unspeakable character of sexual desire, and tells a story of love and desire that is a tale of merging identities but also of irreconcilable differences. In this way Duras dramatises at one and the same time, in the same text, both of the – contradictory – modern myths that govern contemporary understanding of sexual desire: the myth of love as a fusing of self with other, and the myth of sexuality as an inescapable curse of difference and mutual exclusion. Both myths, interestingly, are embodied most convincingly in literary or fictional works, and it is as though there were some secret complicity between writing and desire, literature and love. For her part, Duras in her work merges both myths into one, producing a version of

Proust's *Sodome et Gomorrhe* to the music of Wagner's *Tristan and Isolde*, unless it is the reverse. And by counterposing the one against the other, Duras subjects both these fictional versions of love to a literally catastrophic sense of their own fragility.

Moderato cantabile ends on an ambiguous note. The final scene of the novel provides an explicit echo of the murder scene, but does so in a manner which is difficult to determine as either simply positive or negative. As a result, the ending functions both as the completion of a ritualised enactment and as its deliberate effacement. Within repetition there is also a refusal to repeat; and within the refusal to repeat a new desire for re-enactment begins. The end, like the apocalyptic sunset that Duras is careful to mention as Anne gets up to leave, functions as an opening as well as a closing. And the last exchange between Anne and Chauvin is in the form of a shorthand summary of much of what has taken place in the novel:

> – Je voudrais que vous soyez morte, dit Chauvin.
> – C'est fait, dit Anne Desbaresdes.

> ('I wish you were dead,' Chauvin said.
> 'I am,' said Anne Desbaresdes.)

(*MC*, 84; 119)

Charged as it is with apocalyptic associations of finality and revelation, Anne's phrase is a resonant, if elliptical one, implying completion as well as release. It is a formula that recurs elsewhere, in a number of Duras's early novels, where it functions as a leitmotif signifying intense desire as well as separation or death. Thus, in *La Vie tranquille*, it serves to mark the burial of Jérôme (*VT*, 42), but also the beginning of Françou's intense first love for Tiène ('C'est fait,' she admits. 'J'aime. J'aime Tiène' [*VT*, 130]); in *Le Marin de Gibraltar*, the phrase twice refers to the narrator's decision to leave his girlfriend and go in search of new desires (*MG*, 54, 143; 39, 104); in *Les Petits Chevaux de Tarquinia* (*PC*, 38; 36), it records the last efforts of an elderly couple to piece together the scattered fragments of their son's body after he accidentally steps on a landmine even before the novel begins (and there are obvious echoes here of the inaugural violence that sets *Moderato cantabile* in motion); and in the story 'Des journées entières dans les arbres', Jacques tells his mother how he has made the necessary arrangements for her to leave – and release them both from the effects of their stifling love for one another – with the words: 'C'est fait' ('It's done', *J*, 95; 65), adding only, to himself, a few moments later: 'Qu'elle meure, mais qu'elle meure' ('Let her die, please let her die', *J*, 96; 66).

In these early novels, the formula is used to punctuate the action and introduce at key turns in the narrative an ambivalent mixture of death, violence, desire, love, and aggression. In *Moderato cantabile* the apocalyptic associations of the phrase are made more explicit. But they are not peculiar to this text. In *Le Square*, for instance, the maid uses the phrase to convey her sense of impending disaster, notably her fear that a sudden change in her life might rob her of her innocence (*S*, 41; 29). But she is not to realise, as the novel goes on to show, that her life will not remain untouched; and her only recourse is to greet the disaster of change as a possibility of renewal. And in *Dix heures et demie du soir en été*, in 1960, though the context is very different, the lesson is the same. Against the backdrop of another apocalyptic sunset, from which the novel takes its title, the protagonist Maria contemplates the end of her relationship with Pierre, who has fallen in love with their best friend Claire; her response is to try to salvage from imminent disaster her own sudden but intense desire for Rodrigo, the murderer she glimpses by chance at the very same moment and rescues, only for him in turn to commit suicide in despair at having earlier killed his own wife. And at each turning of the plot, as it interweaves these twin strands of separation and desire, is the same apocalyptic formula in many of its modes and tenses: 'A l'aurore, c'en sera fait' ('At dawn, it will all be over', *DH*, 42, 128); 'Est-ce fait?' ('Was it over?', *DH*, 47; 132); 'Ça va être fait' ('It will soon be over', *DH*, 138; 199); and, finally, once more, as Pierre and Claire consummate their love and bring to a conclusion the process of separation from Maria: 'C'est fait' ('It's done', *DH*, 139; 201).[11]

There is, in addition, another important text by Duras in which the formula: 'C'est fait' is used, and with similar apocalyptic effect. This is an early version of the story *L'Homme assis dans le couloir*, written soon after *Moderato cantabile* and published for the first time in 1962. (The story is of course better known in the rewritten version Duras brought out in 1980, in which the phrase 'C'est fait' no longer appears.[12]) In many respects, as the large number of lexical and thematic echoes indicate, *L'Homme assis dans le couloir* – in both versions – is a reworking of the scene of desire and violence at the centre of *Moderato cantabile*. The story ends, for instance (at any rate in the 1980 text, since the conclusion is lacking in 1962), rather as the novel had begun, with the image of a man lying, weeping, across the woman who is his lover and whom he has perhaps just killed (*HC2*, 36). Some pages earlier, in the same vein, Duras states blandly of the man speaking to the woman: 'Il lui dit qu'il voudrait ne plus l'aimer. [. . .] Il lui dit qu'un jour il va la tuer' ('He tells her that he would like not to love her any more. [. . .] He tells her that one day he is going to kill her', *HC2*, 31–2; 274); and the woman replies to the effect that yes, she would like to die ('elle voudrait mourir', *HC2*, 33; 274). But if *L'Homme assis dans le couloir* re-enacts the scene from *Moderato cantabile* it also makes it more explicit. In the later work, Duras is no longer staging a symbolically veiled, deferred repetition of sexual violence but directly describing the act itself; yet as in the novel Duras still refuses to adopt within her story any moral perspective on the man's brutality as he kicks the woman's body over the stony ground, or on the woman's expressed desire to have her face pummelled and beaten by him (*HC2*, 32; 274).

Mingling sexual pleasure and violence in this way, *L'Homme assis dans le couloir* is a disturbing and provocative text; it has left many readers wondering, like Marcelle Marini, whether the work might not best be described as pornographic. However, as Marini concedes, the rhetorical complexity of the story makes it impossible to attribute the text to any ready-made literary category. This is particularly clear if one compares the 1980 version of the story to the fragmentary 1962 text. The many modifications Duras makes to the work allow one to see how she is at pains to develop a coherent literary strategy to deal with what is easily her most intractable material.

These alterations, affecting every aspect of the text, from vocabulary to sentence structure, narrative voice, setting, and even character, are too numerous to mention in any detail. However, much hinges on the structural changes Duras incorporates into the rewritten version, chief among which is the introduction of an unnamed first-person narrator in the role of supernumerary observer. With the shift in narrative voice comes a shift in mode. The 1962 text had begun in the present tense and concluded, albeit rather oddly, in the narrative past (the French *passé simple*); the 1980 version, however, though also mainly in the present, refers to the main events that punctuate the action in the conditional. Thus, for instance, to the opening sentence of the 1962 version, which reads: 'L'homme assis dans le couloir, à quelques mètres de la porte d'entrée, regarde Anne-Marie Stretter' ('The man seated in the passage, a few yards from the front door, is watching Anne-Marie Stretter', *HC1*, 70), the 1980 text, as though to cite and displace the earlier beginning, responds with the words: 'L'homme aurait été assis dans l'ombre du couloir face à la porte ouverte sur le dehors' ('The man might be said to be seated in the obscurity of the passage facing the front door', *HC2*, 7; 268). This change in tense is more than a figure of style, for it must be remembered that in French, as Duras reminds readers of *Le Camion* (*C*, 89), the conditional is a tense not of definite events, but of conjecture, allegation, unconfirmed report, and theatricality. As it begins, then, the 1980 version, removing the act of looking from the male protagonist to make him first an object of vision before he looks at the woman again, affirms itself not as a representation of events, but more plausibly as an exploration or enactment of fantasy.

A number of consequences flow from this self-presentation of the text as fantasy. The first concerns the status of the narrator. In her introduction to the rewritten text, published in *Les Cahiers du cinéma*, Duras describes the narrative voice as an authorial surrogate, a figure of the author as spectator.[13] But as such, the voice is surprisingly mobile in its positioning throughout the story. At times it sides with the male figure and narrates events from his viewpoint, at other moments it stages the action from the visual perspective of the woman. Referring at one point to the woman's face, the text reads: 'Je ne vois rien que son ovale détourné, le méplat très pur, tendu. Je crois que les yeux fermés devraient être verts. Mais je m'arrête aux yeux' ('I see only the averted oval of her face, the drawn purity of its plane. I think her eyes, though closed, must be green. But I go no further than the eyes', *HA2*, 13; 269); but, a few paragraphs later, the text continues: 'Nous entendons que l'on marche elle et moi. Qu'il a bougé' ('We hear the sound of someone walking, she and I. We hear that he has stirred', *HA2*, 14; 269). From one passage to the next, the narrative voice has shifted its allegiance from the place of the man observing to that of the woman listening. Finally, the voice detaches itself from both these positions to report to each protagonist what the other is doing: 'Je lui parle et je lui dis ce que l'homme fait. Je lui dis aussi ce qu'il advient d'elle' ('I speak to her and tell her what the man is doing. I also tell him what is happening to her', *HA2*, 16–17; 270).

The sliding of narrative viewpoint from male to female and back again is not restricted to the narrative discourse. It is reflected, in the 1980 text, in some of the language Duras uses to name the sexual organs of her two protagonists. Thus the woman's pubic area, as often in French, is referred to as 'le sexe' (*HC2*, 16; 270), in the masculine; while the feminine pronoun 'elle', with no explicit antecedent (but which might plausibly have been, say, *'la verge'), is the term employed for the man's penis and testicles (*HC2*, 24–5; 272). And, similarly, the man's anal cavity is described as 'la caverne de l'homme' (*HC2*, 30; 273). This slippage or transfer of gender marks repeats on the level of textual discourse the sexual mingling of bodies taking place in the diegesis. The merging of identities is consistent, of course, with the fantasy status of the text; but it also challenges the representational stability of the fiction, making it impossible for the reader simply to construe the text as a crudely pornographic depiction of a violent heterosexual encounter.

This mobility of gender position in respect of both vocabulary and narrative voice also militates strongly against voyeurism, if one understands by that a position of controlling subjective anxiety, an attempt to fix what is not there (which, in Freudian terms, would be thematised as the maternal phallus) within a tightly controlled fetishistic scenario in which the role of the missing member is taken by some appropriately stiffened object or signifier.[14] In Duras's text, signalled by the slippages in the narrative voice, there is a fluidity or excess that challenges the constriction of such a representational scene. This excess is crucial; and indeed, when adapting *L'Homme assis dans le couloir* for the stage, Duras emphasised the point herself by dividing up the text among three different actors, two female and one male, each of whom at various points in the story speaks in the first person.

Staging the text in this way also underlines to what extent the story functions as a circulation of differentiated looks, ranging from that of the man gazing commandingly at the woman's body from his place in the shade (*HC2*, 7; 268), to that of the narrator surveying the boundless immensity that surrounds the scene like some indeterminable frame (*HC2*, 26; 272), and, finally, the woman herself, whose half-open or closed eyes resist capture and allow her a peculiarly half-lit vision of the scene around her (*HC2*, 8–9; 268). However, this reference to half-closed eyes does not constitute evidence, as some critics have assumed, of the woman's passivity as the object of a dominant male gaze, for as Duras's text makes clear, though the woman is being looked at intently by the man, she herself knows this, with a knowledge that is itself a powerful form of seeing. As the narrator affirms: 'Elle le sait les yeux fermés comme je le sais moi, moi qui regarde. Il s'agit d'une certitude' ('She knows it with her eyes closed just as I do who am looking.

There's no possible doubt', *HC2*, 9; 268). (Already the 1962 text had asked, rhetorically, along similar lines: 'Les yeux fermés, ne voit-elle pas?' ['Even though her eyes are closed, can't she still see?', *HC1*, 73].)

In addition, the woman's eyes are green (*HC2*, 16; 270) and it is indicative of what is at stake here for Duras that she takes this motif of green eyes (which occurs elsewhere in her work) as emblematic of her own relation to the filmic image and uses the phrase as the title for the issue of *Les Cahiers du cinéma* she edited in June 1980, for which the rewritten version of *L'Homme assis dans le couloir* was initially intended.[15] In the story, the woman's green eyes interact – as a kind of complementary counterpart – with the colour purple (*HC2*, 22; 271) or violet (*HC2*, 35; 275) that Duras uses here (as she does in *Le Ravissement de Lol V. Stein* [*R*, 176]) for the rising haze and impending summer storm; they signal, as elsewhere in Duras, a kind of cinematographic vision in which sight and sound are not joined together under the control of a commanding voyeuristic gaze. Instead, the light is blurred ('brouillée' [*HC2*, 9; 268]), and the scene flickers between extremes of brightness and obscurity; it develops according to the pulsating rhythms of a mode of desire in which it is increasingly difficult to distinguish between subject and object, and thus ever more problematic to subordinate the text to the hierarchical polarity of spectator and screen.

This overturning of perspective is evident in the scene of fellatio at the centre of the text. Here, in a reversal of the opening incident of *Moderato cantabile* (which had shown blood on the man's lips), it is the woman who begins devouring the man's – feminised – genitals in a movement of oral enjoyment and aggression that is neither active nor passive but somehow beyond the power of that distinction. Unlike pornographic representations of oral sex, which turn on the unproblematically superior status of the penis in its role as transcendent phallus, Duras's text gives the woman the decisive, transgressive role. She it is who infringes the taboo relating to the male member and turns it from an untouchable transcendental signifier into a mythical object that no longer belongs to the man and is on the brink of being swallowed up by his partner (*HC2*, 27; 272–3). Similarly, but more painfully, the final episode of *L'Homme assis dans le couloir* is in the form of an extreme sado-masochistic encounter, with the man, at the woman's invitation, hitting her about the face, mouth, and whole body with his hand or fist (and it is here that *L'Homme assis dans le couloir*, in both versions [*HC1*, 76; *HC2*, 34; 274], remembers Chauvin's beating hand at the end of *Moderato cantabile* [*MC*, 84; 120]). The outcome of the process is not just depersonalisation but dehumanisation, too. Once more, distinctions between active and passive, pleasure and pain, self and other, lose their relevance as the two bodies become engulfed in an ecstatic but murderous ritual:

> La main descend, frappe sur les seins, le corps. Elle dit que oui, que c'est ça, oui. Ses yeux pleurent. La main bat, frappe, chaque fois plus sûre elle est en train d'atteindre une vitesse machinale.
>
> Le visage est vidé de toute expression, étourdi, il ne résiste plus du tout, lâché, il se meut autour du cou à volonté comme chose morte.

> (The hand comes down, striking the breasts, the body. She says that yes, that's it, yes. Tears flow from her eyes. The hand beats, strikes with a progressively surer aim, building up to a mechanical rhythm.
>
> The face is drained of all expression. Stunned, dazed, offering no resistance whatever, it dangles listlessly from the neck when released like a dead thing.)

(HC2, 34–5; 274)

The scene is a harrowing one and it is easy to be shocked by its violence, which seems to exceed any common notion of what is normal or acceptable in sexual intercourse. But to read it literally, as a real enactment of murder, would be to disregard the many rhetorical slippages by which Duras prevents the reader from taking up a commanding voyeuristic position. The scene works chiefly as a transposed version of heterosexual intercourse; and in this respect it exactly resembles, in kind if not intensity, the earlier episodes of the woman exposing herself provocatively to the man's gaze in a pose Duras describes as 'obscène, bestiale' ('this obscene animal pose', *HC2*, 12; 269), or of the man brutally pressing his foot down upon the woman's breasts (*HC2*, 18; 270).

Indeed, Duras's story is constructed as a sequence of such transposed scenes of intercourse and it is unclear how the reader may discriminate in these scenes between what is properly and acceptably sexual and what is not. Like *Moderato cantabile*, but more radically and with more disturbing effect, *L'Homme assis dans le couloir* demonstrates the sheer difficulty of delimiting the boundaries of the sexual or erotic. The shifting of such borders is implicit in the writing of the text. What in 1962 was the 'enclave admirable du petit visage' ('marvellous enclave of her small face', *HC1*, 73) belonging to the woman, becomes in 1980 the 'enclave du sexe entre les lèvres écartées' ('enclave of her sex wedged between the open lips', *HC2*, 12; 269). The move from mouth to vagina illustrates the precarious nature of the division between what is sexual and what is not, and, by the same token, between what may be read literally and what is metaphorical.

It would be misleading to argue that Duras, by staging in *L'Homme assis dans le couloir*, as in *Moderato cantabile*, the death of a woman at the hands of her lover, is somehow endorsing violence against women or automatically linking heterosexuality with oppression. (And the point is reinforced by the realisation that, when Duras stages this scene of desire and sexual violence elsewhere, as she does for instance in the script for *Hiroshima mon amour*, it is just as likely for it to be the woman – the film's French actress – who is found lying across the body of her dead male partner – the German soldier who was her lover under the Occupation, and is shot by a sniper; here, it is the tears in her eyes that mingle with the blood from his mouth [*H*, 44], and much the same reversal of roles is to be found, twenty years later, in the play *Agatha* [*AG*, 17].) Rather, the disturbing intensity of Duras's text lies in its refusal to moralise sexuality or normalise the excessive nature of desire. Sexuality, Duras suggests, falls beyond meaning and cannot be rationalised or contained within recognisable limits. As though to press the point home, *L'Homme assis dans le couloir* closes on a familiar mythical or apocalyptic scene as evening begins to fall and a summer storm threatens. Surrounding the scene in an immensity which is geographically indeterminate and embraces the whole of time past and to come, Duras projects her scene of desire into a realm of mythical enactments. Myth here affirms the radically transgressive and original power of desire in Duras's imagination. Desire, it seems, is like some kind of radical disaster that cannot be held within bounds; and it comes into its own when it pushes humans to the very limit of what they are. That limit, as we have seen, has the value of a catastrophic revelation.

3 Scenes of desire

I

Of all Duras's novels the one that is best known and has given rise to the most extensive commentary is without doubt her text of 1964, *Le Ravissement de Lol V. Stein*.[1] The book is also one of Duras's most complex works; it raises in obsessive but tantalising fashion many of the issues that are at the centre of all Duras's writings, among which are questions touching, for instance, on the relationship between repetition and desire, knowledge and sexual difference, madness and reason, fusion and separation, sight and speech. Many of these concerns were already clearly present in Duras's fiction of the 1950s; but with *Le Ravissement de Lol V. Stein* Duras brings to her writing a new, more radically experimental manner.

Le Ravissement de Lol V. Stein occupies an important place in Duras's work in another way. With the first overt or public mention of crucial Durassian names like Anne-Marie Stretter or S. Tahla, it inaugurates an extensive series of fictions in which characters, places, and events recur with baffling regularity and mutability as though in a never-ending round of desire (and it is not for nothing, perhaps, that love in these texts is thematised principally by use of the figure of dancing). From the mid-1960s onwards, Duras's writing becomes increasingly absorbed with the effects of transposing narrative material from one fictional context to another. The rule is one of repetition but also transformation, recurrence but also displacement; and whatever familiarity readers gain from revisiting characters and events already encountered elsewhere is tempered, if not entirely overshadowed, by the sheer perplexity caused by the impossibility of piecing together these many different versions of similar events to produce a stable fictional world.

The figure of Lol V. Stein is a case in point, for Duras's protagonist lives on in much altered form in the author's writing well beyond *Le Ravissement de Lol V. Stein*; she appears again, though now without a name, in the sequel *L'Amour*, published in 1971 and filmed the following year – in a much revised version – as *La Femme du Gange* (in the scenario for which, published a year later, Lol, who never speaks in the film, is referred to throughout as 'L.V.S.', bearing her identity rather like a serial number [*NG*, 109]); and she is also remembered – though never seen – in the dialogue of the play and film text, *India Song* (together with its cinematographic doublet *Son nom de Venise dans Calcutta désert*). There seems also to have existed a film treatment of the story of Lol, a summary of which was published in 1979; and Lol, identified by Duras with her former schoolfriend Hélène Lagonelle, remains an intriguing if ghostly presence both in *L'Amant* and *L'Amant de la Chine du Nord*, which provide, at least in part, a belated autobiographical reading of the text of 1964.[2]

There is a further reason for the celebrity or notoriety enjoyed by *Le Ravissement de Lol V. Stein*. For Duras's novel has been the subject of considerable attention on the part of both psychoanalysis and feminism. This interest in the novel stems in part from a short article published in December 1965 by Jacques Lacan, who at the time, and during the years immediately following, was at the height of his influence as one of the most controversial figures in French psychoanalysis. It seems Lacan was first shown the book by Michèle Montrelay, who went on to give a presentation of the novel at Lacan's seminar in June 1965. Before writing his own essay, the only text he ever published on a living author, Lacan met Duras at midnight in the basement of a local bar for a conversation that went on for over two hours. Duras, on her own admission, understood little of what went on; however, the article, when it appeared, under the grandiloquent title of 'Hommage fait à Marguerite Duras, du ravissement de Lol V. Stein', started from the surprising conviction that 'Marguerite Duras s'avère savoir sans moi ce que j'enseigne' (*MD*, 133; 124), and endeavoured to explain how it was, as Lacan put it, that Duras seemed to know all about Lacanian theory without having had the benefit of ever attending one of his seminars.[3]

As the quip suggests, Lacan enlists the support of Duras's novel as an exemplification and confirmation of Lacanian psychoanalytic theory, much as with Edgar Allan Poe's short story 'The Purloined Letter' in his famous 1955 seminar on the tale. Admittedly, literary

texts, for Lacan, are always paradigmatic; like *Hamlet*, they are
always typical to the precise extent that they are atypical, and
Lacan's approach to *Le Ravissement de Lol V. Stein*, as to Shake-
speare and Poe, relies on the assertion of a necessary convergence
between practising writing and interpreting the unconscious (*MD*,
133; 124).[4] As elsewhere, Lacan rejects the recourse to psychobio-
graphy; his main concern is to articulate the triangular structure
that, for him, underpins the plot of the novel to the extent that it
stages an unconscious fantasy. In the process, Lacan attempts to
supply a theoretical rationale for the relative position of the sexes
within Duras's story of male and female entanglement, madness,
seduction, and speculation.

Since its publication, Lacan's article has generally been taken as
an authoritative explication of Duras's text. It has also enjoyed
some currency not only among readers sympathetic to psychoanalysis, but among feminist readers, too. This arises in part from
Lacan's own interest in questions of female desire and the influence
of Lacanian analysis on some currents of thinking within feminism;
but it also reflects Duras's own perceived allegiance to the women's
movement and *écriture féminine* in the early to mid-1970s. The
question of the usefulness or relevance of Lacan's work to feminism
is an issue that is, of course, still controversial; and in much the
same way feminist reactions to Lacan's interpretation of *Le Ravissement de Lol V. Stein* have also been sharply divided, with some
readers tending to endorse Lacan's – admittedly brilliant – analysis
on the grounds that it offers an accurate theorisation of female
desire and the character of Lol V. Stein as a female subject. Other
readers, however, have challenged this view, seeing Lacan's intervention more as a phallocentric appropriation of the novel that
entirely misses the subversive potential of Duras's work.[5]

In turn, reflecting this wider controversy about the relationship
between psychoanalysis and feminism, *Le Ravissement de Lol V.
Stein* has itself become disputed territory between different groups
of critics, between those proponents of *écriture féminine*, for
instance, like Xavière Gauthier or Marcelle Marini, who argue that
the text gives voice to the radical otherness of female desire, and
those, like Trista Selous, for whom, on the contrary, it represents
an essentialist mystification of the female self, deeply indebted to
traditional views about women and hysteria. The debate has often
been a polemical or ideological one. Duras, for her part, consistently refuses in her writing to assign either morality or meaning to
desire, and as a result *Le Ravissement de Lol V. Stein* endorses

neither of these interpretations, leaving as provocatively undecidable the question whether the novel is compatible or not with the values and objectives of contemporary feminism.

But before going any further, it is worth recalling the main events of Duras's novel. *Le Ravissement de Lol V. Stein* is the story of a doctor, aged 36, by the name of Jacques Hold, who comes to the town of S. Tahla to work in the local hospital with Pierre Beugner. Jacques has an affair with Beugner's wife, Tatiana Karl, who has an old schoolfriend called Lola Valérie Stein. Lol is now married with three daughters; after a long absence she returns to S. Tahla, where, via Tatiana, Jacques makes her acquaintance. He learns that one evening, ten years earlier, Lol, accompanied by Tatiana, had gone to the ball in the nearby seaside resort of T. Beach with her fiancé, Michael Richardson. The evening was interrupted by the entrance of the mysterious figure of Anne-Marie Stretter, in a low-cut black dress. Michael Richardson dances with this older woman, and she and he depart together as dawn breaks, in a familiarly half-lit Durassian moment, leaving Lol behind in the state of *ravissement* to which the title refers: ecstatic with happiness, according to Lol's subsequent testimony, but also beside herself with loss, though not actual grief, in a condition that, for those present, seems more plausibly to border on madness. But the incident was hushed up and Lol eventually married Jean Bedford. Evidently fascinated by Lol, Jacques begins following her in her apparently aimless walks through S. Tahla; at some point Lol starts to do likewise and a strange complicity between the two develops.

Lol and Jacques enter into a mutual pact by which Jacques agrees to continue his affair with Tatiana, during which time his feelings for Lol become more and more intense, while she, for her part, looks on, embarking on what both she and Jacques realise is a metaphorical but nonetheless massive reprise of her own past. Her desire, she says, had always been 'to see' Michael Richardson undressing Anne-Marie Stretter after the ball ('Les voir,' she explains [*R*, 103]); and she subsequently re-enacts the scene by getting Jacques to stand in, as it were, for Michael Richardson, and Tatiana for Anne-Marie Stretter, in an apparently triangular voyeuristic game. She revisits with Jacques the ballroom in T. Beach; this provokes in Lol a crisis that ends with her – seemingly – losing her sanity; but this is averted, perhaps, if only momentarily, in the closing scene as Lol looks on from the rye field at the hotel room in which Jacques and Tatiana prepare to make love in what is to be their final assignation.

Reduced to its rudiments, such is, in the terminology of Russian Formalism, what one might describe as the *fabula* of Duras's novel, the raw material of characters, events, and setting from which the narrative is constructed. Many of the ingredients are familiar ones, and *Le Ravissement de Lol V. Stein* reworks numerous motifs from earlier novels, notably *Moderato cantabile* and *Dix heures et demie du soir en été*. Like these, the novel opens by referring back to a catastrophic epiphany that has already taken place, even before the story begins, and is staged against the backdrop of an emergent apocalyptic light; like other earlier novels, it also has a plot that develops according to a pattern of repetition and transference, set in a world of uncertain geography and indeterminate border zones; and, finally, like other texts by Duras, it has a woman protagonist who fails to discriminate between pleasure and pain, ecstatic enjoyment and loss of self, and for whom desire is like a circular dance played out with a series of constantly changing partners.

But what makes *Le Ravissement de Lol V. Stein* markedly different from earlier texts is the transformation brought about in the *fabula* by the extraordinary narrative discourse that Duras devises in order to tell the story outlined above. Many details are in fact given twice, once in the form of a retrospective reconstruction of the scene of the ball at T. Beach and its aftermath, then as part of an account of how the narrator assembled the information for that reconstruction. This second account takes the story through to its conclusion, which turns out to be a re-enactment of the opening scenes. For the first seven sections of the novel (out of a total of eighteen), slightly more than the first third of the text, the identity of the narrator is withheld, even though the narrative is largely in the first person. Eventually, the narrator is named by the text – in the third person (*R*, 38) – as Jacques Hold; but Duras has Jacques fulfil his duties as represented narrator in a strangely intermittent way. Indeed, once he is identified, the reader quickly realises that in at least two previous episodes, the first when Jacques had passed by Lol's house with Tatiana (*R*, 38), and secondly when he had emerged from the cinema on his way to a rendezvous with her (*R*, 52), the narrative, when describing how Lol had seen a particular, unspecified man, had in fact been referring to Jacques himself. But despite Jacques's presence on the scene on both occasions, there is no explicit indication that he might turn out later to be the narrator of these events. Indeed, on the contrary, the point of view adopted by the narrative had been that of Lol herself, and the narrator even explains that on the first occasion, though Lol had seen them,

Jacques and Tatiana had not been able to see her, as she had concealed herself behind a hedge.

At crucial moments during these opening sections of the novel, the distinction between male narrator and female protagonist, between voice and vision, is challenged and undermined; and it is as though the separate lives of Jacques and Lol have become permeable, subject to obsessive interference from each other. Elsewhere, however, this merging of the two is specifically denied; and the narrator, in the guise of Lol's as yet unnamed admirer, intent on explaining, as the text puts it, 'l'écrasante actualité de cette femme dans ma vie' ('the overwhelming presence of this woman in my life', *R*, 14), continually reminds the reader that what is being narrated is entirely subject to conjecture and based on a largely unverifiable mixture of second-hand testimony and empathic reconstruction (*R*, 14).

As in *Moderato cantabile*, but in a far more radically disorientating manner, Duras refuses here to dissociate the telling of the story – or narration – from the events of the story – or diegesis; instead the narration repeats, in transferential mode, the events it recalls. As a result, it becomes increasingly problematic in the opening chapters to disentangle the male-authored narration from the female-centred diegesis, since each is caught in an unmasterable cycle of repetition, transference, loss of identity, and desire. As the novel proceeds, however, after the narrator is identified, it might seem that Jacques comes to exercise more control over the narrative. However, this reassertion of his authority over the text is only partially sustained, and narrative disturbances continue to affect the second part of the novel too, with the result that the indecision characteristic of the opening sections is increased rather than reduced. Indeed, repeatedly, the character of Jacques Hold, though now identified as the first-person narrator, slips into the position of a third-person character. Thus, for instance, when Jacques goes to his regular assignation at the Hôtel des Bois with Tatiana, and realises, in the half-light of dusk, that Lol is waiting for them to appear in the window, the narrative, as though in sympathy with Jacques's loss of control over events, increasingly being dictated by the 'despotic' Lol (*R*, 112), suddenly and without warning switches from the first person to the third (*R*, 123). Some pages later, a similar dissociation occurs, also under the influence of Lol's gaze, with Jacques being referred to in the third person, while a first-person voice, that of the book's narrator – but somehow not the Jacques of before – carries on narrating the text (*R*, 134).

In instances such as these, the novel is no longer in thrall to any single or unified narrating voice. Instead, the fiction overwhelms its own alleged narrator, and a number of troubling inversions begin to affect the main axes of the text, including the relationship between narrator and protagonist, voice and vision, male and female, lover and loved one. In this way the relationship between the unnamed narrative voice and the position of Lol as focalising character in the early episodes proves in retrospect to be founded on an impossible confusion. All credibility is undermined and the reader is left wondering what gaps in knowledge have been filled in by the narrator in a deceitful attempt to compensate for his own ignorance. But, on the other hand, what at first seems to point to the existence of an unbridgeable divide, like, for instance, the ill-sorted relationship between Jacques (who speaks) and Lol (who sees), changes into a case of such intense – cross-gender – textual identification that it is impossible to disentangle what desire, fantasy, or knowledge might be attributed to which one of these two unlikely, incommensurable partners.

One cannot say, then, within Duras's text, who is responsible for staging the memory of T. Beach that is rehearsed or repeated at the beginning of the text: is it Jacques Hold, the ostensible narrator, or Lol, the focaliser, or some other narrative agency beyond the control of either? The apparent cohesiveness of the text gives way to an impossible split between speaking and seeing, which in turn gives way to a movement of identificatory fusion; and the process of fusion itself proves inseparable from the division it erases. The problem is a general one in Duras's novel, affecting both plot and narrative discourse, which it becomes impossible to hold apart; an inversion or slippage in the one repeats or echoes an indeterminacy in the other, so that, for instance, Lol's wavering between identification and detachment in her memory of the two lovers of T. Beach is itself re-enacted in the oscillation within the narrative voice as it fluctuates from identification with Lol to detachment from her.

There is considerable instability, then, present in, each of the terms of Duras's text, which has the effect of severely disorganising its representational coherence. This is no doubt one reason for the substantial disagreements among critics of the novel; and it is noticeable that most accounts of *Le Ravissement de Lol V. Stein* diverge on the question of the textual function of Duras's part-time narrator, Jacques Hold, who tends to be seen primarily either as a self-effacing, credible investigator and mouthpiece for the author, or as a self-obsessed and ironically blinkered ladies' man. At issue here, of course, is more than just a formal question, for these differences of interpretation touch on an important debate relating to the treatment of gender and sexual difference in the novel.

For Lacan, the case is fairly clear-cut. Only once does he mention Jacques Hold's position as narrator, and it is to dismiss the issue by making Jacques unambiguously into the subject of the novel, in the analytic sense of the term; Jacques, he concludes, 'remplit ici la fonction non du récitant, mais du sujet' ('fulfils the role not of the narrator, but of the subject', *MD*, 136; 128). To make this claim, however, Lacan disregards all the turbulence in Duras's text in order to attribute to Jacques Hold the commanding position of subject and protagonist in the narrative.[6] Lacan is mainly concerned with the way the structure of the original ballroom scene is repeated or re-enacted in the text, and how the network of looks and gazes that proliferate in the novel can be made to fit the assumptions of Lacanian theory (set out in the 1964 seminar, *Les Quatre Concepts fondamentaux de la psychanalyse*). As a result, for Lacan, Jacques's role is primarily – if not exclusively – to be a character, caught up, more than he knows, in the 'remémoration' – in Lacan's word – that the text stages, and which somehow puts him, as Lacan phrases it, into the balance (*MD*, 132; 123). To this extent, Lacan's retelling of *Le Ravissement de Lol V. Stein* features a far less convoluted or ambiguous scenario than Duras's original novel: it mainly turns out to be a story of a man's homage to a female loved one, a tribute paid by captivated masculine authority to captive feminine beauty, more reminiscent of the tales of courtly love to be found in Marguerite de Navarre's *Heptaméron*, which Lacan cites as an intertextual prototype for Duras's novel (*MD*, 136; 128). By framing Duras's book in this way, Lacan's reading eliminates from the text most of its structural indeterminacies or inversions, and Lol is reduced to a kind of unseeing vacancy who may look but sees – and thus desires – nothing and is at the end precipitated into madness (an interpretation that Lacan backs up by deferring – as gallantry requires – to the authority of his conversation with Duras).

If Lacan unifies *Le Ravissement de Lol V. Stein* by largely ignoring the process of narration and constituting Jacques as a psychoanalytic subject, other readers, notably those wishing to give more weight to the gender gap between Jacques and Lol, have tried to resolve the novel's inconsistencies in another way, by attributing them to the arrogance and self-blindness of Jacques Hold. On this account, those episodes that seem to be told by Jacques imagining how Lol saw him failing to see her, are an ironic testimonial to the extent to which he appropriates Lol's story – and her gaze – for himself and uses this as a means of acting out a male fantasy of unchallenged authority and power. As Susan D. Cohen puts it, 'as writer, [Jacques] silences all other voices, discredits the contributions of Lol's mother and of her friend Tatiana, and seizes hold of Lol's story for himself'. This fantasy, however, proves unsustainable, Cohen argues, and Jacques falls victim to a disturbing 'loss of self', with the implication, as Cohen goes on to claim – contradicting her earlier point – that Jacques's narrative is now somehow able to allow the reader access to the 'other silenced discourses' hidden away in the text, which Cohen describes, misleadingly, as all being women's voices. *Le Ravissement de Lol V. Stein*, suggests Martha Noel Evans, in similar vein, 'emerges as Duras's critique of a male literary tradition in the name of another story written from the point of view of the female object of male fiction'; in the course of the novel, she concludes, Duras 'replaces male with female narrative'.[7] The question that is signally not addressed here is the unanswerable conundrum – which Duras's text leaves in suspense – of how the reader is to recognise this other, silenced story behind the words of a male narrator and, having recognised it, by what criteria she or he is to decide that it is a female narrative truthfully giving voice to female desire, sexuality, or experience. Cohen and Evans take this as given in advance; but, in the last resort, as Cohen admits, the only guarantee that anyone in the novel is telling the truth about what it is to be a woman is the presence of the name of a woman writer (or 'signer', as Cohen puts it) on the cover of the book.[8]

I want to argue that none of these readings is satisfactory. What Lacan on the one hand and critics such as Cohen and Evans on the other all have in common is a desire to allocate fixed places and positions to the male or female characters in Duras's text. But this is to pay little attention to the constant difficulties of attribution affecting narrative voice and point of view throughout the novel, the effect of which is to confuse and muddle irretrievably what the respective places of male and female in the text might be. In this regard, both Lacan's analytic reading and the particular feminist interpretation outlined by Cohen and Evans function principally as attempts at rectification, aimed at straightening out the many detours of desire and cross-gender identification in Duras's text and thereby subordinating the fictional ambivalencies of the novel to the prescriptive truths of a pre-given theory of sexual difference.

Truth, however, is a value that is treated throughout *Le Ravisse-ment de Lol V. Stein* with extreme suspicion; and it would seem that any reading of Duras's novel that seeks to establish the veracity of the story of Lol, whether based on Lacanian psychoanalysis or on the certitudes of female experience, is bound to fail. It is not just that the novel lacks consistency in the relations between narra-tive voice, point of view, and text. It is also evident that the narrative voice, though attributed – half-heartedly – to Jacques Hold, is itself not a unified whole but made up of a complex montage of other voices and discourses, including those of Tatiana and Lol's mother, but also the Bedford family governess, Jean Bedford, Pierre Beugner, Jacques Hold and a number of other anonymous sources. What the reader has to contend with is not a stable fictive world to which criteria of truth or falsehood may be applied in the expectation that conflicts of interpretation will be resolved, but a shifting fictional text in which most things that happen are recounted twice, or in at least two different versions, or with at least two different explanations.

The reader of Duras's novel never breaks out of this vicious circle of repetition, conjecture, and speculation. What the novel dramatises is a crisis in knowledge; it is continually citing, juxtapos-ing, and thereby questioning a range of different discourses of interpretation – as represented by each one of the characters in the novel – all of which claim some purchase on the story of Lol, but none of which are finally validated or proven to be adequate by the writing of the text. The only truths available in *Le Ravissement de Lol V. Stein* are indeterminate half-truths; and these have the capacity to contaminate all the discourses of knowledge that readers apply to the text and which, instead of revealing the truth about Lol, are more liable themselves to turn into partial fictions unable to arrest or silence Lol's quest for what she in the novel – without addressing the word to anyone other than herself – calls happiness, 'le bonheur' (*R*, 108).

II

Le Ravissement de Lol V. Stein, for reader and narrator alike, is a story of epistemological frustration. To read the work as a novel bent on dramatising a man's search for knowledge about a deranged women or as an attempt to distinguish between reason and madness, or male and female stories, is to commit oneself to a series of diminishing returns. Crucial questions about Lol's personal history, her sanity or madness are blocked by the text. The quest for knowledge goes astray, and Duras's novel, unlike most other texts that begin by constructing woman as an enigma, refuses finally to equate Lol with the figure of truth. In hindsight, as the ending of the novel begins to repeat its own beginning, it is clear that what has been driving the narrative forwards from the outset is not the pursuit of knowledge at all, but something else, beyond pathology, morality, or sense, which is at work both on the level of plot and of narrative discourse, and which Duras in her text thematises not as understanding but, more radically, as repetition. And repetition here, as in *Le Square* or *Moderato cantabile*, is inseparable from desire. As Lol's story demonstrates, what repeats itself in Duras is desire; and desire in Duras is what repeats itself.

Much has been written about desire and repetition in *Le Ravissement de Lol V. Stein*, primarily from the perspective of Lacanian psychoanalysis. In his 'Hommage' to Duras, Lacan, in an influential move, organises his reading according to a three-fold series of ternary structures, each of which repeats the others and involves two women and a man: first, the original threesome of Lol V. Stein, Michael Richardson, and Anne-Marie Stretter; then their doubles, Lol V. Stein, Jacques Hold, and Tatiana Karl; and finally the trio of writer, reader, and text, played here by Duras, Lacan, and Lol. V. Stein's 'ravissement' (now sublimated, Lacan suggests, into a work of art). As in the seminar on 'The Purloined Letter', Lacan privileges the object of repetition – the structure of the triangle – over the activity of repetition itself; and, partly in sympathy with Lacan's approach, much critical discussion of *Le Ravissement de Lol V. Stein* (and of Duras's work as a whole) has been dominated by this preoccupation with repetitive triangular structures.

Some critics, for instance, take encouragement from the opening pages of *L'Amour*, Duras's 1971 sequel to *Le Ravissement de Lol V. Stein*, to go on to claim that desire in Duras is generally based on the voyeuristic posture of a third-party female observer who is both included in the spectacle and excluded from it.[9] But while it is true that *L'Amour* begins with a description of the triangular patterns made on the beach by three of the characters who appear in the novel, this triangle has a different distribution of roles; it is now made up of two men and a woman, who, if any of the characters in the novel had names, could be identifiable as Michael Richardson ('l'homme qui regarde' or, subsequently, 'le voyageur' [*AM*, 13]), Jacques Hold ('l'homme qui marche'), and Lol V. Stein ('la femme'). So between the triangle described in *L'Amour* and that staged in *Le Ravissement de Lol* V. *Stein* there is no real continuity or isomorphism with respect to the personnel involved or the relationships between them. Moreover, the triangle in *L'Amour* is unstable; it repeatedly slides back and forth upon itself (*AM*, 9), until it finally dissolves, at which point, with a shout or cry ringing out against the background of the sea and light, the story proper begins (*AM*, 13).

So there are several clues here that triangles may not be all they seem. Already in *Le Ravissement de Lol V. Stein* the threesome at the ball was preceded by the same-sex couple of Lol and Tatiana dancing as teenagers in the school playground. And in *L'Amour*, the triangle, at best, is just a phase the text goes through. The more important notation in the opening sequence of the novel is probably not the reference to geometry, however much that may be of interest to devotees of Lacanian diagrams, but to the fading light. Dusk is slowly falling, but then the light suddenly stops. Duras writes: 'Encore la lumière: c'est la lumière. Elle change, puis elle ne change plus tout à coup. Elle grandit, illumine, puis elle reste ainsi, illuminante, égale' ('The light still: the light's there. It changes, then suddenly stops changing. It increases, glows, then remains as it is, glowing, unvarying', *AM*, 16). ' – La lumière s'est arrêtée' ('The light has stopped', *AM*, 17), comments the man walking, and his response is described as one of violent hope. As it unravels, then, the triangle on the beach gives way to an event affecting the light; and it is not difficult to recognise in that event the memory of an apocalyptic enactment of the kind found earlier in *Le Square*.

Motifs of this sort are, of course, not exclusive to *L'Amour*, but may be found in much of *Le Ravissement de Lol V. Stein* as well; so much so, in fact, that it is worth looking again at the section of *Le Ravissement de Lol V. Stein* in which the initial ballroom scene is reconstructed – by now for the second time – by Duras's as yet anonymous narrator. Here is one part of that account, describing Lol's wanderings through S. Tahla in search, it would seem, for an image of the dance at T. Beach:

> Je connais Lol V. Stein de la seule façon que je puisse, d'amour. C'est en raison de cette connaissance que je suis arrivé à croire ceci: dans les multiples aspects du bal de T. Beach, c'est la fin qui retient Lol. C'est l'instant précis de sa fin, quand l'aurore arrive avec une brutalité inouïe et la sépare du couple que for-

maient Michael Richardson et Anne-Marie Stretter, pour toujours, toujours. Lol progresse chaque jour dans la reconstitution de cet instant. Elle arrive même à capter un peu de sa foudroyante rapidité, à l'étaler, à en grillager les secondes dans une immobilité d'une extrême fragilité mais qui est pour elle d'une grâce infinie. [. . .]

Elle se voit, et c'est là sa pensée véritable, à la même place, dans cette fin, toujours, au centre d'une triangulation dont l'aurore et eux deux sont les termes éternels: elle vient d'apercevoir cette aurore alors qu'eux ne l'ont pas encore remarquée. Elle, sait, eux pas encore. Elle est impuissante à les empêcher de savoir.

(*R*, 47)

(I know Lol V. Stein in the only manner that I can, through love. By virtue of that knowledge what I have come to believe is that of all the many aspects of the dance at T. Beach the most important one for Lol is its end, the exact instant of its ending, when the day breaks with unprecedented violence and separates her from the couple that was Michael Richardson and Anne-Marie Stretter, for ever and ever. Lol advances every day towards reconstituting that moment. She even manages to harness a little of its lightning speed, to spread it out and capture each of its moments in a motionlessness of extreme fragility but for her of infinite grace. [. . .]

She sees herself, and that is her genuine belief, in the same spot, in this ending, always, at the centre of a triangulation in which the daybreak and the two others are the never-ending terms: she has just seen the daybreak while they have not yet noticed it. She knows already, the others not yet. She is powerless to prevent them from knowing.)

The triangular structure of this scene, as Lol restages it, is in some ways more apparent than real. Lol is not firmly positioned as a spectator midway between Michael Richardson and Anne-Marie Stretter as a third to their couple, as Lacan's account implies and other critics, like Carol Murphy, have since asserted. Lol is placed at that spot where the first rays of the dawn, illuminating the scene with an exactness of the kind perhaps found only in Murnau's *Nosferatu*, intersect with an imaginary line leading to Lol from Michael Richardson and Anne-Marie Stretter. The relation between these points – to the extent that they are points at all – is not simple. The dawn, belonging to the impending day, functions as a figure of separation; but the couple of Michael Richardson and Anne-Marie Stretter, lingering on in the preceding night, continues to dramatise the possibility of amorous fusion. As it breaks, the dawn signifies a sudden and brutal separation, but what it reveals is a scene in which separation is suspended. Time is poised between what has already happened but not yet taken place. Between day and night, the dawn and the two lovers, between separation and fusion, it is Lol who hangs in the balance; and her gaze is less a static vantage point than an oscillating movement, as Duras puts it, swinging back and forth from the couple to the dawn.

Lol's moment of happiness in the ballroom falls neither before nor after the moment of separation from the two lovers, but at exactly the point when the distinction between separation and fusion is itself hopelessly blurred, when she herself is already detached from her fiancé but at one with the sight of the lovers before her, apparently loving them still, like an ageing mother (*R*, 18). The scene is one of loss and desire, but, as Lol shows when she endeavours to restage it later, with the help of Jacques and Tatiana, its meaning is not fixed; for Lol does not re-enact the scene passively as though it were no more than a pathological or hysterical symptom, but transforms it by substituting for the dawn – as she does in the rye field – a different half-light, the half-light of evening, which, as elsewhere in Duras, promises a return to darkness but also the hope of a different kind of dawn. (As though to deliver this promise, *L'Amour*, seven years later, ends with the coming of dawn and the perplexing news, delivered by the walker, that shortly the woman – a version of Lol herself – will hear the sound of God: 'vous savez . . . ? de Dieu? . . . ce truc . . . ?' ['you know . . . ? of God? . . . that thing . . . ?', *AM*, 143].)

What repeats itself for Lol, as the object of her desire, is less a static triangle, with its unchanging repertoire of male and female participants (as Lacan's analysis contends), than a dynamic, flickering scenario in which there are no fixed positions but a series of mobile relationships. Lol's desire is for an image, a scene, which belongs to the narrative progression of the ball, but also refuses to be contained by it and can carry on being repeated ad infinitum. It is a scene, too, which somehow stands in for the failure of words to describe Lol's moment of happiness, but while recognising that failure of speech gives Lol the possibility of reinventing for herself what, in a suggestive phrase, Duras calls Lol's own cinema, 'le cinéma de Lol V. Stein' (*R*, 49). The reference to cinema here is to something that, by incorporating the phenomenon of the apoca-

lyptic half-light and the spectacle of the two lovers, seems able to
preserve, in timeless fashion, the undecidable moment of fusion
and separation itself. Lol's position in this spectacle is not a predetermined one; indeed what is at stake in the scene of the ballroom,
governing the whole theme of sight in the novel, is the act of
looking not as a means of voyeuristic control but as a mode of
erotic participation or identification, an undecidable interplay of
proximity and distance founded on the constant merging and coming
apart of bodies. (It is worth remembering that already in *Un barrage
contre le Pacifique*, when the heroine first goes to the cinema on
her own, what she sees there, in a description that almost seems
to anticipate the opening shots of *Hiroshima mon amour* – showing
two anonymous and naked torsos, embracing in medium close-up
as their bodies are sprayed with ash, then water (*H*, 21; 17) – is a
similar spectacle of bodily fusion and deathly disarticulation [*B*,
189; 152–3].)

This theme of looking is crucial in all Duras's work, where it is
closely linked, as in the story of Lol, to questions both of fantasy
and of sexual difference. In the scenario of the ball at T. Beach,
there are many elements, for instance, which recall what in Freud
is described as characteristic of the primal scene, those traumatic
memories or fantasies of a child's first sight of adult sexual intercourse.[10] Like a primal scene, the moment of T. Beach enacts or
re-enacts in the form of a visual image what certainly functions for
Lol like her first access to knowledge of sexual difference; it
encrypts a fascinating secret, therefore, that has to do with fusion
and separation, but the origins of that enigma are lost in a cycle
of events in which each prior point is already a repetition of something else, just as the ball itself repeats Lol's dance in the school
playground with Tatiana in the opening pages of the book (*R*, 11).
It operates, too, as a scenario of desire that is capable of perpetual
repetition and constant expansion and is motivated less and less
by the pursuit of sense, and increasingly by the condensations,
displacements, and metamorphoses of desire itself.

Nowhere is this connection between writing and desire in Duras
more evident than in the numerous rewritings or reinscriptions to
which the scene of T. Beach gives rise elsewhere in her work. The
most explicit of these occurs in *L'Amant*, a text in which the name
of Lol V. Stein is nowhere mentioned; however, by the desirous
detour of a reference to the figure of Hélène Lagonelle, Duras
stages a scene that has many similarities with the night at T. Beach
in *Le Ravissement de Lol V. Stein*. It is a scene in which, like Lol

or some other future theatrical impresario, the woman narrator imagines herself giving away the body of her much admired – and keenly desired – girlfriend to her male lover and thrilling at the merging of her own bodily enjoyment with that of her two partners; there exists perhaps no more forceful commentary than this on the desire that inhabits *Le Ravissement de Lol V. Stein*:

> Je veux emmener avec moi Hélène Lagonelle, là où chaque soir, les yeux clos, je me fais donner la jouissance qui fait crier. Je voudrais donner Hélène Lagonelle à cet homme qui fait ça sur moi pour qu'il le fasse à son tour sur elle. Ceci en ma présence, qu'elle le fasse selon mon désir, qu'elle se donne là où moi je me donne. Ce serait par le détour du corps de Hélène Lagonelle, par la traversée de son corps que la jouissance m'arrive de lui, alors définitive.
>
> (I want to take Hélène Lagonelle with me to where every evening, my eyes shut, I have imparted to me the pleasure that makes you cry out. I'd like to give Hélène Lagonelle to the man who does that to me, so he may do it in turn to her. I want it to happen in my presence, I want her to do it as I wish, I want her to give herself where I give myself. It's via Hélène Lagonelle's body, through it, that the ultimate pleasure would pass from him to me.)
>
> (*A*, 91–2; 79)

What is described here is not another triangle to be added to those which Lacan superimposes on to *Le Ravissement de Lol V. Stein*, but a more indeterminate process of simultaneous fusion and division, identification and detachment, a mingling of bodies and sexes by which male and female are no longer discrete positions, but become joined in a round of desire in which neither the subject nor the object of desire can reliably be placed. The narrator delegates her own desires to Hélène Lagonelle, enjoying both the body of her lover – and of Hélène – by the agency of Hélène; she in turn is divided from herself and dispersed, eyes closed, across the space between her gaze and the twin objects of that look, her male partner and her female double, or – equally well – her male double and her female partner. Like the scene at T. Beach, the fantasy is a scenario with different entrances and exits and no single vantage point; rewriting this fantasy, which may be a memory from the past or a retroactive reinvention of the past, the author is both herself, Hélène Lagonelle, her Chinese lover and her text, just as in *Le*

Ravissement de Lol V. Stein, she ghosted as Lol, Tatiana, Jacques, and all the other voices, too. (And, if one were to gloss the scene from *L'Amant* with one from *L'Amant de la Chine du Nord* [*ACN*, 64–6], the cast of characters would also have to include the invisible and always latent figure of Duras's much desired, but now dead brother, Paulo.)

While *L'Amant*, in 1984, gives an autobiographical gloss to *Le Ravissement de Lol V. Stein*, the sequel, *L'Amour*, published in 1971, does so in metatextual mode. The novel, which reads more like a fragmentary film or theatre script than a coherent narrative, imagines a situation that postdates the events of *Le Ravissement de Lol V. Stein* by some years. Much has changed in the interim. An unnamed traveller, presumably Michael Richardson, having abandoned his wife and children and lost everything, returns to S. Thala (as it is now written) to commit suicide. On the beach he finds a woman, resembling Lol V. Stein, who is mad, living in an institution, more like a prison than a hospital, looked after in oddly unassertive or negative style by a man, also mad, possibly related to Jacques Hold, who walks up and down the beach (in *La Femme du Gange* Duras glosses this role of the 'madman' with the words that he is 'la tête-passoire traversée par la mémoire du tout' ['the filter permeated by the memory of everything', *NG*, 148]). Alone, the traveller revisits the ballroom, now located in S. Thala, and decides to stay; he spends the night waiting for the dawn as the town burns, set on fire by a woman escaped from the asylum, understood to be the pregnant Lol, in whom sickness and nausea, externalised in the rise and fall of the sea, seem to embody whatever apocalyptic hopes for the future are concealed in the desire to burn down the town. The novel ends in silence with the promise of a new dawn.

L'Amour is set in a place called S. Thala and this new location is emblematic of the text's relationship to its predecessor. S. Thala, here, is a coastal town, more reminiscent of the town of Trouville (where, Duras explains [*L*, 82; B: 58], *Le Ravissement de Lol V. Stein* was first written) than the pseudo-colonial world depicted in 1964. S. Thala is an area with uncertain and indeterminate limits. Since *Le Ravissement de Lol V. Stein*, it seems to have engulfed the resort of T. Beach; it therefore spreads as far as the river, but also beyond the river: ' – Ici, c'est S. Thala jusqu'à la rivière', points out the walker, but adds: 'Après la rivière c'est encore S. Thala' ('Here it's S. Thala down to the river. Beyond the river it's still S. Thala', *AM*, 19–20). If it has boundaries, S. Thala has internalised them, and in other ways, too, *L'Amour* presents a world turned inside out. Everything here survives on a borderline where non-identity is the solitary principle to be maintained. The beach, for instance, suspended between land and sea, is inhabited only by marginal characters like the mad Lol and the walker, joined by the traveller once he becomes bereft of everything ('C'est vrai,' the woman tells him, with affirmative power, 'vous n'êtes rien' ['It's true, you are nothing', *AM*, 136]). Memory is no longer held within the minds of individuals, but externalised and projected onto the outside environment. The 'cinéma de Lol V. Stein' from *Le Ravissement de Lol V. Stein*, with its quotient of water, sand, and eternity (*R*, 49), has exploded the bounds of Lol's – or Jacques Hold's – imagination to become the décor of Duras's fiction, just as Duras herself has substituted for the fictional universe of *Le Ravissement de Lol V. Stein* the landscape in which it was written. That landscape is an apocalyptic one, characterised by boundless devastation, by fire, storms, and wind, a 'Babylone délaissée' ('derelict Babylon', *AM*, 106) in which the only physical link with the past is the flotsam on the beach, recalling the survival within *L'Amour* of all the textual debris washed up from the earlier story of Lol V. Stein.

In *L'Amour*, the characters confront their own ineradicable madness not in the form of their desires or their past but in the shape of the half-lit world they now inhabit. Thus the traveller, in the foyer of his hotel, plays audience to a ghostly re-enactment of his past, acted out like a deathly mime show by the mad walker: 'Le corps s'emporte, se souvient, il danse sous dictée de la musique, il dévore, il brûle, il est fou de bonheur, il danse, il brûle, une brûlure traverse la nuit de S. Thala' ('His body is in a frenzy, remembers, he dances at the behest of the music, devours, fevers, is mad with happiness, dances, fevers, a fever travels through the S. Thala night', *AM*, 70–1). The memory of the night at T. Beach, renamed, transformed, and almost erased, continues to invade and haunt the present as a kind of mythic ritual testifying both to the apocalyptic devastation wrought by desire and to the illumination the conflagration of desire still affords. Exacerbating its precursor, *L'Amour* pushes the scene of T. Beach to an extreme point of intensity and exhaustion as the catastrophic end of the ball turns into a landscape where demarcation lines can no longer be drawn and Lol's desire for repetition repeats itself endlessly in the motion of the sea, as though the sea itself were Duras's most potent emblem of perpetual fusion and constant separation from itself.

But just as *L'Amour* repeats an earlier text, so it, too, in the

shape of the film *La Femme du Gange*, gives rise to another resta-
ging or reinscription of the story of Lol. New and distinctive here,
of course, is the move to the cinema. But the effect of this shift
from the verbal to the visual is unexpectedly ambivalent. On the
one hand, the film, to the extent that it supplies a visual image,
would seem a logical continuation of *Le Ravissement de Lol V.
Stein* and of Lol's desire for an image of the ball at T. Beach (and
it seems that, had it been made, the projected film of *Le Ravissement de Lol V. Stein* would have been devoted almost exclusively
to providing such an image); but, on the other hand, the move to
film inevitably signals, paradoxically, the impending end of the
desire for images. To supply an image for the story of S. Thala
and thus satisfy this desire is to abolish the desire. Here *La Femme
du Gange*, while repeating *L'Amour*, acts as a kind of final codicil
to it; it cannot do otherwise than provide a definitive final image
for S. Thala, and thus put an end to the cycle as a whole.

   Duras's response to this new threat of closure, much as it was
when first writing *Le Ravissement de Lol V. Stein*, is to sabotage
the representational coherence of the text and open it up again to
internal repetition and desire. To do this, Duras doubles up both
the diegesis and the narrative discourse of the film. When filming
La Femme du Gange, for instance, Duras duplicated several of the
roles in the script by adding a second man on the beach and a
second woman, dressed in black. (Some of this came about more
by chance than by design, when Gérard Depardieu, who plays the
madman, joined the shooting with an actor friend for whom Duras
improvised a part not originally in the script.) And once the film
was edited and virtually completed, Duras reports, she decided to
double the image track with a second soundtrack, spoken off-screen
by two female voices (*NG*, 103).

   These voices, bound together by desire for each other (*NG*, 105)
and by their shared visual investment in the scene, have much the
same relationship to the diegesis as does the narrative voice in *Le
Ravissement de Lol V. Stein*. They comment on events from a
seemingly intradiegetic standpoint; but they also belong to an extradiegetic or heterodiegetic parallel world that is not so much off-
camera as inside the camera. Their mode of existence is in this
respect uniquely cinematographic; they are allowed to see while
remaining totally invisible. In her introductory remarks, Duras
describes them as the inhabitants 'd'un espace nocturne, comme
élevé, d'un balcon au-dessus du vide, du tout' ('of an aerial, noc-
turnal space, of a balcony suspended over the void, over every-

thing', *NG*, 105). What these voices embody is the pure activity of looking. But since this activity cannot be seen, it is impossible to position their gaze in relation to the image on the screen. They ask questions about what viewers also can see on screen and therefore replicate the activity of the viewer; but by surrounding the visual image with a zone of textual invisibility, identifiable as a source of speech but no image, they prevent the viewer from taking up a fixed place in relation to the image. This is made more difficult still by the static camera positions used throughout, which repel the viewer's gaze rather than trapping it in the centre of the image. There is little alternative except to oscillate, in secret sympathy with the memory of Lol, back and forth between the images on the screen and the invisible, extratemporal voices somewhere behind, beside, or in front of them, and gaze on as the image track is doubled by its own repetitive but unrepresentable shadow.

Turning on some of the same constantly repeated and displaced scenes, *L'Amour*, *La Femme du Gange*, and *Le Ravissement de Lol V. Stein* share many characters, motifs, and allusions. They have in common, too, a crisis in representation which threatens the internal stability of each of the texts. As with the figure of Lol in *Le Ravissement de Lol V. Stein*, the effects of this crisis, alternately and undecidably, are described by Duras as displaying both a lack of distinctness and an excess of intensity. Thus Lol is both too vapid and too single-minded a character to sustain a properly constituted narrative with a beginning, a middle, and an end (*R*, 37). But the constant fading of sense is accompanied by the perpetual rebirth of desire (the process is one that affects Duras herself just as much as it does the characters of Lol or Jacques); as Lol's memory of T. Beach demonstrates, words may always fall victim to their inner exhaustion, but the desire to see survives. The one and the other in Duras are always in inverse proportion: seeing and speaking never join together but are constantly played off the one against the other. And it is the inescapable oscillation between these two extremes of effacement and intensification, obliteration and affirmation, that dictates in Duras the savage economy of all apocalyptic revelation.

If Duras's work directs itself towards catastrophic revelation, the object of revelation itself is often described by recourse to the theme of the sublime. The memory of T. Beach, for instance, in *Le Ravissement de Lol V. Stein*, is located against the monotonous backdrop of the falling rain that, like the sea in *L'Amour*, serves as the image of an 'ailleurs, uniforme, fade et sublime' ('uniform, insipid and sublime other place', *R*, 44). As these words suggest, the version of the sublime that is implied here is a state of exception characterised not by overwhelming monumentality or grandeur, but by insipid uniformity, a lack of distinction that makes the sublime doubly resistant to words or representation.

In *L'Amour* and *La Femme du Gange*, many of the same images of blandness return, but they are literalised into a series of indistinct, purely anaphoric references to day or night, the beach and the sea. In *La Femme du Gange* the effect is the same, achieved by an unvarying sequence of static camera shots, in which the only movement, highly stylised that it is, is that conveyed by the patterns traced by Duras's characters on the beach. In *Le Ravissement de Lol V. Stein*, reference was made to the impossibility for Lol of finding a word to name her desire at the ball in T. Beach: 'Manquant, ce mot,' the narrator had explained, 'il gâche tous les autres, les contamine, c'est aussi le chien mort de la plage en plein midi, ce trou de chair' ('The word, being missing, spoils all the others, contaminates them, like it's also the dead dog on the beach at midday, a hole in the flesh', *R*, 48). In *L'Amour*, the dead dog recurs as a physical corpse on the beach, 'chien mort de l'idée' ('dead dog of the idea', *AM*, 125), writes Duras, describing the body of the woman as she lies in the sun, like rotting flesh.

The effect of this process of literalisation is one of insistent repetition and destruction. The world of *Le Ravissement de Lol V. Stein* is drained of diegetic substance and slowly erased; but by being repeated yet again, its force is undeniably accentuated. Desire and separation, fusion and loss merge in a process of sublime, apocalyptic intensification. But the Durassian sublime gestures not towards elevation or erectness, as etymology demands, but towards singularity, paucity, and blankness; it thematises the unrepresentable character of desire as an indictment of the limitations of language and of bodies. Desire is a process of loss of identity, a merging of the body with that of the other, a movement of repetition that repeats itself continually and is constantly pressing on beyond the stage or moment of its own exhaustion. It circulates through all Duras's texts as a sign of muddle and confusion, fusing that which once was separate, separating what once was fused.

4 Crossing genres

I

Throughout Duras's work, desire and repetition are in a relationship of constant reciprocity. Repetition in Duras, however, is not simply a thematic preoccupation, nor just a common form of structural patterning embedded within individual works; rather, from the mid-1960s onwards, as the sequence of works dealing with the figure of Lol V. Stein demonstrates, repetition in Duras gradually begins to exceed the confines of the single text and to function on a larger scale, assuming the status of a process of textual generation. Increasingly, the texts of Duras are produced from and with material deriving from earlier or preceding texts. *Le Vice-consul*, for instance, published in 1966, borrows in this way from *Un barrage contre le Pacifique*, from the early version of *L'Homme assis dans le couloir*, and from *Le Ravissement de Lol V. Stein* itself, as well as reworking material included in the 1964 film script *Nuit noire, Calcutta*. Like *L'Amour* or *La Femme du Gange*, it has as its point of departure the use of repetition as a mode of intertextual transformation.

Such transformations sometimes take place within the bounds of a single genre, as is the case with *Le Ravissement de Lol V. Stein* and *L'Amour*, both narrative texts, albeit of vastly different types. More often, though, the process of repetition or transformation also involves a change of genre and some of Duras's best-known works are the result of this process of generic displacement. *Des journées entières dans les arbres*, for instance, began in 1954 as a short story, was first performed on stage in 1965, and finally filmed by Duras (in 16mm) for French television in 1976, with Madeleine Renaud, Jean-Pierre Aumont, and Bulle Ogier recreating their stage roles. In the case of other works, the transformation was more radical. Thus, *Le Vice-consul*, reworked as the hybrid play text *India Song* in 1973, had by 1976 yielded a radio play as well as both the film *India Song* and its doublet, *Son nom de Venise dans Calcutta désert*; *Les Enfants*, distributed in 1985, was initially derived from Duras's children's story of 1971, *Ah! Ernesto*, before being entirely rewritten by the author as the novel, *La Pluie d'été*, published in 1990. And in May 1978 the magazine *Minuit* published a short text by Duras entitled 'Le Navire Night'. The following March, under the same title, a film version of the story appeared; and the release of the film coincided with the opening of a theatre production also called *Le Navire Night* (featuring Bulle Ogier, as did the film, albeit in a different role). A revised text appeared in the autumn in a volume also containing three versions of the story-cum-film script, *Aurélia Steiner*.[1]

There is here an extraordinary proliferation of different versions and realisations of the same texts that has little in common with what is usually understood by literary adaptation. In general, stage or screen versions of literary texts set out to offer a new audience a fresh presentation of a classic, stable, if unfamiliar narrative; or else they use the original merely as a prop in creating a work that, in the end, bears little resemblance to its precursor. But in either case, whether the outcome most resembles, say, William Wyler's *Wuthering Heights*, or Godard's *Le Mépris*, the aim of the adaptation is to liberate the new work from dependence on its literary predecessor. But Duras's purpose in replicating her own texts follows neither of these paths: her new versions do not maintain the originals intact, but nor do they treat them solely as a convenient pretext. Her adaptations of her own works do not supersede their precursors, but double them with another version of themselves in another genre. To this extent, Duras's strategy of intertextual repetition and displacement is best seen not as a technique of adaptation at all; and as a result, her exploration of the relationship between image and text in her own work for the cinema is strikingly different from the more conventional approach adopted by those early film adaptations of her novels – including, notably, René Clément's *Barrage contre le Pacifique*, Peter Brook's screen version of *Moderato cantabile*, and Jules Dassin's *Dix heures et demie du soir en été* – for which at the time she professed a strong dislike, albeit sometimes after the fact.

It is evident from this constant multiplication of texts and performances across genres that repetition in Duras is not a secondary or external phenomenon, but a primary one, integral to the texts it affects. No one version of any text therefore has precedence over any other. But, equally, texts are no longer entire in themselves, but more like provisional exemplars of an intangible and inaccessible larger work. If one considers the whole of Duras's artistic production, it is rather as though the individual works are always on the point of merging to form an almost seamless, generalised text that exists across genres as an infinitely extendable network of writing, film-making, or theatrical production. But if writing in Duras becomes like a search for its own lost origins, her approach to textuality survives safe in the knowledge that the origin itself is only another fragmentary story calling for another version to be written or filmed. There is no end to the activity of textual repetition; each text turns into a meditation on its own internal limitations, on that which cannot be said or spoken, but which nevertheless remains as the condition of the text's survival and proof of the possibility of its reincarnation in another genre or medium.

Examples from the 1960s and 1970s suggest that Duras's interest in repetition and intertextual transformation found an important outlet in her growing involvement with cinema. The theme of seeing is an important motif in many of Duras's novels of the late 1950s and early 1960s; and what seeing and repeating in Duras have in common is their relationship to desire, and particularly in view of the success of her collaboration with Alain Resnais in 1959, it is not surprising that in the mid-1960s Duras should want to turn to making films directly from her own work. The first film she directed in this way, jointly with Paul Seban, was *La Musica*, based on her own stage play of the same name, first performed the previous year, and originally written for BBC Television; the film, shot in Deauville in June 1966, featured Delphine Seyrig and Robert Hossein in the main roles, with Julie Dassin, in this opened-out version, as the woman with whom the man has a brief affair.

La Musica is a film about doubles; its theme is the apocalyptic aftermath, and repetition, of a love affair. It tells the story of how a freshly divorced couple, Michel Nollet and Anne-Marie Roche, meet up, two years after their original separation, and reflect on their common past and present lives. Each has found a new partner, but is also painfully aware that in the process he or she has already been substituted and supplanted by another. But as they share memories and experiences, the past and the present, ending and beginning, merge together; the past is resurrected as a counterpoint to the present. Desire is rekindled, almost with greater intensity than before, but in the firm knowledge that the two former partners are lost to each other.

But this is why, by a familiar paradox, desire again grows; at the end, in an exchange carried over from the play, Anne-Marie realises that, for her ex-husband, she is now the one woman unavailable to him: 'Regarde-moi,' she says, 'je suis la seule qui te soit interdite' ('Look at me, I'm the only woman now who is forbidden to you', *T1*, 170; 83). Michel replies with the words: 'Ma femme' ('My wife'), as though to confirm that it is precisely in this impossibility of desire that desire itself has its origin (and there is an obvious analogy here with the dialectic of desire and prohibition associated with incest in Duras). Repetition, here, although – or, more likely, because – it signifies finality and exhaustion, also holds out the possibility of apocalyptic renewal, of a desperate intensity refound in the dying moments of love's enactment. It was no doubt to confirm the relevance of this principle to *La Musica* that in 1985 Duras added a second half to the play, under the title *La Musica deuxième*, in which the couple are pushed to the limits of their desires, and rediscover their love for each other at the very moment when they know that it has always already been lost.[2]

Remembering their married past from the perspective of their present divorce, the couple in *La Musica* re-enact their lives as though they were engaged in a self-conscious theatrical perform-ance. This internal doubling of character as well as setting (since the hotel where they meet was where they first lived as a married couple) is strongly emphasised in the mise-en-scène adopted in the film, in which, throughout, windows and mirrors are used to send back reflected images into the camera, and thereby extend and disorient the audience's field of vision. The joint task of directing was divided up so that Seban was responsible for the camera posi-tions, while Duras took charge of the actors; but it was Duras herself who devised the central scene in the hotel lounge, during which Anne-Marie reveals to her ex-husband that she had attempted suicide on hearing of his decision to divorce her.[3] Much of the scene is photographed via a large wall mirror, not unlike the arrangement used for the reception scenes in *India Song*. As a result, the two ex-lovers double up on the screen as both real images and reflected ones, and the viewer is increasingly confused as to which is actually being shown, and which is in fact the more real of the two. The dilemma is naturally one that echoes the uncertainties about desire embodied in the story itself.

After *La Musica*, the first film for which Duras took sole directing

credit was *Détruire, dit-elle*, in 1969. The film was based on a hybrid
novel-cum-play text that appeared earlier in the year. Once again,
it is a work that explores a world of mirror images and merging
identities; and a similar undecidability between the image and its
reflection is duplicated in the relationship between the two works,
the film and the book, both entitled *Détruire, dit-elle*, both published under the name Marguerite Duras (in the film, the position
of Duras as author is both acknowledged and reinforced by an
opening metanarrative exchange, heard off-screen, between Duras
and another female voice). Inevitably, as in all cases where a work
is transferred from page to screen, the film of *Détruire, dit-elle*
limits the book to the extent that it is forced to take determinate
decisions regarding, for instance, the choice of actors or the set,
the style of editing or the selection of camera positions; but at the
same time the film also doubles the book with a reflection of itself
that is recognisably same, yet irreducibly different. The passage of
Détruire, dit-elle from one medium to another invites the audience
to an unending dialogue between two works that share the same
title but display it more as a sign of radical dispersion than as a
badge of identification. Here, then, *Détruire, dit-elle* no longer
simply names a book or a film but, as Blanchot puts it, the interval
between the two.[4] And the significance of *Détruire, dit-elle* for
Duras's relationship to film in general lies in the persistence with
which the work occupies that interval and refuses to allow either
version to be subordinated to its counterpart in the other genre.

As a fiction, *Détruire, dit-elle* drew its immediate inspiration from
the events of May 1968; and, like both *Jaune le soleil* (based on the
book *Abahn, Sabana, David* in 1971) and *Nathalie Granger* (made
in 1972), it is most readily intelligible as an apocalyptic political
allegory. In a hotel bordered by a park and forest, four characters
meet by chance: the mysterious Stein (played in the film by Michel
Lonsdale), who is struggling to be a writer, and is inhabited by
what Duras calls 'ce hurlement intérieur du refus' ('an inner scream
of refusal', *DD*, 20; 10); Max Thor (Henri Garcin), a lecturer and,
like Stein, a Jew (*DD*, 68; 42); Alissa (Nicole Hiss), Max's wife
and former student, whom Stein declares to be insane (*DD*, 36;
21), adding that she is the principal agent of the 'destruction capi-
tale' ('total destruction', *DD*, 59; 36) to which the title refers; and,
finally, Elisabeth Alione (Catherine Sellers), who is in the hotel to
recuperate after giving birth to a dead child (*DD*, 57; 35) and is
also suffering from the end of an unhappy love affair and the

incomprehension of her bourgeois husband (Daniel Gélin) who, in the penultimate scene, comes to visit.

What is at stake in the text is announced most clearly by the names Duras gives her characters. Stein, for instance, as his name implies, is directly related, by cross-gender identification, to the female protagonist of *Le Ravissement de Lol V. Stein*. Like Lol, he is chiefly engaged in watching and looking; his main object of vision, through the open window of the hotel room, is the sight of Max and Alissa making love (*DD*, 52–3; 31). In the act of looking, Stein's identity fuses with that of the pair he espies; to Alissa, for example, he declares: 'Tu fais partie de moi, Alissa. Ton corps fragile fait partie de mon corps' ('You're part of me, Alissa. Your fragile body is part of mine', *DD*, 50; 30). (As he says the words in the film, the scene is shot with Stein seated on the floor to the left of Alissa, while she, dressed in black like him, is bent over on the sofa so that her face is hardly visible; Stein touches her, all the while looking off-screen left, as though to emphasise the anonymity and fusion of the two bodies merged as one, their common body now sustaining a single act of looking.) Later, Max introduces Stein and himself as both being 'les amants d'Alissa' (*DD*, 93; 58), and this interpenetration of the two men is announced in turn by the fact that Elisabeth fails to tell them apart (*DD*, 70; 43). Earlier, in response to Alissa, Max answers that in the book he is writing what he will describe is what Stein sees (*DD*, 47; 28); while, in the film, it is the off-screen narrative voice of Duras herself that explains: 'Max Thor écrit ce que Stein regarde.' And what Stein sees are the bodies of Max and Alissa, and therefore his own, fused together into a shapeless mass: 'Un matin on vous retrouvera,' he tells Alissa, 'informes, ensemble, une masse de goudron, on ne comprendra pas. Sauf moi' ('One morning they'll find you both melted into a shapeless lump like tar, and no one will understand. Except me', *DD*, 53; 32).

In this way, the separate or distinct identities of Stein, Max, and Alissa slowly merge; and what plot remains in *Détruire, dit-elle* entails the extension of this process to Elisabeth Alione. Once more, the name provides a key, for when Stein announces to Max that he was heard in the middle of the night speaking out the name of 'Elisa' (*DD*, 105; 66), it is immediately evident, just as Elisabeth's husband is about to arrive to take her back with him to Grenoble, that Alissa and Elisa have lost their separate identities and become like ghostly reflections of each other.

In the film, so much is already visible from the manner in which the scene immediately preceding is photographed. At 8'20" minutes, it is easily the longest uninterrupted take in *Détruire, dit-elle*, even though, elsewhere in the film, shot lengths of 2'10", 3'50", or even 4'55" minutes, are far from untypical. As the shot begins, the camera is set up at an angle of 45° to the back wall; Elisabeth, dressed in black, is shown in the left-hand side of the screen, beside a wall mirror in which, on the right-hand side, Alissa is reflected, also in black, standing in front of the brightly lit window that looks out onto the park. The camera moves to the right, as does Elisabeth, who now appears in the right-hand side of the screen, while the reflected image of Alissa is visible on the left. Briefly, Alissa is seen doubled up both as a real and a reflected image, before the camera tracks left to show Elisabeth, just visible to the left of the frame, looking at her own reflection (on the right of the screen) and that of Alissa (in the middle). Both women are now visible in the mirror. Alissa comments: 'Nous nous ressemblons', and adds: 'Je vous aime et je vous désire' ('We are alike. I love and desire you'). In the meantime, Alissa has cut her hair to resemble Elisabeth even more closely; and Elisabeth responds, radiantly, that she is no longer afraid. At the end of the shot the camera pans left, revealing both women as real images. Elisabeth exits left, passing in front of Alissa. Throughout the whole sequence, therefore, by mingling real and reflected images and by permutating the relative positions of the two women so that one appears in the place where the other should be, Duras is able to turn the two characters into spectral presences which it is increasingly difficult to tell apart.

Here, then, in *Détruire, dit-elle*, is a portrait of a revolutionary community made up of marginal characters, who do not come weighed down by the burden of any political agenda or programme, but bring tidings of apocalyptic illumination. In the small group made up of Stein, Max, and Alissa, identities have been abandoned, and, with the merging of bodies, desires are left to circulate in an uninhibited, disruptive manner. Duras thematises this transformation as a kind of radical leap. This final, utopian vision is enacted in both book and film by the introduction of a new element: music. (The recourse to music as a concluding non-verbal statement is a device used elsewhere by Duras: the film *Les Enfants*, for instance, ends with a protracted solo for alto saxophone, written by Carlos d'Alessio, which continues to play against the backdrop of the darkened screen long after the image has faded.) In *Détruire, dit-elle*, the music, forming an integral part of the final scene, is a piece from Bach's *Art of the Fugue*. (In *Nathalie Granger*, three years later, at a similarly climactic moment, Duras has her camera wander admiringly over a scattered bundle of scores by Bach and other composers by way of announcing the imminent conflagration of *Le Monde*, the electricity bill, and Nathalie's school report [*NG*, 77], by which Duras signifies the women's refusal at the end of the film to comply with society's oppressive injunctions!)

In *Détruire, dit-elle*, the final scene is shot in a single take of 5'30", during which time the camera holds its position without moving. As evening falls, Stein (standing by the door), Max (seated), and Alissa (slumped forward) are grouped together around the circular table used earlier for the lunch with Bernard Alione. The camera is placed inside the house, facing the open door and windows, beyond which the park and forest can be made out in the mid-distance. The room is in darkness, with no inside lighting. But, reminding the audience of the impending promise of illumination, the sun in the treetops is just visible in the background, in characteristically apocalyptic manner. As the music of Bach becomes audible, it is muffled – but also intensified – by the sound of crashing thunder; and gradually the music becomes louder. Alissa, apparently waking up, announces 'C'est la musique sur le nom de Stein' ('It's the music that goes with the name of Stein'), as though to greet an invisible force flooding in through the door. (The novel has it that, when she delivers this message, Alissa is still asleep, convulsed in a childlike, transgressive 'rire absolu' ['absolute laugh', *DD*, 137; 85].)

As well as imagining the workings of a hieratic revolutionary community, *Détruire, dit-elle*, both as a written text and a film, is concerned with trying to elaborate a similarly radical literary or cinematographic language. In both cases Duras opts for an elemental idiom consistent with the *tabula rasa* of both desire and social organisation depicted in the fiction itself. The book, hesitating between novel, theatre or cinema script, is full of simple declarative or anaphoric statements; subordinate clauses are few. For its part, in parallel manner, the film version of *Détruire, dit-elle* constructs a stylised, theatrical world that falls well short of the conventional requirements regarding dramatic cohesion or continuity. There are, for instance, very few sequences dependent on shot/reverse shot editing, and eyeline matches are also rare. Characters gaze off-screen, but, as with Max Thor, found staring intently to the left, beyond the frame, in the opening scene, that look is not returned, nor does it serve as a cue for action. The result is a process of dramatic disengagement in which the only privileged act of looking is that of the camera itself and, by the same token, the viewer. The effect is accentuated by the slow editing and extreme reliance on the long take (with the result that, with the exception of reaction shots, most images are held well beyond their conventionally expected length); also, fixed camera positions predominate, varied only by occasional, stylised camera movements often coming at the beginning or end of a shot, and by intermittent slow pans surveying the park and its forest boundary.

In its fragmentary, allusive use of off-screen space, its stylised camera movements and non-naturalistic acting, *Détruire, dit-elle* owes something to the influence of a director like Bresson; but in other ways its theatrical mise-en-scène and leisurely editing style are more reminiscent, say, of Dreyer's *Gertrud* (1964). Also important, no doubt, in allowing Duras to develop a distinctive film language of her own, if only by counter-example, was the experience gained from collaborating with other film-makers during the early 1960s; indeed, after the success of *Hiroshima mon amour*, Duras worked on scripts for a number of directors, including Peter Brook (*Moderato cantabile*), Henri Colpi and Jasmine Chesnay (*Une aussi longue absence*), and Georges Franju, for whom she wrote *Les Rideaux blancs*, a short and unmemorable film about the friendship of a teenage boy with a confused, elderly woman during the 1944 Normandy invasion, the theme of which is best summed up in the film's closing words (which explain the title): 'Le ciel est bleu, le soleil brille, à travers les rideaux blancs' ('The sky is blue, the sun is shining, through the white curtains').

But of all her collaborations with other directors, by far the most significant, in the light of Duras's later work, was *Nuit noire, Calcutta*, the short twenty-five-minute film written in 1964 for Marin Karmitz. Karmitz was originally given money by a pharmaceutical company to make a film advertising a drug for use with alcoholics, but, after abandoning the idea of a documentary, suggested to Duras, who had recently undergone treatment for her own alcoholism, that she might like to write a fiction film on the theme. The result was a first (or, more probably, second) draft of what later turned into the novel, *Le Vice-consul*.[5] Though Duras took no part in directing the film, she was present throughout the shooting, which took place largely in Trouville (partly in the author's flat) and on the mudflats along the estuary towards Ouistreham at low tide. The experience gave Duras an invaluable opportunity of seeing at first hand how films could be made quickly and cheaply, with limited resources and a small crew, in the manner pioneered by

Godard, Agnès Varda, and others.[6] (And it is true that, till then, with the exception of *Hiroshima mon amour*, the films in which Duras had been involved as scriptwriter, like the films adapted from her novels, had remained relatively untouched by the inventiveness and iconoclasm of the *nouvelle vague*.)

Nuit noire, Calcutta is the story of a writer, Jean (Maurice Garrel), who has come to the coast to complete a novel about the French vice-consul in Calcutta. He does not find his task an easy one, and he struggles throughout to find adequate words for his story. Convinced, as he puts it, that the words do exist somewhere, he is shown repeatedly working at his manuscript (in which the name Anne-Marie appears), deleting sentences, or tearing up pages in frustration. In the process, he empties several bottles of whisky (hence the connection with the theme of alcoholism!). As he writes, there is a story unfolding in the outside world that seems to parallel the one he is inventing, although it is not clear which of these is mirroring the other. The two series of events refuse to converge; but this enables the film to explore the ironical, metaphorical relationship between the imaginary, speculative world of Calcutta, dominated by the delta of the Ganges, and the dunes and mudflats of the Seine estuary at Ouistreham. As it develops, the film displays a number of familiar Durassian images or motifs: a hotel window that suddenly opens, allowing the protagonist to catch the sight of a woman who might be the female character he is trying to describe; a long shot across a cornfield (perhaps even a rye-field!); a wide expanse of beach with a dog wandering across it at low tide; and a woman caught emerging at night from the casino at Trouville.

Like *India Song* and other later films, *Nuit noire, Calcutta* also effects a marked separation between sound and image. The only characters to speak on screen in the film are two women in a café, overheard talking about a man called Jean who has gone away to write a book; other than this, the virtual entirety of the text is spoken off-screen by the film's protagonist. (During the filming, a working copy of the soundtrack, subsequently erased, was made with Duras herself reading the text, thereby anticipating, as it were, fifteen years in advance, the method adopted later in the two screen versions of *Aurélia Steiner* or *L'Homme atlantique*.) Rather than representing Duras's text in a conventionally mimetic way, Karmitz's film experiments with different relationships between image and sound, founded on similarity and distance, metaphor and irony. And a similar doubleness can also be observed in the use of the camera, with the film alternating throughout between fixed camera positions and fluid sideways tracking shots, between light and dark, interiors and exteriors, the whole modulated, Karmitz explains, according to Cabbalistic constraints.

But if *Nuit noire, Calcutta* in 1964 already pointed to the possibility of a different relationship between image and text from that adopted in *Détruire, dit-elle* and the two films immediately following, it was not until 1972, in *La Femme du Gange*, that Duras began to develop that potential herself. This she did, as I described earlier, by overdubbing at the last moment two – off-screen – women's voices, which comment on the action of the film and, in their erotic relationship with one another, repeat and double the movement of desire acted out on screen; in this way the voices supply the film with a third, purely filmic layer of text, alongside the more usual image track and diegetic soundtrack, which corresponds to a second layer of diegetic activity embedded in the process of cinematographic narration itself. In itself, the extra dimension that Duras introduces remains beyond visual representation and thus cannot be located in time or space; it doubles the audience's gaze with a second, disembodied – ecstatic – act of vision which Duras is somehow able to translate into speech (and the sheer acoustic presence of the voice, detached from any supporting image, is a key factor in bringing about this impossible – imaginary – conversion). And words, as a result, in Duras, begin here to behave like a superior form of seeing, since, unlike images, they have the mysterious and surprising capacity to envision the invisible. For this reason, as far as Duras's relationship to the cinema was concerned, *La Femme du Gange* represents a turning point. In 1974 Duras went on to generalise the technique; the result was the film *India Song*, shot entirely in northern France, loosely based on the 1973 hybrid play text of the same name and probably still Duras's most innovative excursion into film-making.

II

The plot of *India Song* is a condensed and revised version of *Le Vice-consul*; like that novel, it is set in the late 1930s in Calcutta and weaves together, beneath a murky apocalyptic light (described repeatedly as 'crépusculaire' [*VC*, 31; 20]), three parallel but incommensurable strands of narrative.[7] The first deals with a beggar woman from Indochina who has somehow found her way on foot to the delta of the Ganges, where, destitute and infested with disease, she survives living off the scraps left over by wealthy

① ② film-within-the film

European society. In *Le Vice-consul*, what little is known about the woman's past is in the form of a speculative metanarrative (or story-within-the-story) authored by Peter Morgan, a British embassy official with a prurient fascination with what he describes as 'la douleur aux Indes' ('the sufferings of India', *VC*, 157; 124). Between Morgan and the woman who is the subject of his musings runs something of the same relationship of stark antithesis and covert identification as between Jacques Hold and Lol in *Le Ravissement de Lol V. Stein*, with the result that when Duras writes, at the outset, under Morgan's name, that 'je voudrais une indication pour me perdre' ('I need some signpost to lead me astray', *VC*, 9; 1), it is impossible to decide whether the first-person pronoun refers to Morgan or the beggar woman, if not indeed both. By the end of the novel, though, it is the woman who scares off her colonial pursuer, Charles Rossett, not the reverse. And accordingly, while in the 1974 film Peter Morgan all but disappears from the story, the figure of the beggar woman lives on to haunt the film as the necessarily fictional embodiment of an apocalyptic state *sans* (or *post*) everything; but she does so without ever being seen on screen (only in the 1973 play does Duras envisage making the beggar woman visible on stage). The result is that the only sign of the women's existence is in the form of a strange, unintelligible Laotian song, heard periodically on the soundtrack, immediately followed by peals of laughter seeming to imply innocence and gaiety. But because she is reduced to the status of an unseen, unrepresentable phantom, it is the beggar woman, somehow surviving the loss of all the usual fixtures of humanity, including home, family, child, country, even language, who speaks most intensely in the film of exclusion, despair, and desire.

If the beggar woman suggests everything that white colonial society casts out beyond its own carefully policed borders as a means of ensuring its own survival, the remaining threads of the plot have more to do with the grim and embarrassing secret that the European élite harbours within its ranks. Typical in this respect is the story of the virginal (*VC*, 76; 58) – possibly homosexual – former French Vice-Consul in Lahore, who returns in disgrace to Calcutta (the capital of India according to Duras's imaginary geography [*VC*, 35; 23]) after a series of obscure incidents in which he seems to have taken to shooting up the mirrors in his own residence as a way of destroying his own reflected self, as well as firing at the lepers and beggars congregating in the Shalimar Gardens in order to put an end, as it were, to the scandal of colonial misery.

The Vice-Consul, however, refuses to repudiate or explain away his behaviour in Lahore; on the contrary, Lahore, he maintains in *Le Vice-consul*, 'c'était encore une forme de l'espoir' ('was still a form of hope', *VC*, 126; 99). (Interestingly, by 1973, as Duras develops the theme of the Vice-Consul's love for the French ambassador's wife, Anne-Marie Stretter, Calcutta is the word that is invested by him with hope [*IS*, 96; 93]; yet what is most worth noting here is how place names in Duras function consistently – particularly, say, in *Hiroshima mon amour* – as shorthand ciphers for a series of catastrophic events that have somehow broken loose from the confines of geography and history.) Hope, in *Le Vice-consul*, as in *Le Square* ten years before, is violently apocalyptic in tenor; what it signifies is catastrophic destruction as a condition for a fresh beginning and new innocence.

In Calcutta, in order to realise this hope, though in a manner that must dispense with the narrative structure of a love story, the Vice-Consul embarks on a possible (or impossible) liaison with Anne-Marie Stretter. (She of course is transported to India by Duras from the opening pages of *Le Ravissement de Lol V. Stein*, together with her lover, Michael Richardson, who appears in *Le Vice-consul* as the truncated Michael Richard, only to revert to his former name in *India Song*.) Like the Vice-Consul, Anne-Marie Stretter is possessed of a strongly depressive, if also erotic intensity. Known formerly (in *India Song*) as Anna Maria Guardi from Venice, she is an enigmatic, melancholy figure, a pianist (*VC*, 186–7; 149) who, in *India Song*, has slowly abandoned playing because of a vague feeling of pain ('une certaine douleur' [*IS*, 85; 81]) now associated for her with music. She is allowed much sexual freedom by her husband, but languishes in an emotional limbo; of life in India, for example, she remarks in *Le Vice-consul* that 'ce n'est ni facile ni difficile, ce n'est rien' ('it is neither easy nor difficult, it's nothing', *VC*, 109; 85); and in *India Song* the words are the same (*IS*, 82; 77). Though her love for Michael Richard (or Richardson) is described as binding, it remains largely self-destructive; after an evening spent at the Blue Moon club, the reader is told, it would be no surprise to find they had attempted suicide together (which is in fact what they do, unsuccessfully, in the film version of *India Song*):

Quelque chose les lie, se dit Charles Rossett, de stable, de définitif, mais ce n'est plus, dirait-on, un amour dans son devenir. [. . .] On pense qu'il n'est pas impossible qu'un soir, ils soient retrouvés morts ensemble dans un hôtel de Chandernagor, après le *Blue Moon*. Ce serait pendant la mousson d'été. On dirait: pour rien, par indifférence à la vie.

(There is some bond between them, Charles Rossett says to himself. Some lasting and stable bond, but they don't strike one as being in love, at least not any longer. [. . .] No one would be suprised if they were found dead in bed together one morning in a hotel in Chandernagore, after a night at the Blue Moon. If it were to happen, it would be during the summer monsoon. People would say: 'No reason at all. They simply lacked the will to live.')

(VC, 152; 120)

In the course of *Le Vice-consul* and *India Song*, despite the many discrepancies between the texts, as Duras explores her three main characters, she develops a series of implicit parallels between them. Some of these depend on verbal leitmotifs or symbolism, others on intricacies of plot. Peter Morgan speculates, for instance, that a story he was told by Anne-Marie, recounting the adoption of a native girl by a European woman in Savannakhet, Laos (which Duras elsewhere claims to be an incident from her own childhood[8]), may have involved the beggar; but the dates do not coincide (*VC*, 72; 54). Earlier, Anne-Marie is seen by the Vice-Consul giving instructions for water to be left out for the local beggars (*VC*, 36; 24); and a phrase applied in *Le Vice-consul* to the adopted child ('Cette belle enfant est à qui la voudra' ['This fine child can go with whoever wants her', *VC*, 54; 39]) crops up again in *India Song*, in modified form, in relation to Anne-Marie's sexual infidelity: 'Elle est à qui veut d'elle' ('She goes with whoever wants her', *IS*, 46; 38). The beggar woman herself, when first mentioned in the main narrative of *Le Vice-consul*, is found sleeping outside the residence of the former Vice-Consul (*VC*, 29; 18); and when he provokes a scandal at the reception by shouting his desire to stay behind at the end, his cries merge into the chanting of the beggar woman outside the Embassy (*VC*, 151; 120). And a phrase that in *Le Vice-consul* he uses to describe the beggar woman returns, slightly altered, to be applied to him by one of the members of the Embassy party in *India Song* (but only in the film, not the play!): 'La mort dans une vie en cours, [. . .] mais qui ne vous rejoindrait jamais' ('Like a kind of living death [. . .] forever out of reach', *VC*, 174; 139). Towards the end, Charles Rossett (the Young Attaché of *India Song*) wonders: 'Au fait, à qui ressemblait-il, le vice-consul de Lahore?' The answer is unambiguous: 'A moi, dit Anne-Marie Stretter' (' "In point of fact, who did the Vice-Consul from Lahore most remind you of?" "Me," says Anne-Marie Stretter', *VC*, 204; 162), who thus confirms the complicity between the Vice-Consul and herself.

In this and numerous other ways Duras points to underlying similarities between the beggar, the Vice-Consul, and Anne-Marie Stretter. What the three characters have in common, however, is less a positive predicament than a negative state; each is an exile, but from a world that bears little resemblance to the society from which either of the others has been banished. As a result, the convergence of the fate of the three is suggested not by recourse to the sentimental theme of universal human solidarity, but by a rhetoric of metonymic contagion. This is mirrored, *en abyme* as it were, in Duras's use of the motif of leprosy, prominent throughout both *Le Vice-consul* and *India Song*. Leprosy, here, of course, is a figure of infection by touch; those it contaminates it changes into untouchable pariahs, outcasts who bear in their flesh the sores of the social and metaphysical malady that is Duras's India.

In both *Le Vice-consul* and *India Song*, what all three main characters display (rather like the figure of the mother in *L'Amant*) is a mixture of passivity and relentlessness, a submission to their lot coupled with an unflinching determination to affirm their fate by pursuing it to its logical, bitter end. Despite their impossible lives, suicide, for all three, though envisaged, is deferred to the last; but only for the realisation then to dawn, at this remote point of apocalyptic extremity, that the difference between life and death, suicide and survival has dwindled almost to nothing. At this stage of desperation, however, desire, for Duras, reaches the intensity of a pure affirmation; as such, she insists, it is profoundly subversive of European social order. This turns the beggar woman, Anne-Marie Stretter, and the Vice-Consul into the carriers of an apocalyptic insight, which, if generalised, as Duras would do through her own writing, would have the power to shake society to its foundations; and, extravagant though it may sound if set alongside the programmes and agendas of everyday party politics, this is the claim being made by Duras when she asserts the status of her work as a political act.

Writing *India Song* in 1973, and subsequently filming it in 1974, Duras's purpose was evidently not to rewrite *Le Vice-consul* for the stage or screen (or even, in the case of the film, simply to supply a faithful adaptation of the 1973 play text). Instead, *India Song*, both as play and film, is more a rearticulation and intensification of elements drawn from the earlier novel. Duras introduces many changes. First, she rebuilds the plot around the reception scene at the French Embassy in Calcutta. This had occupied little more than a quarter of the length of the 1966 novel, but in the film of *India Song*, at fifty-seven minutes (out of a total of nearly two hours), it grows to take up nearly half the length; and, flanked by a prologue of thirty minutes and an epilogue of twenty-three minutes, it now functions as the main narrative crux of the story. As the scene expands, *India Song* takes its place within a series of works by Duras in which dance scenes are paramount (including, of course, the sequence of texts featuring Lol V. Stein, whose memory is evoked at the beginning of *India Song* [*IS*, 15–16; 13]). In *India Song*, as in *Le Ravissement de Lol V. Stein*, dancing is a figure that dramatises desire as a continual process of fusion and separation (in the 1973 text, for example, a stage direction has it of Anne-Marie Stretter and Michael Richardson that 'ils se rapprochent dans la danse jusqu'à ne faire qu'un' ['they dance so close together as to melt into one', *IS*, 20; 17]; but in the course of *India Song* Anne-Marie also dances with her unnamed house guest – the Peter Morgan of earlier – the Young Attaché, and the Vice-Consul). Sustained by this figure of dance, a familiar scenario of projective identification ensues, with the Vice-Consul declaring his love to Anne-Marie with the words: 'Je vous aime ainsi, dans l'amour de Michael Richardson' ('I love you as you are, in your love for Michael Richardson', *IS*, 96; 93).

The relationship between *India Song* and *Le Vice-consul* is not contemporaneous, but, as befits the delay of some eight years between them, posthumous or retrospective. In *India Song* Anne-Marie Stretter, now the dominant figure in the story, is dead, having drowned herself in the delta of the Ganges at the end of the weekend on the islands; but by revealing this information at the beginning of the film (and play) Duras stages *India Song* not as a mimetic representation of the death of Anne-Marie Stretter, but a ritualised memorial to her. This is the primary, diegetic reason for Duras's decision to systematise what she had first attempted in *La Femme du Gange* and thus radically divorce the image from the soundtrack, with the result that, throughout the entirety of the film of *India Song*, no character is seen to speak on screen. Instead, during the prologue and epilogue, responsibility for the narrative is given over to five unidentified speakers (Nicole Hiss, Monique Simonet, Viviane Forrester, Dionys Mascolo, Duras herself), who fulfil a similar function to the off-screen voices used in *La Femme du Gange*; while during the reception scene, the only sequence that even approximates to a conventionally visualised re-enactment of the story, voices belonging to the actors seen on screen – the Young Attaché (Mathieu Carrière), Anne-Marie Stretter (Delphine Seyrig), the Vice-Consul (Michel Lonsdale), and others – are heard as in a conventional dramatic performance, with the crucial difference that, while being heard on the soundtrack, none of these characters is seen to open his or her lips. Instead, they gaze, allowing their eyes to wander, usually off-screen, with Duras making little attempt, as in *Détruire, dit-elle*, to integrate the space of the film by the use of shot/reverse shot editing or eyeline matches. (In addition to these main protagonists, there are numerous other voices that remain without any visual counterpart, and one character, Michael Richardson [Claude Mann], who, though seen on screen, is never heard to speak; and a major role is played in the film by music, ranging from 1930s dance music to Beethoven's Diabelli Variations, played in covert homage to Anne-Marie's past career as a pianist.)

By dividing image and sound in this way, Duras transforms what the audience sees and hears into something more complex and disorientating than the usual sequence of conventionalised cinematographic signs. Images are displaced one stage further, and turn into signs of signs, images of images; while recorded sound is no longer controlled by visual criteria such as the distinction between on and off-screen, diegetic and non-diegetic.[9] Instead, such boundaries become permeable; and what one expects to hear on-screen is mysteriously relegated to invisible, unlocated off-screen space, while, similarly, those sounds or voices that would conventionally have remained off-screen are denied the extradiegetic authority usually associated with the voice-over to become part of the fiction, which thus doubles up, as in *Le Ravissement de Lol V. Stein*, to include the story of its own narrative re-enactment.

But if, in *India Song*, Duras manages to treat image and sound as autonomous levels proceeding in parallel, it is important to realise that the film as a whole is an effect of the dynamic interplay – symbolic, ironical, referential, or intertextual – between the image track and soundtrack. But though there is frequent overlap between what is visible on screen at any one moment and what is heard on the soundtrack, the two are never fully or consistently integrated, and much of the fascination and difficulty of *India Song* for the viewer derives from this need constantly to reinvent the relationship between image and sound as one watches and listens. (Oddly, as a result, nothing is more disappointing than viewing *India Song* with foreign subtitles, since the appearance on screen of information conveyed only by the soundtrack creates an entirely false coincidence between eye and ear.)

While *India Song* breaks new ground in its treatment of the relation between text and image, the film, in other respects, follows closely the pattern established in earlier films. Here, too, as in *Détruire, dit-elle*, Duras resists the conventions of continuity editing, and, relying extensively on the long take, tends to conceive of each shot as a discrete, autonomous unit. Also, in *India Song*, the camera alternates between a limited number of fixed positions from which events are staged and photographed in consciously theatrical manner, and a series of fluid pans or tracking shots, often taken in the gloomy half-light, that serve as an anti-mimetic counterweight to the overriding theatricality of the main scenes. To an extent, the absence or presence of camera movement is dictated by the contrast between the memory of Anne-Marie Stretter and the aftermath of her death, between the animated interiors and largely abandoned exteriors; but the formalism is only relative, allowing Duras to achieve dramatic effect by establishing, then disrupting audience expectations.

India Song opens with a static long shot that, after the credits, combines two familiar apocalyptic motifs: the setting sun slowly dipping behind the horizon, and, off-screen, the song and cries of the beggar woman. Even before the end of the shot, the two off-screen voices have made the link with Anne-Marie Stretter, a photograph of whom is seen in the next shot, on the piano, lit by a small Chinese lamp that stands out against the general gloom; six shots later (shot 9), at the conclusion of a slow left-hand pan of the reception room (lasting 3'2"), Anne-Marie Stretter herself is seen for the first time, dancing with Michael Richardson. To the right of the frame, the Stretters' house guest (Didier Flamand), leaning against a large wall mirror, gazes off-screen right, evidently looking, if somewhat aimlessly, at the couple dancing; however, the pair are visible to the viewer only in the left of the frame, as reflections in the mirror.[10]

In this way, the mirror, already seen as a darkened surface in two earlier shots, becomes animated with the memory of the reception; and, from this point on, as the film resurrects that story, the mirror, dominating many of the interior shots, functions as a sign of narrativity, of the possibility of joining image to text in the construction of a story. But it is symptomatic that, towards the end of the shot, as the two dancers are fully framed in the mirror for the first time, one of the two off-screen female voices is heard to say to the other: 'Je vous aime jusqu'à ne plus voir, ne plus entendre, mourir' ('I love you so much I can't see any more, can't hear, can't live', *IS*, 21; 18); at the very moment that desire is embodied in the image of the two dancers, already construed as an object of vision by the gaze of the third character in the shot, love is also portrayed off-screen as a fusional intensity which is always liable to overwhelm the distance between subject and object that the act of looking requires (and on-screen, too, by refusing shot/reverse shot editing and showing the guest and what he sees as two images side-by-side in the frame, Duras disorganises the spatial relationship between viewer and object and fuses them together within the same plane).

Desire, in *India Song*, is a force that is always beyond the limitations of visual representation; this is clearly the reason for Duras's refusal to construct the film according to the conventions of shot/reverse shot editing (throughout the whole film there is only one such sequence [shots 23–5], staging the Vice-Consul's first sight of Anne-Marie Stretter). As the invisible, acoustic presence of the film's off-screen voices implies from the outset, the possibility of representation symbolised by the wall mirror is only a provisional one, which the rest of the film puts into parentheses and thus casts into doubt. The mirror itself, of course, is visible in many shots as an internal cinematographic screen, an image-within-the-image incorporated within the film; it functions not just as a symbol of narrativity, but also as a mirror image of *India Song* itself in its search for a – possible – image with which to represent the text. So, what is true of the mirror in *India Song* is also true of the film *India Song* as a whole: the relationship between image and word is incommensurable; the only possible representation of the text is a representation that represents the impossibility of representation.

In the climactic last scene between the Vice-Consul and Anne-Marie Stretter, which, at 10′17″, is the longest single take in the film, Duras demonstrates this paradox by abandoning the device of the mirror in mid-shot. (From this point on, though it is seen twice more in the film, the mirror becomes conspicuously empty, and is used by Duras to show the lingering departure of Anne-Marie Stretter and other guests as they leave by the stairs, and thus disappear, as it were, into the mirror itself.) The scene (shot 52) is filmed as an extended inverse reprise of the mirror sequence described earlier (the two scenes are also the only shots of the reception during which the camera does not remain totally static). The camera, positioned so close to the mirror that the mirror and film frame fuse together as one, picks up – as reflected images – first the piano (with the 'India Song' score visible on it), then Anne-Marie, then the Vice-Consul; after about two minutes, the camera pans slowly to the right through 180°, passing by Michael Richardson, smoking at the open window, until it encounters the couple again, dancing, now shown as real images. It is at this point that the Vice-Consul is heard to tell Anne-Marie of his love for her in by now familiar fusional terms: 'Vous êtes avec moi devant Lahore,' he declares. 'Vous êtes en moi. [. . .] Nous n'avons rien à nous dire. Nous sommes les mêmes. [. . .] Les histoires d'amour vous les vivez avec d'autres' ('You are by my side facing Lahore. You are inside me. [. . .] We have no words for each other. We are the same. [. . .] A love story is something you keep for others', *IS*, 97–8; 94–5).

However, as the Vice-Consul realises the impossibility of his position in society, the pair disappear out of the frame. The camera holds its location; and the Vice-Consul reappears alone, then exits to the left. All that remains of his outburst are his cries, heard off-screen; his place by the side of Anne-Marie is taken by Michael Richardson. At the end of the shot, the film has been returned to the position occupied at the end of the earlier mirror shot, but with the crucial difference that the mirror is now no longer visible. Something in the story has been exhausted by the excess and extremity of the Vice-Consul's apocalyptic desire for Anne-Marie Stretter. It is as though the Vice-Consul, whose story began, in *India Song* (and *Le Vice-consul*), with him shooting at his own reflection in the mirrors in his residence at Lahore, has found a way finally to shatter that reflection. At this point, though he is seen once more in the film, arriving at the islands, the Vice-Consul leaves the story (and screen) that he has never properly inhabited, followed shortly after by Anne-Marie, whose death comes towards the end, as she too exits to the left, leaving the film to conclude as it had begun, with an evocation of the unseen, unrepresentable beggar woman from Savannakhet.

'Les miroirs sont les portes par lesquelles la mort vient et va' ('Mirrors are the doors through which death comes and goes'), says Heurtebise in Cocteau's *Orphée*; and the mirror in *India Song* ends up performing much the same function, seemingly able to stage events as though they were present before the viewer's eyes, but secretly aware that such images imply only the absence of what they seem to embody. Like the mirror, the image track of *India Song* as a whole does not deliver the spectacle of real presences, but enacts a failure of representation. The gap between image and text cannot be bridged. As a result, the relationship between image and text inevitably becomes tenuous, almost arbitrary; and even the ironically provisional images of Anne-Marie Stretter and the Vice-Consul that are shown in *India Song* may be redundant. Such images, one might argue, are unnecessary, and could in principle be replaced by other images; and those other images need not even attempt to illustrate the text, as *India Song* still does in part, but might prefer simply to double the text in such a way that all they would display would be their own failure to represent this unrepresentable story. In due course, such alternative images would constitute a further textual gloss on the narrative, which they would inevitably signify, by metaphor or metonymy, but without even attempting to represent it and thus exhaust its endless potentiality.

In some ways, then, it comes as no surprise that, within two years of making *India Song*, pausing only to film *Des journées entières dans les arbres* after her own stage production, Duras was at work on a second version of *India Song*. This she entitled *Son nom de Venise dans Calcutta désert*, after the phrase first spoken on the soundtrack of *India Song* by the voice of Duras herself (and which owes its peculiar resonance to the fact that it scans as a classical French twelve-syllable alexandrine). *Son nom de Venise dans Calcutta désert* uses almost exactly the same soundtrack as *India Song* but contains none of the same images; throughout the whole film, virtually no human figures appear on screen, except in two scenes, the first (shot 6), in which two bodies may just be made out in the gloom of a darkened room, and the second (shots 73–7), towards the end, when two women in ordinary dress (Delphine Seyrig and Nicole Hiss) are seen behind a bay window, as though they, too, had just seen the film with the audience.

In other respects, the film develops and radicalises the procedures adopted in *India Song*, and alternates between a recurrent series of static shots of windows or mirrors, most of them – appropriately enough – broken or cracked, and an extensive repertoire of dimly lit and disorientating forays with a hand-held camera through the abandoned rooms and cellars of the palais Rothschild near Rheims (which Duras had already used in *India Song* for the exteriors of the French Embassy in Calcutta). Also, *Son nom de Venise dans Calcutta désert* necessarily redoubles and cites *India Song*, but it tends to do so by inverting rather than replicating the earlier film. For the final scene between the Vice-Consul and Anne-Marie Stretter (shot 52 of *India Song*), for instance, Duras uses three shots, of 1'7", 7'41", and 1'40" respectively (shots 49–51). The first of these is a high-angle counter-clockwise pan, passing through almost 360°, that shows the irregular, gravelly surface of the terrace (a similar shot is used to open the film); cutting at the point when in *India Song* the camera began panning to the right, Duras follows up this first shot with a slow left-hand tracking shot showing the base of the disaffected building, its closed-up windows, iron railings and balustrade, before ending with a view of the park. Having replaced, in both these shots, the right-handed movement of shot 52 of *India Song* with left-handed shots, Duras now tracks and pans with the camera in a right-hand direction across the darkened surface of a lake, in which one can see the inverted reflections of the trees, shown previously (in shot 48) lit with the intense blue and orange glow of the evening sky ('Regardez le ciel, malade, cette épaisseur, cette crasse, à travers la nuit' ['Look at the sky, you'd think it was sick, like a thick layer of filth through the darkness'], as the voice of one woman guest had commented); and the sequence ends with this covert, apocalyptic evocation of the mirror previously abandoned in *India Song*.

III

Son nom de Venise dans Calcutta désert showed Duras that if mirror images, as in *India Song*, could be taken to enshrine the death or absence of what they seemed to represent, then the same principle could be applied more generally to other film images as well (if not, in fact, to all film images as such, as the *Aurélia Steiner* films and *L'Homme atlantique* were subsequently to confirm). This provided Duras with the starting point for her next important film, *Le Camion*, made in 1977 immediately after the abortive *Baxter, Véra Baxter*, which Duras later rejected.[11] The lesson that Duras drew from *Son nom de Venise dans Calcutta désert* was an obvious, if idiosyncratic one, for it ended with Duras partially abandoning fiction and fictional images to opt for a film form that was beyond easy generic distinctions and stood midway between fiction film, documentary, media talkshow, and improvised theatre. The main novelty of *Le Camion* was that it showed Duras, alongside Gérard Depardieu, playing the part of herself as narrator and author. In the film Duras reverted once more to apocalyptic political allegory;

the character she chose this time as a vehicle of catastrophic political affirmation was a nomadic middle-aged woman hitchhiker, possibly a refugee from a mental asylum, who, like Duras herself, though not a Jew, has a passionate commitment to Judaism. The political point of the film lay in its emphasis on the irreconcilable differences between this woman's radicalism and the arrogance and conservatism displayed by the lorry driver, a traditionalist PCF member, who offers her a lift.

The film itself crosscuts consistently between two parallel series of images, each of which subdivides into two further contrasted series. First, the film follows the movements of a 32-ton blue Saviem HGV, alternating slow pans of the outside of the HGV as it travels across the industrial suburban or rural landscape with a sequence of faster tracking shots taken with the camera mounted inside the cabin. (The unreality conveyed in many of these shots, once the credit sequence finishes, derives from the replacement of direct sound of the road with the music of Beethoven's Diabelli Variations or Duras's own voice-over.) Throughout the film, these exteriors alternate with a series of largely static interior shots, taken in one or other of two locations in Duras's flat; these show Duras and Depardieu, separately or together, reading or improvising the story of the woman hitchhiker and the communist driver. Common to both series of shots is the inevitable – apocalyptic – progression from afternoon light to evening gloom and then once more towards illumination, together with three of Beethoven's Diabelli Variations, which act as a bridge between the two sequences, as do the words of Duras herself, heard in- and off-screen at various moments throughout.

The two series of shots are clearly calculated to mirror each other. The panning shots of the HGV as it moves across the country might be showing the HGV which Duras and Depardieu are describing in their story (though the locations are different); and the inside of the room might be the cab of the HGV with its two inhabitants, one male and one female (but Duras and Depardieu are inventing a road movie, not actually working as truckers). The two diegetic spaces remain distinct, but in the course of the film also implicitly fuse together. Duras confirms this when she compares the situation of Depardieu and herself with that of the two unseen characters:

> J'ai l'impression que vous et moi aussi, nous sommes comme menacés par cette même lumière dont ils ont peur: la crainte

que d'un seul coup s'engouffre dans la cabine du camion, dans la chambre noire, un flot de lumière, voyez. . . . La peur de la catastrophe: L'intelligence politique.

(*C*, 41–2)

(I feel as though you and I are also threatened by the same light as they are afraid of: the fear that all of a sudden the cab of the truck, the dark chamber, might be engulfed by a flood of light, d'you see. . . . The fear of catastrophe: political understanding.)

There is here a peculiar merging of actuality and potentiality, of what is visible on screen and what may be imagined on that basis, between what is and what might be, and this equivalence provides the film with one of its most characteristic traits. Duras puts the principle clearly from the outset, in response to a question from Depardieu: 'Ç'aurait été un film. C'est un film, oui' ('It would have been a film. It is a film, yes', *C*, 12).

The two separate series of shots are not autonomous, but closely interwoven. But they exchange attributes – to great dramatic effect – only at the end of *Le Camion*, when Duras stages a climax somewhat reminiscent of the ending of *Détruire, dit-elle*. Four shots before the end, as on two previous occasions in the film, the camera remains motionless as the HGV passes by on one of its forays through the countryside. Then, in the shot immediately following, for almost the first time in *Le Camion*, the camera abandons its fixed position during an interior shot and tracks forwards, towards and beyond Duras and Depardieu to frame the bright afternoon sun visible through the net curtains, with the result that the central panel of the frame is over-exposed and almost burnt out; but again, in the next, penultimate shot, as the two actors sit in semi-darkness, the camera once more tracks towards them, then pans to the right to show, through an open window, the outline of the trees against the luminous blue of the evening sky. The film cuts to black, while, for sixteen seconds longer, the off-screen voice of Duras continues, carried by the music of the 31st Diabelli Variation; as both fall silent, without transition, the waltz theme starts up again to greet the final credits. In these closing shots *Le Camion* crosses immobility with mobility, afternoon sun with evening light, exterior with interior, in a mimetically incoherent sequence of images that is resolved at the end only by the cut to black; and it is as though the final frame, sustained just by the voice of Duras and the piano of Beethoven, by refusing to provide a determinate image, is somehow the sublime embodiment of everything in Duras – from desire and madness to apocalyptic revolution – that transgresses or exceeds visual representation.

Le Camion is a film that demonstrates the inevitable – if also necessary – limitations of vision when compared with the sublime invisibility of voice or music, which perhaps only an entirely blackened image can match. Duras writes in explanation that: 'Le cinéma arrête le texte, frappe de mort sa descendance: l'imaginaire. C'est même là sa vertu même: de fermer. D'arrêter l'imaginaire' ('Cinema freezes the text, kills its progeny: the imagination. That's even what it does best. To close, put a stop to the imagination', *C*, 75). Film, by providing determinate images, puts an end to the infinite possibility of images. In strangely contrary fashion, it seems that for Duras only the invisible, unseeing written text can safeguard the possibility of the infinite proliferation of images and thus somehow save cinema from itself; but if writing preserves the possibility of cinema in this way, it does so by pushing it to a limit that is ruinous of cinema as such. The paradox is a powerful one, and it affects all Duras's work on film after *Le Camion* (even when, as with *Les Enfants* in 1985, she reverts to the theatrical manner of *Détruire, dit-elle* and *Nathalie Granger*). It finds particularly forceful expression in *Le Navire Night* of 1979, a film that is both a recapitulation and a radical restatement of all Duras's work for the cinema in the 1970s.

The plot of *Le Navire Night* concerns a love affair between a young man and a woman, F., who first make contact by telephone one night, quite by chance. They have never seen each other or met before, but a relationship begins as a result of the conversation; F. continues telephoning. He, however, never learns F.'s full name, telephone number or address, and all initiative for the relationship falls to her. The affair unfolds purely as an affair of the human voice, but this adds to the sexual intensity of the relationship rather than detracting from it: 'C'est un orgasme noir,' one hears the voice of Bulle Ogier saying. 'Sans toucher réciproque. Ni visage. Les yeux fermés. Ta voix, seule' ('It's a dark orgasm. Without mutual touching. Nor a face. Eyes closed. Just your voice', *N*, 27–8). Three years go by, and the pair agree to meet. (In the 1978 magazine version the meeting is F.'s idea, while, in the later version, it is the man who insists on seeing F., but only as a way of putting an end to his fear of seeing her [*N*, 33]; in this respect it is as though the desire to see belongs to neither her nor him, but circulates between them as a necessary step that must continually be envisaged yet constantly deferred.) F. goes to the meeting, sees her lover, but fails to show herself. He subsequently receives several photo-graphs of F., which he sends back; having finally succeeded in forgetting them, he rediscovers his very first and only desirable image of F. – 'l'image noire' (*N*, 75) Duras calls it – given to him by F. herself, verbally, over the telephone. Towards the end, F., who claims to be suffering from leukaemia, announces that he is the only man she has ever loved (*N*, 77), but also informs him of her forthcoming marriage; the story ends in suspense, without F.'s lover knowing whether she is dead or still alive.

Whatever the origins of the film, which Duras claims to be based on a true story, it is clear that for Duras *Le Navire Night* functions primarily as a cinematographic parable on the relationship between desire, voice, and vision. As such, the film has an evident mythic dimension, which is reinforced by implicit references to the story of Orpheus and Eurydice, as well as the Sirens; in turn, these allusions to Greek myths are re-enacted, as often in Duras, in a parallel story, framing the soundtrack of the film at both beginning and end, which recounts a visit to Athens by Duras and her former cameraman, the film director Benoît Jacquot. In this frame story, the two friends find themselves enjoying each other's presence at a distance, having been in the same place at different times; in sim-ilar, but converse fashion, the lovers in the film's other story – '*l'autre histoire*' (*N*, 20) of the telephone network – act out their passion bonded to each other in time, if not in space, by the calls they make. The telephone works here as a powerful metaphor for desire: for, like desire, it suspends the distance between bodies, but also maintains separateness; it enables intimacy, yet preserves difference. Satisfaction is balanced by frustration, and desire is able to produce the conditions for its own survival. So, as they listen to each other on the telephone, the protagonists of *Le Navire Night* are allowed a relationship of desire that is founded simultaneously and without contradiction on bodily fusion and bodily difference.

Filming *Le Navire Night*, Duras, for obvious reasons, abandoned all attempt at mimetic figuration. The only concession the film makes in this respect is to provide a series of empty shots taken inside the Bois de Boulogne, perhaps on the grounds that the area is mentioned in the lovers' story, and of the Père Lachaise cemetery which F. also mentions, telling her lover that he might find out her name by going there (which he fails to do [*N*, 60]). The visit to Greece at the very beginning, for instance, is illustrated antithet-ically, by shots of blue sky over Paris, while the story of the wounded statue of Athena (*N*, 61–4) is read during a static medium shot (lasting 3'15") showing Bulle Ogier having make-up applied to her face for a cinema or theatre performance that is never seen to take place. There are similar shots of the other actors in the film. Dominique Sanda, for instance, during the long evocation of F.'s illness (*N*, 40–3), is shown earlier, having her eyes and cheeks made up, in a single prolonged take of 7'4". Similarly, as the story of F.'s love for a priest is being read off-screen, the audience is left looking (for 2'50") at Mathieu Carrière also being made ready for a performance. (This reference to a deferred or absent performance is constant throughout; the story of the lovers, after the prologue and credit sequence, is framed visually by two almost identical shots, each over six minutes long, in which the camera, starting from a darkened mirror, moves slowly left, in front of an array of windows looking out over a garden, to a pianist playing in a room to the left, before retracing its course to the right, till, in the far corner, it frames a set of three chandeliers that, though lit at the beginning, are finally extinguished just before the closing reference to Greece and the film that has not been made. And at the heart of the film, the camera, in a long circular movement through virtually 360°, done in a single take of 7'30", reveals that the location is in fact a stage set, with spotlights, cue boards, and the rest.)

But despite the presence of three actors in *Le Navire Night* the relationship between them and the story of the lovers remains strangely indeterminate. None of the actors speaks on screen; they are only heard to ask occasional questions on the soundtrack, since the bulk of the text is read off-screen by Duras herself, aided by Benoît Jacquot. If the actors are preparing for a performance of *Le Navire Night*, it is not self-evident what role each will take, since the script seems to call for two characters, not three. In the make-up sequences, close attention is paid – almost painfully so – to the actors' eyes; and this insistence on the vulnerability of vision is a reminder not only of the self-imposed blindness of the two lovers but also of the viewer's own inability to see, given that none of the characters in the fiction is ever visible on screen. In each case, too, as they are being made up, the actors gaze off-screen, without the viewer being shown what they are looking at, though there is a suggestion earlier, in one sequence which shows them grouped together looking off-screen to the left, as though transfixed by an absent or impossible image, that they are somehow able to see the same film as the viewer, in which case, of course, they would in fact be looking at themselves.

A curious circularity, then, affects the problem of vision in *Le*

Navire Night. The only desired object of vision is one which is somehow unavailable or invisible. As a result, for both the actors shown on screen and the film's spectator, looking is like an intransitive process; it is an activity with no determinate object. Seeing or looking turns into an act of patient martyrdom, as the film's three make-up sequences demonstrate. The attention to make-up also underlines the fact that in the film, as far as Bulle Ogier, Dominique Sanda, and Mathieu Carrière are concerned, seeing is itself indistinguishable from the fact of being seen. For them, seeing and being seen are like two sides of the same coin; as far as they are concerned, the distinction between subject and object is therefore lost. The relationship between F. and her lover in the story is affected in a similar way. Indeed, one of the reasons for the intensity of F.'s desire, the spectator is told, is precisely that it is no longer held within a voyeuristic scenario that couples a seeing subject with a silent object in a hierarchical relation that privileges vision over speech. As the film tells us: 'Elle dit n'avoir pas su avant lui être désirable d'un désir d'elle-même qu'elle-même pouvait partager. Et que cela fait peur' ('She says that before him she didn't know what it was like to be desirable with a desire for herself that herself could share. And that it is frightening', *N*, 25).

There is no voyeurism, therefore, between F. and her lover, but rather a fusion of bodies which suspends identity without abolishing difference. The same is true of the relationship between the images of the actors on screen and the story being recounted off-screen. The tendency may be generalised to apply to the film as a whole. Indeed, throughout, image and text never coincide; but by the very fact of their co-existence during the screening of the film they become inseparably fused together. The film invents what is in the history of cinema a new and intriguing mode of cinematographic vision. Watching the film, the spectator sees determinate images; but, hearing the text running parallel to the image, the spectator is also witness to the fundamental invisibility that surrounds the image as its very condition of possibility. The images do not illustrate the text but interact with it across the gap opened by the incommensurable difference between speech and sight; and in the process, the images transform the text, making visible all that is necessarily unspoken by it, just as words themselves, beyond the cinema screen, continue to embody the strange privilege that invisibility confers upon them.

In her later films, by refusing to join image and sound together in a relation of hierarchical mimetic unity, Duras inevitably fails to provide her audience with the fantasy satisfaction of that impression of reality that has long been associated with cinema as a narrative medium. But instead, Duras undertakes to liberate both image and sound from the demands of specular coherence. In the process, image and sound lose the power to control each other, and Duras's cinema becomes an infinite exploration of the differences and interactions between the two. As in *Le Navire Night*, it constitutes an unending tribute to the potential of the invisible and the unspoken, for these are the forces that sustain desire, the desire to see as well as the desire to speak. And desire in Duras's films becomes a quest that has as its goal the dissolution of the spectator into an affirmation of the pure, ecstatic difference that exists in the unrepresentable gap between image and word.

5 The limits of fiction

By 1980, as a result of almost fifteen years spent making films, Duras found herself in a curious predicament. Though she was still known primarily as a novelist, she had not published a single narrative work, except for screenplays, since *L'Amour* in 1971. And the last text that she had not reworked almost immediately, within a year or two of publication, as a play or film, was *Le Vice-consul* in 1966 (which, of course, merely had to wait a few years longer before reaching the screen). Prior to that, Duras's most recent novel to be content with remaining a novel, as it were, was *Le Ravissement de Lol V. Stein* (although even this was more by chance than by design, once Duras had abandoned the idea of making the book into a film).

From the evidence available it does seem that this apparent retreat from narrative fiction was the cause of some disquiet to the author herself; and it is with obvious relief that, in 'Les Yeux verts', the special issue of *Les Cahiers du cinéma* she edited in June 1980, she tells of rediscovering writing and literature through the fictional figure of Aurélia Steiner (though even before she had finished work on the magazine, two of the three *Aurélia Steiner* stories had in fact already been made into films).[1] This rediscovery of literature, though, was fragile and provisional; for if *Aurélia Steiner* represented a new beginning for Duras, it also forced her to confront intractable material of the most extreme kind, since the subject that all three narratives attempt to deal with is the theme of Auschwitz and the fate of the Jews in the Second World War.

Aurélia Steiner, Duras explains (*YV*, 4), began as a letter to an unnamed distant acquaintance (probably, in fact, Yann Andréa [*YA*, 9–11]), and this structure of an appeal addressed to an absent interlocutor supplied the author with the means of achieving some necessary literary distance with regard to the theme of the death camps. Admittedly, the idea of writing as a call to an unknown other was not altogether new; Duras uses it as a fictional framework both in *Le Navire Night* and in *Les Mains négatives*, one of the texts she had written to accompany the discarded footage left over from the previous film. It was a strategy she also adopted when bringing together the various different materials included in 'Les Yeux verts'; here, as in the other texts, the recourse to the idea of an implicit dialogue taking place between the writer and an unnamed addressee helped to give the collection a more cohesive overall structure.

But perhaps more importantly, using the format of the letter to an absent addressee also allowed Duras to begin experimenting with a mode of writing which, because it was no longer subject to the requirement of narrative coherence, could not easily be classified either as fiction or non-fiction. Beyond story-telling, Duras was more interested in breaking down barriers between genres in order to arrive at a kind of generalised textuality that was not inhibited or constrained by the need to deal with a predetermined subject in a predetermined manner. In 'Les Yeux verts', for instance, Duras touches on a broad variety of topics: the relationship between cinema and literature, her own films and the films of other directors, various likes and dislikes, left-wing politics, and much else besides. At the same time, the style or tone of her pieces is markedly heterogeneous: there are journalistic items, statements of personal political principle, jottings from her diary, anecdotes, memories, reports of conversations with friends, imaginary interviews, snatches of improvised literature, and, on a different plane, a selection of stills taken from her own films, as well as production shots of plays and films, and a collection of family photographs. Across all this material Duras develops a characteristically insistent voice that mixes both personal and public and is by turns polemical, paradoxical, lyrical, anecdotal, and discursive, as well as emphatic, portentous, incisive, and apocalyptic; she combines a simplicity and immediacy of oral delivery in her writing with a stylistic casualness that borders at times on the opaque and the contorted.

Shortly after 'Les Yeux verts' appeared, Duras agreed to contribute – also under the title 'Les Yeux verts' – a regular weekly column to *Libération*, the fledgling left-wing daily which at the time was still being run along radical co-operative lines. Later the same year the articles appeared as a book, entitled *L'Eté 80*. Though Duras's involvement, at her own insistence, lasted only ten weeks through the summer, the arrangement provided her with a further opportunity to experiment with a mode of writing that lay outside of narrative (the word 'outside' is the one Duras herself used in 1981 for a collection of earlier journalistic pieces). To an extent this was not á new departure. Duras had written regularly in the press before; and, now as then, writing in *Libération* gave Duras a political platform that allowed her to express her views on most of the issues of the day (including the Soviet invasion of Afghanistan, the revolution in Iran, the rise of Solidarity in Poland, the terrorism of the Italian Red Brigades, as well as, in France, the problems of the Giscard d'Estaing presidency as it entered its final year).

At the same time, though, having to address the unknown readership of the paper on a series of topics of her own choosing closely mirrored what she had attempted to do in both *Aurélia Steiner* and *Les Cahiers du cinéma* (and eventually Duras herself recognised the connection by appealing to the reader of *Libération* in much the same terms as she had done to the addressee of *Aurélia Steiner* [*E*, 63–5]). The result was to turn the attempt at journalism into an altogether more wide-ranging and hybrid activity; for what the *Libération* articles exemplify is a mode of writing that belongs to no established genre (novel, screenplay, or stage play) and is closer in spirit to the impromptu letter or personal diary. For the most part, Duras concentrates her attention on the unpredictability of day-to-day events and the inherent formlessness of everyday existence. But writing every week for an unknown audience clearly stimulated Duras's narrative imagination as well, and much of what she put into her column, together with lengthy accounts of the weather, is in the form of a weekly serial about a Jewish boy called David and the young female holiday camp monitor who befriends him. As a result, the sequence of articles as a whole creates a curious mix of themes and topics by virtue of which everything – international politics, the local weather, the story of David, the state of the sea – somehow merges with everything else, and there is no longer any viable method of distinguishing the important from the unimportant, or the essential from the incidental.

L'Eté 80 represents an important moment in Duras's return to regular journalism in the 1980s. But the impact on Duras's writing as a whole was arguably more radical. For *L'Eté 80* begins to explore a new manner of writing and a new relationship between textuality and experience. The book occupies a space that is somehow beneath or prior to literature in the received sense; but, paradoxically, for that very reason, Duras's text remains closer to the original – catastrophic – movement of writing as an experience of exteriority and dispossession. By refusing to become literature, as it were, *L'Eté 80* remains more faithful to the idea of literature as a mode of apocalyptic revelation; and by falling short of established literature it is more responsive to the violence and innocence in which, for Duras, writing has its origin and which – at any rate in Duras's view – provide the only basis for the value of literature as such.

Like 'Les Yeux verts', what unifies *L'Eté 80* is not so much a set of themes or generic conventions as the name or signature of the author that appears above or below the actual text. In Duras's case, the signature, being a pseudonym, names a persona who is both real and fictitious, both a citizen of France and an invention of the author's own imagination. In both *L'Eté 80* and 'Les Yeux verts' the distinction between the two was gradually eroded and the boundary between fiction and autobiography, journalism and prose narrative rendered permeable and uncertain. A shifting signature is all that authorises Duras's texts; and on numerous later occasions, following a tactic invented in the 1970s by Roland Barthes, the author's name itself reduces to a magical pair of initials, turning Marguerite Duras – or 'M.D.' – into the almost mythical embodiment of her own writing.[2]

This investment of Duras's personal signature with textual significance had a double effect. On the one hand, in the early and mid-1980s it served to promote the figure of the author as a media personality and, in the eyes of some readers, the result was simply to inflate – and thus devalue – the worth of Duras's name. But the implication also was that the author no longer had any autonomous existence outside of her writing, even though the only authority the writing enjoyed was the authority it derived from the author's name. The relationship between the author's name and the writing it signs is affected by an inescapable circularity. Each exists purely as an effect of the other; text and author thus fuse together and lose their autonomy. Any type of writing could be authorised as a text by Duras provided it carried the author's name; but the name Duras, being only a word, might also be used to sign anything. So if, as in *La Vie matérielle* of 1987, a shopping list might be included in a text akin to a work of literature, it was because literature itself was always already akin to a shopping list (*VM*, 57; 49–50). Everyday experience and written text are woven together in Duras like the threads of a single, endlessly variegated fabric. The domestic and the literary, the private and the public, the personal and the political, the trivial and the serious, living and writing are no longer opposed, but function more as different-handed extensions of each other.

In terms of Duras's earlier work this was an important, but not entirely unexpected development. However, the end product, four years after *L'Eté 80*, surprised everybody. For it turned out to be Duras's greatest commercial success, and an international bestseller as well: the autobiographical text, *L'Amant*. Within two to three years of publication this pseudo-confessional rewriting of the story already told in *Un barrage contre le Pacifique*, and reworked in 1977 in the play, *L'Eden Cinéma*, had won Duras both the Prix Goncourt and considerable critical esteem in France, as well as worldwide sales in excess of a million copies (and in 1992, amid some controversy, a creakingly wooden, exotically voyeuristic screen adaptation of the book followed, made on location in Vietnam by Jean-Jacques Annaud).

Notwithstanding its enormous success, *L'Amant*, like both 'Les Yeux verts' and *L'Eté 80*, maintains an uneasy relationship with literature. The book, which cannot be classed unambiguously either as a novel or a personal memoir, hovers uncertainly between the autobiographical and the fictitious. While it claims, in part, to give an autobiographical explanation for specific motifs from Duras's earlier, explicitly fictional works, like, for instance, the story of the beggar woman from *Le Vice-consul* or *India Song* (*A*, 103–8; 89–93), *L'Amant* does no more than repeat these episodes rather than account for them, and Duras often uses the same words or terms as in previous fictional texts, making it impossible to distinguish the allegedly real version from the fictionalised one. Self-exposure shades undecidably into self-concealment, clarification into obfuscation. Moreover, Duras in *L'Amant* refuses to supply the reader with a reliable life story, and narrative structure in the book is more often in the form of digression than progression. Narrative continuity is constantly offset by rhapsodic discontinuity and Duras's writing oscillates constantly between past and present tenses, first- and third-person narration.

Like 'Les Yeux verts', *L'Amant* was originally intended to be a commentary on a collection of family photographs.[3] But as the photographs fell away, they were replaced by a series of verbal scenes or portraits. And, as though to dramatise the incommensurability inherent in the relationship between seeing and speaking and the final impossibility of matching image with text, the book incorporates allusions to both a non-existent image and an invisible cinematographic subtext. The non-existent image is the 'absolute' photograph that, as Duras explains (*A*, 16–17; 13–14), was never taken, but – were it to exist – would show her as a 15-year-old girl embarking on a mythic journey across the Mekong river, travelling irreversibly down the path toward desire, sexual knowledge, prostitution, and subsequent exile. For its part, the invisible cinematographic subtext (to which Duras refers several times in passing [*A*, 12, 67, 122, 126; 10, 57, 105–6, 109]), is a favourite film from 1955, Charles Laughton's *The Night of the Hunter*, which ends with a desperate journey down the Mississippi by a young boy, John, and his sister, Pearl, who are all the while being hunted down by a false preacher – now their murderous stepfather – who aims to steal from them the money entrusted to them by their dead father, only for John at the end, once the preacher is captured, to rush forward to offer him the money and beg forgiveness.[4]

Each in its own way, from either the centre or the margins of Duras's text, these two absent images surround *L'Amant* with an invisible and unrepresentable shadow. On the one side they charge Duras's writing with ambivalence, in the image of the preacher's two fists, the right tattooed with the letters LOVE, the left with the letters HATE; while on the other they suffuse the text with all the familiar paradoxes of fusion and separation, intimacy and distance, as a result of which love in Duras is only ever made possible – but simultaneously impossible – by the recognition of difference, death, and loss. To give expression to what is at stake in these enigmatic states of desire a Chopin waltz is on hand to commemorate – in apocalyptic mode – a young man's suicide by drowning and a woman's realisation of the love she has for the man she has just left: 'et la musique s'était répandue partout dans le paquebot noir, comme une injonction du ciel dont on ne savait pas à quoi elle avait trait, comme un ordre de Dieu dont on ignorait la teneur' ('and the music spread all over the dark boat, like a heavenly injunction whose import was unknown, like an order from God whose meaning was inscrutable', *A*, 138; 120).

L'Amant is a work about ambivalence, desire, and loss. The temporality of Duras's text, however, is never progressive, but retroactive and discontinuous. Each of the emotions that Duras describes in the book is always immediately contemporaneous with all the others. Experience develops as a series of recurrent moments suspended in time; events repeat themselves and have inevitably always been anticipated long before they actually happen. In the story of Duras's life, therefore, as she recounts it, it is always already too late (*A*, 9; 7); and whatever takes place in the book –

like the initiation into desire, the discovery of alcohol, even the collapse of Duras's features with age (*A*, 15; 12) – has always already happened in advance of itself. In turn, writing *L'Amant*, Duras herself is not engaged in an act of fond remembrance of events that, in the main, are more than fifty years distant, but involved in a dramatic repetition or re-enactment of her past. To that extent Duras is right to stress that the central concern of the text is not the author's adolescence in itself but its future transformation into the present act of writing (*A*, 29; 24). But if *L'Amant* is a story of initiation, the secret revealed at the end is not so much the inherent and paradoxical ambivalence of desire, but more the realisation that writing itself is the only and best enactment of the dual dynamic of fusion and separation mobilised in desire.

Writing, however, in *L'Amant*, entertains an ambivalent relationship with narrative. 'L'histoire de ma vie n'existe pas' ('The story of my life doesn't exist', *A*, 14; 11), suggests Duras, and it is evident that, in *L'Amant*, as in *Le Ravissement de Lol V. Stein*, twenty years before, a subterranean force is operating to disorganise the text, as though from the inside, compromising the coherence of the writing and subjecting it to disturbances at almost every level, syntactic, discursive, and thematic. The result is a mode of writing possessed of a peculiar and distinctive intensity in which correctness or clarity of expression is often sacrificed in the cause of greater emotional density or immediacy. Like other late texts by Duras, *L'Amant* relies on a manner of writing which gives increasing prominence to emphatic accumulation, insistent repetition, dramatic amplification, and severe lexical ellipsis.

Evidence of syntactic disequilibrium in *L'Amant*, for example, is intermittent, but compelling. From time to time, in the course of the text, Duras writes sentences which take surprising liberties with the standard conventions governing French prose, and which few other novelists of Duras's age and experience would probably be willing to leave uncorrected. The following sentence, from the beginning of *L'Amant*, in which Duras is explaining her urge to kill her elder brother, is arguably one such case. Duras writes:

C'était pour enlever de devant ma mère l'objet de son amour, ce fils, la punir de l'aimer si fort, si mal, et surtout pour sauver mon petit frère, je le croyais aussi, mon petit frère, mon enfant, de la vie vivante de ce frère aîné posée au-dessus de la sienne, de ce voile noir sur le jour, de cette loi représentée par lui, édictée par lui, un être humain, et qui était une loi animale, et qui à chaque instant de chaque jour de la vie de ce petit frère faisait la peur dans cette vie, peur qui une fois a atteint son cœur et l'a fait mourir.

(I wanted to do it to remove from my mother's sight the object of her love, that son of hers, to punish her for loving him so much, so badly, and above all to save my younger brother, my younger brother whom I took also to be my child, from the living life of that elder brother ranked above his own, from that black veil over the light, from the law represented by him, decreed by him, a human being, which was an animal law, and which at every moment of every day of the younger brother's life filled that life with fear, a fear that one day reached his heart and killed him.)

(*A*, 13–14; 10–11)

Elsewhere in *L'Amant*, Duras writes with simplicity, directness, brevity, even lyricism. Here, however, as in other passages in which the author struggles to disentangle the ambivalent relations of love and hate, identification and revulsion, that bind her to her mother and two brothers, it is as though syntax itself is on the point of giving way under the pressure of the task. Instead of a detached and lucid account of family interactions, what the reader is given is a dramatic – even melodramatic – re-enactment of the relentless violence of the emotions at work within the family group. In the process, the sentence itself almost disintegrates into a series of repetitive assertions and continual amplifications that owes less to the carefully balanced periods of traditional French prose than it does to the oral rhythms of a tirade or a harangue. 'Nous sommes ensemble dans une honte de principe d'avoir à vivre la vie' ('We are side by side in our shame in principle at having to live life', *A*, 69; 59), comments Duras later, referring to herself and her family, and the effect is much the same: of defiance and vulnerability, violence and hopelessness abruptly colliding to create not just an unstable family situation, but also, as Duras re-enacts it in 1984, a sentence that manages to err on the very edge of ungrammaticality.

In cases like this Duras seems deliberately to sabotage the clarity of her text. It is not just the syntax of individual sentences that is affected. She behaves in a similar way when dealing with narrative structures. She begins *L'Amant* in the first person, referring to herself in the third only when this is warranted by the conventions of free indirect speech: 'Ma mère, institutrice', we are told, 'veut le secondaire pour sa petite fille. [. . .] Ce qui était suffisant pour elle ne l'est plus pour la petite' ('My mother's a teacher and wants her girl to have a secondary education. [. . .] What was enough for her is not enough for her daughter', *A*, 11; 9). Some pages later, however, the same term, 'la petite', recurs (*A*, 19; 15), no longer supported by the mother's discourse; and this trend towards third-person narration becomes gradually more widespread throughout the book (*A*, 29, 33, 42, 45–50; 25, 28, 33, 42, 45–50, etc.). To an extent, the third person is justified here because Duras is referring to a external photographic image – albeit a non-existent one – from the perspective of the belated spectator that, with over fifty years of hindsight, she herself has become. At other times it is because the text adopts the point of view of, say, Duras's mother or her lover, so that, for instance, when one reads of a well-dressed man gazing at 'la jeune fille au feutre d'homme et aux chaussures d'or' ('the girl in the man's fedora and the gold shoes', *A*, 42; 36), the effect is to transform her into an erotic image glimpsed by a passing spectator, who is of course not only the Chinese lover, but also the ageing narrator herself, and the reader.

But as the text proceeds, this convention remains far from self-evident. True, Duras reverts to the first person immediately after her third-person account of the girl's first experience of love-making (*A*, 45–50; 39–42) since this aftermath is no longer contained in the non-existent image of the journey across the Mekong; whereas the love-making itself, by virtue of the retroactive logic of Duras's text, was somehow already embodied in the encounter on the ferry. But the distinction between what does belong to the 'absolute' image and what is external to it is never clearly defined, and at the end of *L'Amant* (*A*, 135–42; 117–23), as the heroine leaves Saigon to return to France, the writing slips back into the third person, as though the account of the narrator's journey across the ocean had suddenly been contaminated by the image of an adolescent girl crossing the Mekong some eighteen months earlier. Of course, if one follows the paradoxical logic of desire in Duras, it is clear that this final leave-taking was itself also contained in the image of the ferry crossing. But prior to this concluding episode, the text of *L'Amant* had lingered for some time in the first person, with the result that the return to the third person in the closing pages, rounding the text off as in a circle, functions in *L'Amant* like a last memorial to the inextricable entanglement of fusion with separation, loss with enjoyment, mourning with desire.

Duras's manipulation of narrative voice and personal pronouns in *L'Amant* disrupts the narrative linearity of the text. The narrator-protagonist doubles up as the third-person heroine of a mythic narrative and the first-person witness of an apocalyptic enactment. But the text refuses to mediate between these two positions, and merely shifts back and forth between them. This serves to emphasise the unbridgeable gap between the first and the third person, between 'I' and 'she', but the difference between them in Duras's text can seem almost secondary, if not entirely gratuitous. The two pronouns are irreducibly distinct but also oddly interchangeable, with the result that the relationship between the narrator and her text, like much else in *L'Amant*, oscillates ceaselessly between separation and fusion.

Duras's stance with regard to her own text is therefore not one of sober detachment dominated by a commitment to telling the truth, but of desire rediscovered and relived in retrospect. A similar movement of simultaneous fusion and separation also dictates her relationship to all the other characters who appear in *L'Amant*, none of whom remains autonomous, but all of whom at some point merge together with all the others just like the various bodies deployed in the imaginary scenario staged by the narrator involving Hélène Lagonelle and the Chinese (*A*, 91–2; 79). Thus, the lover, for instance, as he gazes across the bed at the young girl's body next to his, is unable to see where hers ends and his own begins (*A*, 121; 105); and so, too, the narrator, as she mourns her younger brother, realises that, though he is dead, her body and his are still the same (*A*, 128; 111). Similarly, in the bedroom in which the narrator and the Chinese make love, she imagines not only the figure of Hélène Lagonelle passing through, but also the ghost of each of her two brothers, the loved one, Paulo, as well as Pierre, the hunter after children (*A*, 122; 105–6). Here, once again in Duras, threatening the possibility of proper narrative progress and of transparent textual meanings, it is incest that provides the model for the very ecstasy of love.

'Je vois la guerre sous les mêmes couleurs que mon enfance' ('I see the war as I see my childhood', *A*, 78; 67), wrote Duras in *L'Amant*, and there is an evident, if unpremeditated logic to the fact that Duras's next published work, immediately after *L'Amant*, was a group of writings dealing with the Occupation. Under the overall title of *La Douleur*, the collection contains six separate texts. These include a wartime diary or memoir, recounting the events following the arrest and imprisonment of Robert Antelme, to whom Duras was still married at the time, and four short stories, all based on actual events, according to the author, together with the 1984 stage version of *Aurélia Steiner*. With the exception of this very last text, there is considerable uncertainty about the actual date of composition of the material collected in *La Douleur*. The four stories are all revised or rewritten versions of texts dating from much earlier; as for the diary, the most important part of the book, the author claims in her brief preface not even to remember writing it, though internal evidence suggests it was probably completed in the latter part of 1946 or 1947. Introducing it in 1985, Duras also wondered, rhetorically, how she could have come to leave the diary in a cupboard in her house at Neauphle (just outside Paris), even though the house, as she puts it, is frequently affected during the winter by flooding (*D*, 10; 4).

This last remark, like the failure to remember the existence of the text at all, is no doubt best understood as a symptom – if not in fact a conscious symbol – of the necessary inadequacy of memory and the guilt associated with forgetting. Throughout Duras's work, from *La Vie tranquille* or *Un barrage contre le Pacifique* onwards, water is by definition that which overwhelms and overpowers; it jeopardises the possibility of maintaining limits and borders and is emblematic of the forces that threaten any attempt to establish the meaning of past events. In much the same way, in both *L'Amant* and *La Douleur*, water serves consistently as a figure for the catastrophic loss of boundaries, irrespective of whether what is at stake is desire or anxiety. In *L'Amant*, for instance, as the girl with the felt hat prepares to cross to the other side, the narrator is aware in retrospect of the powerful underwater current driving the Mekong river, as it plunges towards the Pacific, indiscriminately carrying everything before it (*A*, 30–1; 25–6); similarly, in *La Douleur*, once the narrator realises the full extent of her doubts and fears, she voices her distress by remarking: 'L'horreur monte lentement dans une inondation, je me noie' ('Horror mounts in a slow flood, I'm drowning', *D*, 45; 37).

Remembering the past, then, in both *L'Amant* and *La Douleur*, is a precarious undertaking, thrown into doubt not only by the passage of time but also by the fact that what has to be remembered cannot be adequately contained within the available boundaries; and to this extent the precarious survival of the diary in *La Douleur* does no more than reflect the haphazard and fragile nature of memory itself. But at the same time, the diary owes its existence to the indestructible quality of writing as an act of witness. This realisation, for Duras, is of course what gives the diary its particular importance as an apocalyptic document, for it is a text that embod-

ies in the fact of its own chance survival its own status as a catastrophic revelation. The diary not only tells of catastrophe, but, by
its miraculous and unexpected survival, also alludes to the possibility of catastrophe which it has itself just narrowly escaped. For
Duras, *La Douleur* is a work that, like *L'Eté 80*, has value precisely
to the extent that it precedes – and thus exceeds – literature in the
received sense. Rereading the diary almost forty years to the day
after the events it records, Duras was confronted, as she puts it,
with 'un désordre phénoménal de la pensée et du sentiment auquel
je n'ai pas osé toucher et au regard de quoi la littérature m'a fait
honte' ('a tremendous chaos of thought and feeling that I couldn't
bring myself to tamper with, and beside which literature was something of which I felt ashamed', *D*, 10; 4).

But this stated preference for the raw immediacy of a seemingly
pre-literary text does not mean that the diary as it stands is a
spontaneous and unconsidered document. On the contrary, when
La Douleur was published in 1985 Duras spoke of rewriting the
original 1940s text and making substantial cuts to it; and, so far as
one can judge from the fragments published – anonymously – in
the feminist magazine *Sorcières* in 1976, the revisions to the diary
were in fact quite extensive.[5] In particular, Duras seems to have
consistently edited and condensed the text in order to heighten its
dramatic intensity. Two other changes are also worth noting. First
is the transformation of the figure of Robert Antelme, who in the
anonymous 1976 text is named throughout by use of the initials
'R.A.', into the part-fictional character, Robert L. (with Duras the
narrator being referred to, on at least one occasion, as 'madame
L.' [*D*, 13; 7]). Secondly, at crucial moments in the narrative,
Duras replaces the first person with the third, so that, for instance,
when in 1976 the reader was told: 'J'ai acheté du miel, du sucre,
du riz, des pâtes' ('I bought honey, sugar, rice, pasta'), the corresponding passage, in 1985, runs: 'On achète du miel, du sucre, des
pâtes' ('Honey, sugar, pasta are bought', *D*, 43; 34). Similarly, in
1976, the narrator had assuaged her anxiety with the words: 'D. . . .
sait qui je suis. [. . .] Je veux le voir et lui demander des explications' ('D. . . . knows who I am. [. . .] I want to see him and
ask him to explain'); but by 1985 this had become: 'Qui elle est,
D. le sait. [. . .] Elle le sait, elle peut le voir et lui demander des
explications' ('Who she is, D. knows. [. . .] She knows she can see
him and ask him to explain', *D*, 46; 37).

The effect of these changes is to generalise what was in any case
already implicit in the original diary. But, as a result, the text is

further depersonalised, and the act of bearing witness is no longer a private act, authorised solely by personal experience. Coming forty years after the events it records, *La Douleur* is naturally unable to add anything of importance to public knowledge of the Resistance and the fate of those prisoners who were sent to concentration camps, and, in any case, the whole premise of the diary is the narrator's inability to find out what was happening to her husband during the time he was held in Germany. To this extent *La Douleur* has little to offer the reader by way of a recitation of unfamiliar facts. Instead, what Duras does is to dramatise her own experience of grief, shock, and loss, thereby re-enacting in graphic terms the moment of her own discovery – in 1945 – of the existence of the Nazi concentration camps (and in 1985, at a time when, in France, so-called revisionist accounts of the war were becoming more current, claiming the Holocaust to be a myth created by Allied propaganda, this was an act that was not without its particular political point).

This recourse to dramatisation inevitably necessitated a detour into fiction, and it is this no doubt that is signalled by the use of the term, Robert L., which, as far as Duras was concerned, was reminiscent less of historical fact than of the main character from her 1961 screenplay, *Une aussi longue absence*. This is the story of a tramp, named as Robert Landais – though the local café-owner Thérèse Langlois is convinced he may be her deported husband, Albert – who is found wandering through the town of Puteaux having lost all memory of the past. He spends his days cutting pictures from magazines, searching, as it were, for an image that might represent his sunken past life; and to that extent *Une aussi longue absence* is clearly already an attempt on Duras's part to fictionalise the real story of Antelme's return and the difficulties of retrieving the past. But by simply transposing Antelme's story into a conventional narrative plot, the screenplay (and the ensuing film) are unable to do more than cite one isolated case of a man losing the thread connecting him to his own previous life; in this respect the film is at best little more than a somewhat implausible melodrama on the theme of amnesia and the Occupation. In *La Douleur*, by contrast, the reliance on fictional techniques is only partial; Duras concentrates instead on the uncertain middle ground that lies between historical document and retrospective fiction. As a result, Duras in *La Douleur* is able to explore not so much the events of 1944 and 1945 in themselves, but, more pertinently in 1985, the question of the very possibility of representing those events in language.

This question of representation is a central one, since at every turn *La Douleur* is haunted by the fragile and speculative character of those boundaries that make stable representation possible. The text of the diary oscillates painfully between the narrator's hope that Robert L. is still alive and the fear that he may already be dead; in the process, the narrator realises, of course, that to pronounce him dead in anticipation is paradoxically also to save him from dying, while also proving in advance that her concern and distress achieve nothing and are without object or purpose. Contradictory and endless conjecture is the only recourse in *La Douleur* (*D*, 11; 5); and it is in secret accord with the boundless uncertainty attaching to the fate of Robert L. that the state of mind of the narrator fluctuates ceaselessly between the desire to survive – in order to know the truth – and the desire to die – in order not to have to confront the agonising prospect of knowledge. But the pain of waiting is so great that, were Robert L. to return, she would have nothing left to do but die (*D*, 36; 28).

Loving Robert L. becomes indistinguishable from hating the Germans (*D*, 35; 27), but those emotions contaminate each other and become interchangeable, as they do also, for instance, in *Hiroshima mon amour*, where Duras converts this story of grief for a man who might have been thrown into a ditch and killed by a German bullet into a story of love for a dead German soldier. In either case, the cruel separation from the body of the loved one is denied, outstripped, and yet reinforced by the sense that, in grief as in love, distinctions between bodies are annulled and abolished. The narrator of *La Douleur* dies as Robert L. dies (*D*, 15; 8); but the urge towards identification is both intensified and undermined by the painful awareness that the bread she has in her hand is bread he cannot eat (*D*, 17; 10). Desire for a loved one and the grief of enforced separation merge as one. Earlier, the actress in *Hiroshima mon amour* had implied much the same when, speaking of her German lover's dead body, she had explained: 'Je n'arrivais pas à trouver la moindre différence entre ce corps mort et le mien. . . . Je ne pouvais trouver entre ce corps et le mien que des ressemblances. . . . hurlantes' ('I couldn't find the slightest difference between this dead body and mine. All I could see were the similarities between this dead body and mine. . . . screaming at me', *H*, 100; 65). And when Robert L. does return, he, too, like the German soldier, floats mysteriously between life and death (*D*,

66; 55), between a state of survival that is a kind of life-within-death and an otherworldly state of almost apocalyptic happiness or grace, marked only by a smile signifying dim familiarity and disembodied strangeness (*D*, 65; 53).

Throughout *La Douleur*, borderlines prove to be fragile and unreliable; relations between self and other, reality and fiction, living and dying are subject to constant disturbance and redefinition. The only subject of certainty is that about which there can be no certainty, so when the narrator declares: 'je tiens une certitude' ('I'm certain of it', *D*, 14; 7), the phrase turns out to be immediately self-cancelling. 'Tout ce qu'on peut savoir quand on ne sait rien, je le sais' ('I know all one can know when one knows nothing', *D*, 14; 8), adds the narrator, recalling similar words by Jacques Hold on the subject of Lol V. Stein. The principle is one of confusion and uncertainty and rests on the impossibility of establishing reliable boundaries between any one thing and its presumed opposite. As such, it extends beyond the diary in *La Douleur* to each of the short stories contained in the volume. In 'Monsieur X. dit ici Pierre Rabier', for instance, the reader sees the narrator – Duras herself, according to the author – being courted and toyed with by a particularly seductive German collaborator, with the full agreement of the Resistance; in 'Albert des Capitales', the author, under the pseudonym of Thérèse, indulges in a gratuitous, vengeful, and militarily indefensible act of torture which produces nothing of value to the Resistance group and simply discredits them in their own eyes; while in 'Ter le milicien' Duras explores the theme of her own admiration and desire for an attractive young member of the much reviled collaborationist *milice*.

In all these cases, Duras's disrespect for time-honoured polarities and divisions is thoroughgoing and at times shocking. Historical testimony of the kind Duras appears to be offering in *La Douleur* normally – and necessarily – takes for granted the exemplary status, veracity, and communicability of the personal experience of the witness. But the reliability of each one of these assumptions is thrown into question in *La Douleur*, with the result that the texts in the volume as a whole function less as a testimony to the truth of what happened in 1944 or 1945 than as a means of questioning the terms on which testimony in general is possible.[6] Instead of giving an objective account of historical events it suggests in effect that there is no stable place or position from which neutral testimony can be offered. In other words, from the perspective of *La Douleur*, it seems that the experience of war, internment, and the camps cannot be enclosed within boundaries and thus delimited. Historical catastrophe on that scale threatens not only the survival of its own immediate victims, but also the very possibility of establishing a secure frame of reference within which catastrophe as such might be understood or rendered meaningful. *La Douleur*, in this respect, is not only a testimony to the ravages of war but, more radically, a work that bears witness to the sheer impossibility of bearing witness.

At the end of *La Douleur* is not moral outrage as such, nor condemnation of the Nazi camps in the name of already established humanistic verities. These can no longer be taken for granted. The potential for violence, as the story 'Albert des Capitales' shows, is inherent in all human beings, even when they are on the side of social justice and the Resistance. So what is implicit in *La Douleur*, for Duras, is not an assertive moral position, but an ethics of attention, the first move of which is to acknowledge the relationship of reciprocal inclusion or identification that exists between the judges and those being judged. The aim is to refuse to treat the camps as an inexplicable aberration resulting from the inherent perversity of a particular race or people (*D*, 63; 52). As Duras points out: 'Nous sommes de la race de ceux qui sont brûlés dans les crématoires et des gazés de Maïdenek, nous sommes aussi de la race des nazis' ('We are the same race as those who were burned in the crematoriums or gassed at Maidenek, and we're also the same race as the Nazis', *D*, 57; 46–7); and she goes on to explain:

> Si l'on fait un sort allemand à l'horreur nazie, et non pas un sort collectif, on réduira l'homme de Belsen aux dimensions du ressortissant régional. La seule réponse à faire à ce crime est d'en faire un crime de tous. De le partager. De même que l'idée d'égalité, de fraternité. Pour le supporter, pour en tolérer l'idée, partager le crime.

> (If you see the Nazi horror as a German and not a collective responsibility, you reduce the man in Belsen to regional dimensions. The only possible answer to this crime is to turn it into a crime committed by everyone. To share it. Just like the idea of equality and fraternity. In order to bear it, to tolerate the idea of it, we must share the crime.)

> (*D*, 60–1; 50)

Put in these terms, Duras's reponse to the discovery of the existence of the camps accords perhaps most clearly with the view expressed by Antelme himself in his own memoir, *L'Espèce humaine*. Writing of the daily struggle for survival in Buchenwald, Antelme affirms that, as far as he and his fellow detainees are concerned, despite appearances to the contrary:

> il n'y a pas d'ambiguïté, nous restons des hommes, nous ne finirons qu'en hommes. [. . .] C'est un rêve SS de croire que nous avons pour mission historique de changer d'espèce, et comme cette mutation se fait trop lentement, ils tuent. Non, cette maladie extraordinaire n'est autre chose qu'un moment culminant de l'histoire des hommes. Et cela peut signifier deux choses: d'abord que l'on fait l'épreuve de la solidité de cette espèce, de sa fixité. Ensuite, que la variété des rapports entre les hommes, leur couleur, leurs coutumes, leurs formations en classes masquent une vérité qui apparaît ici éclatante, au bord de la nature, à l'approche de nos limites: il n'y a pas des espèces humaines, il y a une espèce humaine. C'est parce que nous sommes des hommes comme eux que les SS seront en définitive impuissants devant nous.[7]

> (There is no ambiguity, we are still human, we shall end our lives as humans. [. . .] It's a dream of the SS to believe that our historical mission is for us to change species, and as the mutation is too slow in coming, they kill. No, this extraordinary disease is a culminating moment in human history and not anything different. And this can mean two things: first that we are testing out how solid, how fixed this species is. And second that the variety of relations between human beings, their different colour, customs, class groupings mask a truth that is plain to see, at the edge of nature, as we near our limits: there are not several different human species, but only the one. It is because we are as human as they are that ultimately the SS will be powerless over us.)

The everyday reality of the camp exists at the very margin of what is still recognisable as human. But even at this extreme limit, Antelme suggests, the power of the Nazi state is necessarily confronted with the indestructible human reality of those it has set out to destroy. 'L'homme est l'indestructible qui peut être détruit' ('Humanity is that which is indestructible but may be destroyed'), Blanchot puts it by way of commentary on Antelme's text; and it is evident, as Blanchot notes, that even though the SS may have succeeded in suppressing the existence of human beings without number, survival is nonetheless vouchsafed by the tenuous, eerie, almost inhuman possibility of language that Antelme displays in writing *L'Espèce humaine*. Writing here is not the expression of ready-made humanistic values; rather, it is constrained to occupy the impossible, incommensurable gap that exists between the available words and the experience that can find no place in them. 'A peine commencions-nous à raconter,' admits Antelme, referring to himself and his fellow returnees, 'que nous suffoquions' ('We had hardly started to tell our story before we began to suffocate'). But as Antelme writes this, it is as though, by allowing him to formulate disaster, albeit in terms that, inevitably, cannot even claim to be adequate, language itself has always already preceded the disaster of the camps; somehow, therefore, without it being able to overcome or prevent such catastrophe, the act of writing is able yet, if only perhaps in solidarity, to associate with the possibility of survival embodied in Antelme's text its own desperate capacity for apocalyptic affirmation.[8]

Writing, then, is always already transgressive of authority; it always exceeds the law that seeks to impose limits and to police borders. The law, for it to be promulgated, must first be written down; and writing retains from this precedence or priority an excess and an affirmative value that cannot be negated. If it is true that *L'Espèce humaine* is a story of catastrophe, it is also the case that, in Antelme's text, as in all apocalyptic writing, that selfsame catastrophe functions as a moment of disastrous revelation. Even at the most extreme point of dereliction and despair there is room for the possibility of affirmation; and it is that chance of apocalyptic grace that is in some ways the most shocking moment of all. Duras records it as a telephone message from D., announcing Robert L.'s return: 'c'est plus terrible que ce qu'on a imaginé,' says D. 'Il est heureux' ('it's more terrible than anything we imagined. . . . He's happy', *D*, 64; 53). And writing to Mascolo himself, shortly after his return, Antelme described the limbo-like world in which he suddenly found himself as more akin to paradise than hell: 'Eh bien,' he writes, 'dans ce qui chez d'autres représentait pour moi l'enfer, tout dire, c'est là que j'ai vécu mon paradis' ('What others took to be my own private hell, having to tell the whole thing, that for me was my version of paradise').[9]

As these words suggest, the ethics implied in *L'Espèce humaine* is an ethics founded on the transgressive value of writing, and much the same is arguably also true of Duras's texts in *La Douleur*. Writing, here, has a strange status. It precedes the law of division and exclusion, and undermines the authority of the law by fusing together apparently irreconcilable opposites; and it dissolves all fixity of meaning by virtue of the fact that words always exceed whatever it is they appear to say. Writing here takes on the role of a radical force that overwhelms identity, and disperses all monolithic authority or power. It continually outlives its own finite character and survives as pure affirmation, as an attentiveness to otherness that eschews moral dogmatism and refuses to enclose meaning or alterity within the circular equations of dialectical identity.

The connection between this account of writing as a mode of radical or fundamental transgression and Duras's rejection of authoritarian or humanistic politics is not difficult to see. Among the casualties, by the end of the 1940s, while Duras was probably still writing some of the texts eventually published in *La Douleur*, was her membership of the French Communist Party, from which she resigned after an acrimonious debate touching precisely on the relationship between culture and politics. In *L'Amant*, many years later, Duras reiterated her repudiation of the PCF in terms that had lost none of their violence. Working as a Communist Party activist after the war, she wrote, was tantamount to collaborating with the Nazis. Both the one and the other, she suggested, reflected the same quasi-religious nostalgia for external authority: 'C'est la même chose,' Duras wrote, 'la même pitié, le même appel au secours, la même débilité du jugement, la même superstition, disons, qui consiste à croire à la solution politique du problème personnel' ('The two things are the same, the same pity, the same call for help, the same lack of judgement, the same superstition, if you like, that consists in believing in a political solution to the personal problem', *A*, 85; 73). Here, for Duras, the only politics consistent with the ethics of writing is a politics that rejects all forms of representation or external authority; it is a politics that is simultaneously a refusal of politics.

In the wake of May 1968, the relationship to politics in Duras's fiction writing is often mediated by the figure of the Jew (relayed elsewhere, as I have suggested, by women, children, music, or writing itself). Judaism in Duras is a consistent political, ethical, even aesthetic reference point. What it offers is the figure of a relationship to the law that precedes the law; what it embodies for Duras, as it were, is that which has always already been excluded from history and politics. So the reference to Judaism is fundament-ally apocalyptic, not only in the sense that, for Duras, Judaism is inseparable from the unspeakable catastrophe of Auschwitz, but also because Judaism, as she sees it, both reveals and affirms the values of innocence, despair, and nomadic transgression that – like writing itself – have always already been repressed by history, technology, and rationalism. The place of the Jew, for Duras, is to be ever present in the margins of discourse as a force of nomadic exteriority and radical questioning that challenges all identity or authority.[10]

This image of the Jew as the only truly radical revolutionary, dedicated not to the construction and edification of state power but to exile, anonymity, and failure, is a frequent one in many of Duras's texts from the late 1960s onwards. Already in *Détruire, dit-elle*, of course, Stein and Max Thor had been portrayed as German Jews (*DD*, 111; 70), in memory of those students who in May 1968 answered anti-Semitic attacks on Daniel Cohn-Bendit by chanting: 'Nous sommes tous des juifs allemands.' More explicit still among Duras's works in its endorsement of the Jew as an exemplary embodiment of authentic revolutionary energy is *Abahn, Sabana, David*, dedicated to Antelme and Blanchot in 1970 and turned into the film *Jaune le soleil* the following year. Like *Détruire, dit-elle*, *Abahn, Sabana, David* is mainly to be understood as an apocalyptic political allegory. It tells how David, a *lumpen* building worker, together with Sabana, who is friend, wife, and mother to him, arrives at the house of Abahn, the Jew, with the purpose of assassinating him. This David has been ordered to do by Gringo (Grinsky in the film), the local Communist Party boss who has reached an understanding on this issue with the local traders or capitalists. Abahn's crime is to have challenged the authority of the Party regarding questions such as the fate of the Jews in the Soviet labour camps (*ASD*, 130), and to have reminded both the Party and their capitalist partners of the transgressive power of political despair and nomadic freedom (*ASD*, 28).

But the identity of Abahn is nowhere guaranteed in Duras's story, and he immediately doubles up, from the very outset, as both Abahn and another man whose name in the text is given only as 'le juif', i.e. the Jew (*ASD*, 18). (In the film version, the process is reiterated for a second time, with two characters [Sami Frey and Dionys Mascolo] doubling up in the role of this newcomer, as though to emphasise still further the association between Judaism and proliferating multiplicity.) As the text proceeds, all the other divisions in the plot, particularly those between the two versions of Abahn and the two other main characters, are gradually eroded, too. Sabana, for example, ends up identifying with the Jew; David, in turn, is also drawn into a relationship with him because of their shared love of dogs, and is forced to realise that the Jew is a threat only to the authoritarian power of the Stalinist Gringo. In a moment of joyous – apocalyptic – illumination (*ASD*, 141), David abandons his mission and, taking the Jew's dogs with him, embarks on a future of nomadic exile in the forest beyond the town of Staadt. In the process, his own identity merges with that of the Jew. Revolutionary values are thus reaffirmed in the text, but with the understanding that the only valid politics is a refusal of politics, the only communism is an impossible one (*ASD*, 94), and thus the only response to party or state authority is to say: 'NON', the word the Jew has tattooed on his wrist instead of a concentration camp serial number (*ASD*, 123). For its part, the film endorses the claim by showing, in its final sequence, the assembled company of actors all babbling musically in a heap, as though to acknowledge the demand for an ecstatic community that the film makes throughout, and as a token embodiment of the promised revolution that it wills into being as it ends.

While in *Abahn, Sabana, David* or *Jaune le soleil* Judaism provides Duras with a model for messianic revolution, elsewhere it serves as a focus for her concern with the ethics of memory, desire, and writing. Clearest expression of this is to be found in Duras's recurrent preoccupation with the Holocaust; and this in turn is most firmly in evidence in the three texts Duras published in 1979 under the title, *Aurélia Steiner*.[11] The three texts all attempt, in slightly differing ways, to fictionalise aspects of the story of Auschwitz. The issues at stake in the endeavour are naturally immense, and they are sufficient to impose on Duras a new manner of writing, since for the first time since the 1950s, in these three stories, she chooses to write, pseudo-autobiographically, with the voice of a first-person woman narrator, called Aurélia Steiner. But this apparent movement beyond fiction into documentary is doubled by a backwards turn to literature, given that Duras in the *Aurélia Steiner* stories cannot avoid fictionalising what is being narrated (and, in any case, crucial aspects of the narratives, like the father's hanging related in 'Aurélia Vancouver', are borrowed from other texts, such as Elie Wiesel's Auschwitz memoir, *La Nuit*, or from the living testimony of other survivors).[12] This fictional recourse to other texts is reenacted by the fact that 'Aurélia Melbourne' and 'Aurélia Vancouver', the titles of the first two stories, are also the titles of two films, shot by Duras in 1979, in which the author, like many a traditional documentary film-maker, reads the texts aloud as an invisible off-screen voice; but, by rejecting the possibility of mimetic figuration, the films transform this documentary convention into the point of departure for something else, more nearly akin to the apocalyptic fictionality explored in *Le Camion* or *Le Navire Night*.

Aurélia Steiner names a whole population of texts, both literary and cinematographic, which exist on the boundary between – and thus beyond – fiction, autobiography, and documentary. This proliferation of the name is not purely circumstantial, for it affects narrative content as well. In 'Aurélia Melbourne' the name Aurélia Steiner refers only to the narrator; in 'Aurélia Vancouver', however, in addition to the narrator, it also refers to the young woman on the seafront (who has a liaison with the sailor with blue eyes and black hair who reminds her of her father) and her mother who died in childbirth in Auschwitz; while, in 'Aurélia Paris', the name belongs to both the narrator and the young Jewish orphan in the flat, in addition to her mother as well. But in all these instances, though the actual referent constantly changes, the words 'Aurélia Steiner' continue to name the same condition of exile and transgression, but this is a state of proliferation and dispersion that is without unity or identity; Aurélia Steiner, writes Duras, is in this respect a name without a subject, a 'nom sans sujet' (*N*, 130).

As well as the constant reference to Judaism and the camps, the common element in all the *Aurélia Steiner* texts is the theme of love or desire; and, as elsewhere in Duras, this is dramatised principally in the form of a merging or fusing of identities. Love, here, is an overcoming of fragmentation or separation, and the question at the heart of all the texts is the one voiced most clearly in 'Aurélia Melbourne': 'Comment nous faire nous rapprocher ensemble de cet amour, annuler cette apparente fragmentation des temps qui nous séparent l'un de l'autre?' ('How can we draw closer to this love together and annul the apparent fragmentation of time which holds us apart?', *N*, 106). The question is addressed, in turn, in 'Aurélia Melbourne', to an anonymous interlocutor, of unknown gender, and, in 'Aurélia Vancouver', to the narrator's dead father, and dead mother. In the process, it becomes clear that the desire for fusion, here, is also a desire for redemption; by addressing the place of loss itself, writing can overwhelm death by means of the sublime affirmative force in which textuality has its origin: 'lorsque je vous écris', says Aurélia Steiner, 'personne n'est mort' ('when I write to you, no-one is dead', *N*, 107).

Writing here is a mode of apocalyptic testimony whose most

dramatic emblem, in 'Aurélia Vancouver', is the action of the sea as it rises up and floods the town (*N*, 133–7). As it does so, vast quantities of salt are accidentally released into the sea and – as though to remind the audience of *Un barrage contre le Pacifique* – disseminate death and sterility all about. Like a catastrophic disaster, writing too reduces life to an original petrified mass; but as it records such disaster, it enacts love and fusion, renewal and beginning. Desire returns; mourning the past is now a possibility, and writing becomes an affirmation of the undifferentiated immensity of the sea: 'la différence,' writes Duras, 'inexistait' ('difference was non-existent', *N*, 139).

What this original, apocalyptic immensity represents is totality without totalising identity, an image that is affirmed for a final time in the shots of water that conclude both film versions of *Aurélia Steiner*. In 'Aurélia Melbourne', the camera throughout is mounted on a Seine river barge, and the final frames are of the river and sky lit up at nightfall by the orange sunset, reflecting in the water and colouring the blue sky pink; the closing shot (3'22"), as the barge constantly tracks forwards, concludes with the camera tilting back as it pans to the right and left to capture the darkness beneath the bridge, the dark sky, and, finally, the rippling waters of the Seine. In 'Aurélia Vancouver', shot in monochrome along the Normandy coast, the end comes with three shots, the first (1'5") a static shot of the sky and clouds, the second (1'30") a slow right-hand pan of the beach with the waves lapping against the pebbles, and the final take (1'28") a gradual right-hand pan of the distant horizon that frames the sky, the opposite side of the bay, the waves, and the beach, all of which appear like barely distinct horizontal layers of grey; and here, as in the preceding film, the trace of the skyline bears silent witness to the boundless immensity of water and sky.

At this extreme edge, literature and film-making in Duras are pushed to the limit, in terms both of the genre to which they belong and the reality to which they refer. Writing is dispossessed of all authority and thereby loses its predetermined structure. Its fate, here, is to dissolve into the world at large like an endless murmur preceding meaning, sense, and discourse; and what it figures at this point of apocalyptic exteriority is a moment of sublime excess that, as far as Duras is concerned, can just as easily stand for the beginning as well as the end of the world.

6 Writing sexual relations

In her texts of the 1980s and 1990s Duras embarked on what amounts to a complex restatement of many of the concerns that were at the centre of her earlier work.[1] Once again, as in the 1950s and 1960s, the theme of the couple predominates. But in the prose and theatre of the 1980s, the couple, though still usually made up of a woman and a man, is in many respects more unconventional and irregular than ever before. In her play *Agatha*, for instance, written in 1981, and filmed the same year under the title *Agatha et les lectures illimitées*, Duras stages a story explicitly devoted to an incestuous relationship between brother and sister. In the piece, sexual desire, hovering perpetually on the brink of ecstatic consummation, albeit only by proxy or in retrospect, prepares to enact that which, in normal circumstances, and in most known human societies, lies far beyond the pale of exclusion. *Savannah Bay*, Duras's next play, produced in 1983, though not concerned with incest, is in other respects very similar; what it shows, mediated and refracted through the words of two women, separated by two generations, is a mythically conjectural love story, part fiction, part remembrance, involving a man and a woman, both of whom commit suicide as an expression of the intensity of their desire for each other. Here, as elsewhere, even despite the birth of the couple's daughter – if not in fact as a direct consequence of it – no marital or familial institution seems adequate to contain their overpowering love for each other (*SB*, 60). And much the same theme, though framed in more conventionally melodramatic terms, is in evidence in *La Musica deuxième* (1985) with its story of two recent divorcees lingering nostalgically but dangerously in the vivid afterglow of their now spent and impossible relationship.

But perhaps more provocative – at any event more controversial – than any of these tales of thwarted but overwhelming heterosexual passion is Duras's short *récit*, halfway between a novel and a play-script, entitled *La Maladie de la mort* (1982), together with the longer narrative that amplifies and reworks it, *Les Yeux bleus cheveux noirs*, written in 1986.[2] In both these texts, Duras explores the sexual relationship between a homosexual man – though not explicitly named as such in either text – and a compliant hetero-sexual woman; the two are joined together in a contract that could well be described as prostitutional, were the pair, at least in the 1986 text, not also to be bound by their common – though mutually exclusive – desire for the inaccessible stranger to whom the words in the title refer. Duras also makes it clear that the woman in the first story is not primarily in search of money (*MM*, 23), but that something more is at stake that has to do with the question of the relation between sickness, death, and desire which the words, *La Maladie de la mort*, seem to suggest. But in turn, Duras implies, that relation itself hangs on the more radical conundrum of the very possibility of sexual relation between the two differentiated, adversarial bodies whose mutual dealings Duras in her narrative nonetheless endeavours to articulate or relate.

In all Duras's writings of the 1980s, relations between the sexes are of vital importance, but they also prove to be intensely fraught and precarious. In many instances, the prospect of union seems out of the question from the outset; and for some of the partners even the possibility of a shared present or future is excluded. To this extent, these stories of incest, suicidal passion, male homosexuality, separation, or divorce all display a prolonged and deep-seated crisis affecting the inner logic of sexual relations; and what Duras's texts describe, rather than a sequence of euphorically transgressive love idylls, is a series of sexual relations that seem to be like so many failures of sexual relation. The simple bliss of unencumbered happiness is nowhere apparent, and each text tends instead to inscribe or retrace a sexual or affective catastrophe culminating only in irreparable loss, mourning, solitude, aggression, or despair.

But throughout Duras's work, states such as these function less as signs of bodily fiasco than as figures of sublime or catastrophic disclosure. As such, they obey what in Duras is a familiar logic of apocalyptic inversion or reversal. For desire here survives un-deterred by the cultural taboos that, for instance, forbid sexual relations between brother and sister; and it refuses to be intimidated by the puzzling asymmetry produced by the co-existence of diver-gent, mutually antagonistic sexual orientations or object choices within the same couple. On the contrary, such difficulties seem inseparable from the very origin of desire itself; and their effect is not to diminish the power of love but rather to provoke, sustain, and radically intensify it. Thus, the bars on sexual satisfaction encountered by Duras's couples seem rarely imposed on them from the outside; on the contrary, desire itself in Duras is always already animated by the inaccessibility of the object it seeks and the necessary impossibility of ultimate gratification.

What is most clearly common to all the love relations that Duras describes in her late texts is an abiding, though paradoxical, sense that relations of desire between sexually differentiated bodies are somehow founded on the very impossibility of such relations.[3] Bodies in Duras remain irreducibly separate and irreconcilably different; but in so far as the goal of sexual desire is to erase these boundaries between bodies, and thus fuse self with other in an undecidable merging of identities, it is evident that the absence of relation between self and other, like the separateness of bodies themselves, instead of blunting desire, is its necessary and indispensable precondition. It is only ever when there is no possibility of relation between self and other that the other may be grasped as radically different, and thus genuinely desirable. Desire here is no longer regulated by received notions of sex or gender identity or by criteria of crude orgasmic efficiency; instead, in Duras, it often turns out, as *L'Amant* most clearly shows, that the most sexually desirable of other bodies is that very body with which, for reasons of cultural custom, social or personal circumstances, or even sexual orientation, no relationship is possible.

The logic of desire at work here is an ecstatic and often violent one, and one of the most incisive demonstrations of what it entails is provided, among Duras's works of the 1980s, by her two films of 1981, *Agatha et les lectures illimitées* and *L'Homme atlantique*. The first of these, a version of her – by then still unperformed – play *Agatha*, is in the form of a dramatic reading of the dialogue from that text, spoken off-screen by the voices of Duras and Yann Andréa;[4] while on the image track, amidst a series of largely static shots of the beach, sea, and sky at Trouville, punctuated periodically by the intervention of an empty black (or blank) frame, Bulle Ogier and Andréa are seen to embody, intermittently and without ever speaking on screen, the roles of the two protagonists. For these interior shots, the film uses the empty entrance hall in the Hôtel des Roches noires in Trouville (where Duras's own flat is situated and where, a decade before, she had already set *L'Amour* and *La Femme du Gange*).

Having finished *Agatha et les lectures illimitées* in May, Duras followed it, only six months later, with the release of a second film based on the same visual material, *L'Homme atlantique*. The text was subsequently published, with minor variations, early the following year. This second film, which at forty-one minutes is less than half the length of its predecessor, is made up of an off-screen commentary spoken solely by Duras, while in the role of the eponymous *L'Homme atlantique* Duras casts none other than Yann Andréa, to whose image the film is seemingly addressed, and who, of course, opposite the author, had read the part of the incestuous brother in *Agatha et les lectures illimitées* and had appeared in the earlier film, though for no more than a few frames, wearing the same black sou'wester as he does in *L'Homme atlantique*. Using the same tactic as when making *Césarée* from the abandoned footage belonging to *Le Navire Night* in 1979, Duras did not film any new material specially for *L'Homme atlantique*, but decided to utilise the shots jettisoned after the final editing of *Agatha et les lectures illimitées* earlier in the year. As in the previous film, these shots are intercut with a series of empty black frames, but in *L'Homme atlantique* these interruptions are far more extensive than before. Their duration is extremely variable, and while in some cases the empty frame is held for little more than one or two seconds, at other moments the state of invisibility is imposed on the film for considerably longer; and Duras ends the film with a black empty frame which is held for 14′40″, during which time the author's off-screen voice reads the equivalent of nine and a half pages of published text (*HA*, 22–31).

As this brief description suggests, the relationship between the two films is a complex one. The many points of visual similarity between the movies are offset by striking divergences between the two spoken texts. In this respect, though in a different register from before, the making of *L'Homme atlantique* recalls the apocalyptic rewriting of *India Song* as *Son nom de Venise dans Calcutta désert* in the mid-1970s. As with the earlier film, there are a number of specific ways in which *L'Homme atlantique* both recapitulates and radicalises its predecessor. In *Agatha et les lectures illimitées*, for instance, one key sequence, interrupted and resumed several times over, shows the figure of Bulle Ogier, doubling on the image track in the role of the sister, as she enters from the left, and crosses the hall of the Hôtel des Roches noires on her way towards the windows positioned to the right of the screen, which face out to sea; behind her, the camera, just before it begins to pan to the right to keep her in shot, can be seen reflected, together with the film crew, in the large wall mirror at the back of the frame. Ogier herself, like the room's many empty chairs and internal pillars, is also replicated as an image in the mirror, in which, some minutes later, it becomes clear that a second, parallel mirror, mounted on the opposite wall, is also visible; meanwhile, between these two sightings of mirrors, the camera lingers on the windows that overlook the beach, positioning the sea as a distant image within their rectangular frame.

Throughout this whole sequence the effect is a disorientating one of infinite visual regress (not unlike the scene described ten years earlier in *L'Amour* [*AM*, 56]). The use of the two parallel mirrors, showing the camera photographing itself photographing itself, invites the sense that the object being viewed is vertiginously out of control, no longer properly contained or held in place by the frame that surrounds it. Moreover, there is a dizzying sense of the abysmal uncertainty affecting the status of the images on the cinema screen, and it is at times unclear whether these are real images, or simply reflections of images, or indeed reflections of reflections of images (at one point, for instance, there are three different versions of Bulle Ogier visible simultaneously within the same frame). From the very outset, too, Duras uses the frequently opaque or dimly translucent windows as a visual frame-within-the-frame, drawing attention to the failure of the camera to reach beyond the severely imposed limitations of its own monocular vision. The result is a peculiar tension between the frame itself and the object – often the sea – that it aims to enclose. And in the end, it is as though the camera, frustrated at the possibility of being able to record only a plethora of narcissistic reflections, is appealing, beyond the frame, to some other dimension invisible to the human eye. That other dimension, as far as *Agatha et les lectures illimitées* is concerned, is not hard to find: it is the dimension of the human voice.

Speech, clearly, is not subject to constraints of visibility; and it is thus inevitable that it should be in the voices delivering Duras's text that the difficulties of vision explored in the sequence described above are overcome, albeit on the condition that what the voices enact should itself remain hidden from sight, like some clandestine secret that ought not to be disclosed. This, of course, is exactly what is at issue in the film. For throughout this whole interrupted sequence, as Bulle Ogier passes from the mirror to the windows and to the second mirror and back again, what the voices of Duras and Andréa are reading – from the play *Agatha* – is a story of incestuous identification between brother and sister. In the story, each of the two siblings, independently, visits the converted château – or house of assignation – that reminds them of their childhood, in part because it overlooks a river and has a piano (*AG*, 24–35); as the woman begins playing a favourite Brahms waltz on this piano, she is aware of her brother listening from the floor above. Unable to play the waltz correctly, she abandons the attempt (reminding viewers of Anne-Marie Stretter, that other musician in Duras who also despaired of her piano-playing). As she gives up, her brother appears – unseen by the viewer – in the doorway, and resumes the waltz on the piano in her stead, while she, in turn, now leaves the room, only to find herself in the reception hall a little further off, gazing at her own reflection in a mirror; as she listens, it is as though she can see their two bodies merging simultaneously in the glass. Music, as often in Duras, becomes a vehicle for displaced erotic communion, and the woman's body is overwhelmed by a surge of ecstatic physical desire: for a few moments, she says, 'j'ai perdu la connaissance de vivre' ('I lost all sense of being alive', *AG*, 30).

The story offers a pointed commentary on the relationship between sound and image in Duras's film. For just as the scene recounted by Duras and Andréa off-screen tells a story of literal separation and metaphoric fusion, so the film, overlaying the mirror image on screen with the theme of the mirror on the soundtrack, is able to create in the viewer a powerful, if imaginary sense of the metaphorical identification taking place in the film between the body of Bulle Ogier and that of the fictional Agatha, even though all that is shown on camera is the isolated figure of Ogier facing the mirror. Image and spoken word refuse to match, but they do converge metaphorically; so the film is able temporarily to suspend the effect of their separation without annulling it. What the film does, therefore, is to enact or re-enact the impact of the Brahms waltz on the sister recalling her bodily identity with her own brother. Though the violence of the desire between brother and sister is not displayed on screen directly, it is performed invisibly by the impossible merger between screen and sound effected within the film itself. To the extent that it can articulate that which escapes representation, speech here is given priority over image; but what is more important is that all realist coincidence between vision and sound is withheld, its very possibility denied, even as Duras invites her spectator to imagine their impossible conjunction. And it is that impossibility which gives incestuous desire its awesome power, its 'force si terrible' (*AG*, 12). As the text later puts it, spoken to the brother by his sister's voice: 'Je vous aime comme il n'est pas possible d'aimer' ('I love you as it is not possible to love', *AG*, 30).

Some five minutes after the beginning of *L'Homme atlantique* there is a scene similar to the one from *Agatha et les lectures illimitées* that I have been describing. A human figure enters from the left, is filmed against a wall mirror by the camera that is visible as a reflection within the image that it is itself recording. The camera pans to the right, showing a silhouette looking out to sea through the windows; and it then turns to the left, where it encounters the mirror again. Throughout, unlike before, the figure on screen is not that of Bulle Ogier, but of Yann Andréa, and it is in part as though Andréa is still continuing – though in the wrong film – in his earlier role of the incestuous brother from *Agatha et les lectures illimitées*, revisiting the hall of the Hôtel des Roches noires and retracing his sister's steps in a belated lover's homage to her. Separate sequences from different movies fuse together even as they remain at a distance. Cinema, Duras's voice announces on the soundtrack, is at the limit here of what it is capable of recording (*HA*, 12–13), and it is certainly the case that the shot, at 3'15" the longest genuine take in the film (if one excludes the black frames), is initially as confusing as the sequence from *Agatha et les lectures illimitées* which it cites and largely reproduces.

This reprise of one film by another provides, of course, another neat allegorical fable of incest as a merging of two siblings as one, but in some respects the reworking of desire implicit in *L'Homme atlantique* is more disorientating than this. For in the film, unlike its predecessor, there is no recognisable narrative structure with which to make sense of the image of Andréa replicated in the mirror alongside the abysmal reflection of the camera and crew. Though the text of the film, as read by the voice of Duras, is addressed to an unnamed second person – 'vous' – with a precise date – 15 June 1981 – it is impossible to tell who this addressee is. Even within the film itself there is no reliable match between the image of Yann Andréa and the person eferred to by the text, so that, when the voice declares: 'La mer est à votre gauche en ce moment' ('The sea is now to your left', *HA*, 14), this turns out conspicuously not to be the case. As a result, no reliable subject-object axis sustains the relation between spoken text and image, and the shifting transferential dynamic of desire in Duras is such that it is impossible to decide, when viewing the film, whether

Andréa is still doubling up as Agatha's brother, or whether, alternatively, he is acting out his own biographical role as Duras's publicly
accredited companion, or whether he is not simply an extra appearing in an experimental film. What is important about the image of
Andréa in *L'Homme atlantique* is that it fulfils all these possibilities
at one and the same time; Andréa's role, like an ocean breaker,
so to speak, is to stand in for himself amidst the multiplicity of
other men he both is and is not. This, at any rate, is what the viewer
is told by the voice of Duras: 'dans le déferlement milliardaire des
hommes autour de vous,' she says, 'vous êtes le seul à tenir lieu
de vous-même auprès de moi' ('amidst the surging millions of men
around you, you are the only one to take the place of yourself
beside me', *HA*, 10).

In this way, if *L'Homme atlantique* reprises *Agatha et les lectures
illimitées*, it does so only with the effect of ruining its precursor's
residual claims to narrativity. Projecting desire beyond the realm
of story-telling, it amplifies its apocalyptic, catastrophic intensity.
As a result, what Duras articulates in *L'Homme atlantique* is no
longer in the form of a recognisable narrative, save possibly a
private scenario of desire, abandonment, and loss, but rather in the
shape of an impossible dialogue between an invisible speaking voice
and a silent – often absent – screen image. To an extent, this
asymmetry was already implicit in *Agatha et les lectures illimitées*,
but here, with *L'Homme atlantique*, the separation of image and
voice becomes more radical than ever before, since for the first
time in Duras's cinema the gap between image and sound is now
aligned with the fissure of sexual difference itself.

In *L'Homme atlantique*, the divorce between female and male
lapses into an impossible, failed dialogue between voice and image.
All communion between the sexes, as between text and screen, is
found to be desperately lacking or wanting; but this is a clue that
the very impossibility of such communion is itself a spur for turning
it into a miraculous actuality, the name for which, in Duras, is love
itself. In *L'Homme atlantique*, one might say, it is the impossibility
of the relationship between sight and sound that paradoxically
makes such a relationship possible, even though, at the very same
time, it has the effect of deferring that possibility and making it
perpetually unavailable. The paradox is one that applies not just to
Duras's film but also to relations between the sexes. (And this
convergence between cinema and sexuality is no doubt the reason
why, later in *L'Homme atlantique*, life is described by Duras as a
photographic phenomenon, ['ce phénomène photographique, la

vie', *HA*, 25].) The voice of Duras puts it as follows in the film, addressing an empty, black frame in which, immediately after, the image of Yann Andréa reappears: 'C'est à votre incompréhension que je m'adresse toujours. Sans cela, vous voyez, ce ne serait pas la peine' ('It is your failure to understand that I am appealing to. Otherwise, do you see, it would all be pointless', *HA*, 18).

While the asymmetrical, failed relationship between image and voice in the film places male and female on either side of an unbridgeable divide, other elements of the film point to the fact that this apparently irreconcilable state of opposition between the sexes is only one aspect of the economy of desire *L'Homme atlantique* strives to articulate. This is evident at various moments in the film when Duras has recourse to the theme of the ocean, as she does, for instance, at the end of the film, when, during the final empty frame (lasting 14'40''), in the gaps between her own spoken words, the sound of the sea is heard on the soundtrack, building first to a roar and then fading away. The effect is repeated four times. With regard to *L'Homme atlantique* as a whole, the motif is not unlike the use of thunder at the end of *Détruire, dit-elle*, and here, as there, what it announces is the promise or arrival of an unnamed force which seemingly has the power to fuse bodies together and overwhelm the state of separation that exists between them. By introducing into the film a third element, the ocean, which is neither male nor female and without identity or determinate shape, Duras unsettles the binary opposition between the sexes which the film otherwise appears to endorse. Faced with the presence of the ocean on both the soundtrack and image track, the viewer is invited, also, to reflect on the title of the film, which shortly after the unexpected sound of the ocean ends – though not in the 1982 published version – with the words: 'Vous êtes l'homme atlantique. Vous l'ignorez' ('You are the Atlantic man. You are unaware of this').

But who or what is this Atlantic man? Part of the answer has evidently to do with what, earlier in her text, the author names as the Atlantic object, 'l'objet atlantique' (*HA*, 12), which is none other than the ocean itself. Readers of Duras will remember that this is not the first occurrence of the Atlantic ocean in her work, nor is it the first occasion there has been an unnamed Atlantic man. Already in the author's second novel, *La Vie tranquille*, published in 1944, there is an Atlantic man, or at any rate an anonymous man who drowns in the Atlantic (*VT*, 172–5). The incident happens while the narrator, Françou, is in a small town called T . . . on the

Atlantic coast, where she has gone to grieve for her brother, Nicolas, who earlier in the book committed suicide in remorse at causing the death of his uncle (*VT*, 111–15). (Shortly after her arrival, as though in anticipation of *Agatha*, almost forty years later, Françou finds herself staring at herself in a mirror; the person she sees is like some alien character, both brotherly and malevolent ['à la fois fraternel et haineux', *VT*, 122], silently challenging her identity.) Some days later, lying on the beach, Françou watches a man swimming, and sees him laugh; later she realises that her grief for her brother has begun to subside, and she returns to her hotel, to discover the following day that the man has disappeared, presumed drowned, at which point she is obliged by the hotel proprietor to leave the resort.

In the novel in which it figures, the episode may seem at first sight to have little connection with the rest of the plot; but it is clear that the scene serves as a belated, transferential frame for the ambivalent feelings of desire, guilt, and loss, associated for Françou with the death of her brother, Nicolas. As such, the episode is more than just an isolated reference in Duras's work to the dangers of submersion. On the contrary, it seems to have set in motion, throughout a series of texts, a remarkable spate of deaths by drowning, many of which are suicides, and among the victims of which may be counted characters like Anne-Marie Stretter in *India Song*, or the two desperate lovers in the play *Savannah Bay*, and several others. Even more common than deaths by drowning in Duras are references to the fear of drowning, which recur with surprising frequency, and are particularly in evidence in the texts of the 1980s, notably *Agatha*, *Savannah Bay*, *L'Amant*, and *La Douleur*.

The Atlantic ocean, for Duras, seems to fuse together two conflicting yet equally compelling motifs: the theme of incestuous identification with the brother, and the theme of death, loss, and guilt. Both meanings lie at the centre of *L'Homme atlantique*, as they did in *Agatha et les lectures illimitées*; and it is no doubt because the two are never properly disentangled by Duras in the film that *L'Homme atlantique* presents the viewer with such a problematic and disconcerting impression of desire fused with aggression, or violence with amorous intensity. 'Je suis dans un amour entre vivre et mourir' ('I am in a state of love between living and dying', *HA*, 31), affirms the voice of Duras towards the end, and if it is true that *L'Homme atlantique* records the narrator's abandonment by the man to whom the film is addressed, the film also constitutes an ecstatic message delivered to that inaccessible other. Desire here is nothing other than the very process of its own exhaustion or extinction; as Duras's voice puts it to her lover: 'Tandis que je ne vous aime plus je n'aime plus rien, rien, que vous, encore' ('Even as I no longer love you I no longer love anything, not anything, except for you, still', *HA*, 27).

Slightly earlier in the film, by way of glossing its title, Duras, in her role as narrator, suggested that, for her part, she saw no difference between her lover and the sea; she tells him:

> Vous et la mer, vous ne faites qu'un pour moi, qu'un seul objet, celui de mon rôle dans cette aventure. Je la regarde moi aussi. Vous devez la regarder comme moi, comme moi je la regarde, de toutes mes forces, à votre place.
>
> (*HA*, 14)

> (You and the sea are as one for me, a single object, corresponding to my part in this adventure. I am looking at it too. You must be looking at it just as I am, just as I am looking, with all my strength, from where you are standing.)

Coming as it does at the end of the mirror sequence described above, the passage condenses the many transformations of desire at work in the film: the identification of the narrator's lover (in the masculine) with the sea (in the feminine); her fusion with him as she takes his place and both are bound together in a common predicament, facing this undifferentiated element, the sea, to which they both already belong yet which still remains somehow separate from them, and inaccessible; and, with this motif of the sea, the implied equivalence of desire and death, love and mourning. Yet none of the mergers promised here seems as yet to be complete, and something still resists the imperious and assertive violence of Duras's prose. The result is a dual, contradictory dynamic by which the libidinal loss of self is constantly offset by the irreducible singularity of the film's differentiated bodies and the asymmetry of their possible relations.

In *L'Homme atlantique*, as in the *Aurélia Steiner* stories, what the theme of the sea serves to articulate is both the engulfment of bodily difference and the perpetual reaffirmation of that difference. Much the same sense of oscillation is implicit in the rise and fall of the waves heard on the soundtrack of the film. It follows that the sea, if it is an object of desire, is arguably not a determinable object from which the narrator or lover may be detached; and that if it is a body, it is a body with which the only relation is one grounded in ambivalence, with the result that the narrator is left moving back and forth, irreconcilably, without the possibility of a stable position, between a fear of death by drowning and a yearning for bodily submersion. Here, the sea is no doubt itself already no more than a metaphor for that most primal and archaic of all ambivalent love objects in Duras's writing, one that, throughout the whole of her work, she describes with an equal measure of violent anger and intense desire, as she made plain herself, barely three years after *L'Homme atlantique*, in *L'Amant*: the body of the mother.[5] In Duras's case, as *Un barrage contre le Pacifique* had established in 1950, the identification between the sea and the mother (in French, 'la mer' and 'la mère') is no idle pun; and its re-emergence in many of the texts of the late 1970s and early 1980s confirms that, in *L'Homme atlantique*, as in several of the texts that follow, what is at stake for Duras is not the success or failure of desire for this or that body in preference to another, but, more radically, the very ground on which these choices are made, the enigma of what it is that drives bodies to separate at all from each other, only for those selfsame bodies then to struggle endlessly and painfully to reverse the process in the pursuit of impossible love.

As this association with the mother suggests, the sea in *L'Homme atlantique*, though it is named in the text as an object, is less an object than a kind of ever-changing, indeterminate environment which necessarily escapes all properly mimetic representation. But, at least in the film version of *L'Homme atlantique*, it nonetheless retains its own distinct and persuasive visual emblem. This is clear when, at the point corresponding to the passage cited above, a cut in the image track of the film intervenes just before the viewer hears the second sentence: 'je la regarde.' The frame that follows immediately after is an empty black image lacking in all definition. Such frames, by the end of *L'Homme atlantique*, entirely overwhelm the film and submerge it in darkness. As they do so, they seem to signify in a double manner: they point on the one hand to the absolute separation of bodies, of male and female, image and voice, and lament the loss of all properly cinematographic space in which the two might have been joined together; but they also promise, in apocalyptic mode, the possibility of a catastrophic merger of the unseen with the unspoken, of the visible with the invisible, and thus, at last, of male with female. (It comes as no surprise to realise that, in almost all Duras's texts of the 1980s, erotic communion is signified by the motif of characters intently looking, with their eyes closed.) What is accomplished at the close of *L'Homme atlantique*, is an act of erotic fusion, in which intense libidinal engulfment becomes inseparable from deathly submersion.

In *L'Homme atlantique*, all images except absent ones are pushed to a point of exhaustion; all that survives, functioning precariously as a sign of bodily and sexual difference but also, if it were to fall silent, presaging the imminent loss of difference, is the sound of the human voice, itself, in this guise, working arguably as yet another avatar of the maternal body. But less, here, is also more, and this rediscovery of the radical extremity of the human voice, towards which the ending of *L'Homme atlantique* points, is a feature central to much of Duras's later work. Indeed, following on from her experience with films like *La Femme du Gange* and *India Song*, Duras seems, in the latter half of the 1970s, to have taken a renewed interest in the aesthetic possibilities of the speaking voice. This in turn was instrumental in persuading her to resume writing for the theatre after an interruption of nearly ten years, with the result that, from 1977 onwards, Duras became increasingly involved in work for the stage, publishing *L'Eden Cinéma* in 1977 and *Le Navire Night* two years later (though this second piece was also a film script); *Agatha*, *Savannah Bay*, and *La Musica deuxième* followed in quick succession. These last two plays Duras also directed, to mixed reviews, for their Paris opening; in 1981 she provided Sami Frey and Delphine Seyrig with a new version of her adaptation of *La Bête dans la jungle* (based on the Henry James short story *The Beast in the Jungle*),[6] and in 1985 brought out a French version of Chekhov's *Seagull*. Earlier, in January 1984, at the Théâtre du Rond-Point, Duras organised a series of dramatic readings from her work, in the course of which a number of non-theatrical texts – including *L'Homme atlantique*, *L'Homme assis dans le couloir*, the three versions of *Aurélia Steiner*, and four other short pieces – were read on stage by a small group of actors.[7]

Surprisingly, the common thread that runs through all these different theatrical activities, whether on the level of the texts themselves or the mode and manner of their performance, is a concern in Duras's work that seems to be at the opposite extreme to what the theatre is usually held to offer: the act and theme of reading. Admittedly, the term is used by Duras in a rather idiosyncratic way, and the particular significance of reading in relation to the theatre is perhaps best revealed by the unusual, elongated title given to the film *Agatha et les lectures illimitées*. 'Unlimited' readings, the audience is told, are 'personal' readings (*AG*, 63); and in the text of the film (and play) this is explained by the acknowledgement that the names of the characters, Agatha and Ulrich, are borrowed from Robert Musil's novel, *The Man Without Qualities*: the unnamed brother and sister of Duras's text, the explanation runs, reading Musil or some other story while still children, seem immediately to have recognised themselves as the incestuous siblings in the text and thereby, so to speak, become a direct embodiment of the text they were reading.[8]

If incest in Duras is a merger of two into one, then the act of reading, as dramatised in *Agatha et les lectures illimitées*, constitutes a similar loss of boundaries and a process of fusion between reader and writer, with both mingling their bodies in the text they share as though in an ecstatic union exactly parallel to incest itself. The process is one that *Agatha et les lectures illimitées* endeavours not only to describe but also to enact. For Duras's film reminds the viewer from the outset that it, too, is based on a reading – an off-screen recitation of the play *Agatha* by Marguerite Duras and Yann Andréa – and to that extent is itself constituted as an act of apocalyptic fusion with its own text. As though to demonstrate the fact, the opening shot of Duras's film, presenting itself as an ecstatic re-embodiment of the author's own writing, is taken up with the movement of the camera scrolling down the first page of the printed Minuit text of *Agatha* (and the same gesture is repeated, with later pages, three times more in the film).

In the stage directions given in *Agatha*, the two protagonists (who, in the film, are never visible on screen) are described at one point as having to appear, stiffly, with closed eyes, as the 'récitants imbéciles de leur passion' ('mindless narrators of their own passion', *AG*, 19). The phrase describes exactly what is at stake here; for what it affirms is that Duras's actors, in the course of the performance, are themselves transformed into depersonalised vehicles for the sublime intensity of the text. Their fate is to be dissolved, as they speak, into the act of reading that alone sustains their existence as performers. The act of reading, for Duras, is an act of powerful fusional identification, yet it stands at the opposite extreme to any naturalistic, psychological representation of sexual passion. What it affirms, instead, for Duras, with regard to both theatre and cinema, against all forms of realism, is an apocalyptic refusal of representation. The plays Duras writes may at times resemble love stories, but their aim is to disable any psychology of desire; exploding the bounds of inwardness, they therefore promise – and enact – the catastrophic ruin of psychological explanations. And it is in accordance with the ensuing overwhelming devastation that, in all her later plays, from *L'Eden Cinéma* to *Savannah Bay* or *La Musica deuxième*, Duras points to the need for stage sets that are open, empty spaces, lacking in intimacy or detail, allowing the intensity of the text being read to touch each last corner of the theatre with its incandescent power.

Reading, as Duras understands or practises it, is an embodiment of the written text that aims – impossibly – to dispense with both representation and performance, and, reaching beyond theatrical illusion, to arrive at a mode of textuality that is pure affirmation or event, shunning all ready-made, prior narrative space or temporality, reliant only on its own sublime virtuosity. Implicit in the endeavour is Duras's rejection of theatre in its conventional form; and this refusal of stage representation is itself a concern that lies at the centre of her two most controversial works of the 1980s, the *récit* entitled *La Maladie de la mort*, together with the longer narrative that reprises and reworks it, *Les Yeux bleus cheveux noirs*. Both texts explore the effects of a sexual contract by which a woman, explicitly said not to be a prostitute, agrees, in return for money, to spend a given number of nights with an unknown man who explains he has never had experience of desire for a woman; in both versions the story culminates in an ecstatic moment of sexual intercourse, the result of what the woman in *La Maladie de la mort* terms 'une faille soudaine dans la logique de l'univers' ('a sudden fissure in the logic of the universe', *MM*, 52), while, in the later book, as the woman cries out, it is not only logic, but Duras's own prose as well that falters in its attempt to describe the intensity of the woman's orgasm (*YB*, 132; 101). Duras concludes in both cases with a familiar apocalyptic motto: 'Cela est fait' ('It is done', *MM*, 53), or, alternatively: 'Tout était fait. Autour d'eux la chambre détruite' ('It was all over. Around them, the room, destroyed', *YB*, 143; 110).

Common to both *La Maladie de la mort* and *Les Yeux bleus cheveux noirs*, in addition to their obvious similarities of character and plot, is the contradictory relationship each entertains with the theatre. Initially, neither text was written for the stage. But, at the end of *La Maladie de la mort*, Duras suggests in a note, as she had earlier with the published versions of *Détruire, dit-elle* and *India Song*, that this work, too, might be done on stage (*MM*, 59–61); Duras stipulates, however, that the text be performed as a reading by a male narrator (distinct from the – absent – male protagonist), while the woman in the story would speak her text from memory in the usual way. But despite the recommendation, the text as it stands is in the form less of a stage script than a peremptory address in the style of *L'Homme atlantique*, delivered by an anonymous first-person voice ('je' [*MM*, 15]) to the man (addressed as 'Vous') decreed by the woman who agrees to sleep with him to be suffering from the malady of death mentioned in the title; the woman herself is referred to throughout in the third person (as 'elle').

The published text of *La Maladie de la mort* makes little concession, then, to the possibility of a future stage performance of the work. Duras's note in this respect appears to have been no more than an afterthought or, at best, a statement of intent; and it is perhaps not surprising therefore that, in reality, though *La Maladie de la mort*, when first published, seemed already to have taken into account the eventuality of a stage version, no such adaptation in fact occurred. Duras explained why, when, in an article in *Libération* in November 1986, entitled 'La Pute de la côte normande', she described her difficulties in devising a satisfactory stage adaptation of the text, which she eventually abandoned, and went on to insist that the text as published could not be represented, only read on stage (*PCN*, 7). Eighteen months later, during a television interview with Luce Perrot, she reiterated her refusal to commit herself to a stage adaptation of the text and illustrated her point by reading *La Maladie de la mort* aloud to camera on her own.

If *La Maladie de la mort* is a text that promises itself to the theatre only ultimately to withdraw from the arrangement, *Les Yeux bleus cheveux noirs* questions the possibility of stage representation in more explicit textual terms. For though the book is in the form of a continuous narrative, almost three times the length of *La Maladie de la mort*, the story it recounts is that of a stage performance, interspersed with hypothetical stage directions, as though to suggest that the published text could in fact be used as a script for a real theatrical production. But that performance, it is implied, would only ever occur in the sense that reading the book already, in advance, renders it redundant, if not in fact null and void. To read *Les Yeux bleus cheveux noirs* is to be a spectator at an event which is already both more and less than a theatrical occasion in the conventional sense: 'La lecture du livre,' writes Duras, 'se proposerait donc comme le théâtre de l'histoire' ('The reading of the book will act as theatre for the story', *YB*, 38; 25).

Duras's qualifications of the possibility or impossibility of theatrical representation of *La Maladie de la mort* and *Les Yeux bleus cheveux noirs* may seem anecdotal. But an important series of issues is at stake. The contradictory relationship that exists between Duras's two texts and the question of their theatrical adaptation re-enacts a paradox that goes to the heart of Duras's writing. For if Duras, as she reports in 'La Pute de la côte normande', eventually failed to honour the agreement to provide theatre director Luc Bondy with an adaptation of *La Maladie de la mort*, it is because text and theatre for Duras, despite their reciprocal fascination, resist one another according to a relationship of mutual exteriority; and if no theatrical adaptation of *La Maladie de la mort* proves to be adequate to the written text, it is because Duras's own writing denies the possibility of any preconceived or ready-made – and, thus, theatrical – space of representation in which male and female might appear together and thus allow a stage performance to take place. As far as the lovers in Duras's text are concerned, given their asymmetrical object choices, the situation is of course much the same; and though the contract they conclude obligates them to one another, what it primarily serves to demonstrate – more readily than any sense of prior community – is their radical incompatibility. The relationship between text and theatre in *La Maladie de la mort*, then, provides an implicit gloss on the question of relations between the sexes in Duras. The encounter between them, whether sexual or textual, is arguably always already a missed encounter; the only mode of relationship that Duras's text allows one to envisage is in fact a non-relationship.

But while *La Maladie de la mort* and *Les Yeux bleus cheveux noirs* both fall short of – or exceed – the possibility of theatrical representation, they survive nonetheless as written texts that, though irreducible to theatrical representation, may at times be read on stage in a place which may be a theatre. To this extent, both texts include the possibility of theatre while also outstripping it. The theatre functions here for Duras as an internal limit, one which it is the role of writing, like the unlimited readings referred to in *Agatha*, constantly to subvert or overwhelm. Writing here functions as an apocalyptic refusal of all generic closure or specification; so, while allowing the possibility of theatre, it also disallows it as an unwarranted limitation if not in fact a return to some earlier state. And when Duras does eventually come to posit – in a fictional, written text – a theatrical space in which the relation of male and female might occur, as she does in *Les Yeux bleus cheveux noirs* (*YB*, 151–2; 116–17), it follows that the theatre in question should turn out to be inspired by an indestructible concrete wall, set amidst the Normandy cliffs like a relic from the last war, surrounded by the violence of the sea raging below, as though to suggest that the inescapable impasse of relations between the sexes will always be overwhelmed by the unrelenting, oceanic fury of desire itself, but also that no final reconciliation will ever be on hand to resolve this antagonism between elemental force and human architecture.

Duras refuses to adhere to the conventions and limitations required by stage production by affirming the apocalyptic violence of her texts. To that extent, the relationship between writing in Duras and the theatre is a transgressive one. In *La Maladie de la mort* and *Les Yeux bleus cheveux noirs*, however, the writer goes one step further in transgressing the apparent object and purpose of her own narrative. For by articulating in fictional terms an account of the libidinal asymmetry of the sexes and the non-relationship that exists between them, Duras's writing has already forged a relationship between the sexes, albeit one ultimately founded on the impossibility of unification or identity, and in so doing her own text already exceeds and contradicts the position it had initially aimed to establish. Thus, even while Duras explores a situation of radical incompatibility between the sexes, that separation is simultaneously already in the process of being questioned and effaced by the very fact of writing itself.

Writing therefore, by virtue of its existence, is an act that constantly transgresses its own boundaries and divisions. It is towards the end of *La Maladie de la mort* that this becomes most clearly evident. For in closing, as the series of meetings between the male protagonist and the woman come to an end with the woman's anticipated but nevertheless abrupt departure, *La Maladie de la mort* alludes to the possibility that the protagonist might somehow be able to fashion their time together into some coherent narrative. But the tale he tells, that very evening, in some bar, remains a dubious and uncertain one, which he subsequently abandons, or retells with a laugh, as though to indicate that it could not possibly have taken place, or simply that the whole saga was mere fabrication (*MM*, 54–5). Much the same comments, of course, might be seen to apply to Duras's own text, but by affirming them within her own writing, as a set of possibilities which the text itself incorporates, Duras's text outstrips or transgresses them too, and the result is a mode of textuality that is uncontrollably in excess of whatever it may itself be saying. To write in Duras is already to affirm the excess and extremity of desire, if only in the form of the desire to write. Embodied in *La Maladie de la mort* is a writing that enables theatre yet overwhelms it, just as it allows narrative but steps beyond it; and as it does so, by virtue of its own existence, it affirms the inescapable necessity of love, desire, and communion at the very moment that it may be suggesting their radical impossibility.

In this way, then, as Blanchot argues in his account of *La Maladie de la mort* in *La Communauté inavouable*, if Duras's text describes a sexual impasse, it also offers the prospect of a lovers' community.[9] Such a community would rely on no prior institution or legislative order, but merely on a singular, unrepeatable contract between two antagonistic, asymmetrical bodies. To this extent, the sexual contract between Duras's two protagonists in both *La Maladie de la mort* and *Les Yeux bleus cheveux noirs* is not a simple external circumstance, to be read primarily as a moral indictment of prostitution or, more broadly, of the inequality of relations between men and women in contemporary society, as some readers have perhaps too quickly assumed. Rather, it functions as a metaphor for the possibility that has somehow enabled these texts to be written even in the absence of any prior, ready-made code governing relations between the sexes. What it figures therefore is the necessary price paid and the debt exacted in order that a sexual relation might in fact take place; it signals difference as well as negotiation, separation as well as transaction, loss of self as well as mutual positioning; it binds together that which resists all binding, and fuses as one that which cannot ever be fused.

The sexual contract enacted in *La Maladie de la mort* and *Les Yeux bleus cheveux noirs* is not unique in Duras. It resembles all the other sexual contracts in Duras's work, of which there are many, as for instance between Suzanne and the philanderer Agosti in *Un barrage contre le Pacifique*, between Anne-Marie Stretter and her admirers in *India Song*, between the youthful Duras and her Chinese lover in *L'Amant*, between Véra and Michel Cayre in *Véra Baxter*, or between the two lovers in *Le Navire Night*. 'L'essentiel c'est l'argent' ('The crucial thing is money', *NN*, 49), declares the narrative voice in this last work, referring to the extravagant presents given to the young man by his unseen lover; and there, as in *La Maladie de la mort*, it is clear that the sexual bargain is more nearly akin to an unaccountable gift than an act of exploitation, and that it serves to stimulate desire rather than to inhibit it. It supplies a provisional structure to love that ensures relationship while also limiting its terms. What the contract enables is the impossible – ecstatic – relation of terms that are themselves without relation.

In *La Maladie de la mort*, the sexual contract that makes the text possible seems inseparable from the title of the work, for it is by seeing the signs of that so-called malady on the man's body that the woman in the text initially agrees to the bargain her future partner proposes (*MM*, 23). But what is this 'malady of death'? At first, what the phrase seems to dramatise most clearly is the sexual gulf between the two partners in the story. The man, the reader is told, has never touched a woman before (*MM*, 9–10, 34); and it is in response to this lack of desire that the woman whom he requires to sleep with him summarily pronounces him dead, declaring, disdainfully, twice over: 'C'est curieux un mort' ('It's strange, being dead', *MM*, 35, 45). A page later, Duras confirms this association between death and sexual difference by writing of the man: 'Vous fermez les yeux pour vous retrouver dans votre différence, dans votre mort' ('You close your eyes to return to your difference, your death', *MM*, 36). But when asked by the man to explain what she means by 'la maladie de la mort', she replies that the malady is deadly in two important respects:

> En ceci que celui qui en est atteint ne sait pas qu'il est porteur d'elle, de la mort. Et en ceci aussi qu'il serait mort sans vie au préalable à laquelle mourir, sans connaissance aucune de mourir à aucune vie.
>
> (*MM*, 24)

> (In that whoever is suffering from it does not know that he is carrying it, death, that is. And also in that he would be dead with no previous life to die to, with no knowledge at all of dying to any life.)

Though it evokes ignorance and sterility, death in Duras resists being enclosed in any simple binary paradigm. It is not the crude opposite of life; it is arguably more like an indeterminate state of existence that precedes life or death in the usual sense, and is inherent in both living and dying as the precondition and final destination of both. Moreover, though it names sexual difference, death in Duras's text does not belong simply on the side of the male body, for the man sees it, too, displayed on the woman (*MM*, 36), while in turn it is the woman who repeatedly uses the figure of death to describe the jealous intensity of her desire. Towards

the end, just before she delivers her second verdict to the man, the
woman asks him:

> L'envie d'être au bord de tuer un amant, de le garder pour vous,
> pour vous seul, de le prendre, de le voler contre toutes les lois,
> contre tous les empires de la morale, vous ne la connaissez pas,
> vous ne l'avez jamais connue?

> (*MM*, 45)

> (Do you not know, have you never known the wish to be on
> the brink of killing a lover, keeping him for yourself, yourself
> alone, taking him, stealing him, in the face of all laws and
> systems of morality?)

To be filled, as is this woman, with murderous desires like these,
to be sensitive, as she is, to all the symptoms of death indelibly
written on her partner's body, is not to be opposed to the malady
of death, but to be profoundly and irrevocably contaminated by it.
To this extent, the only malady that death evokes in Duras's text
is none other than the malady of desire itself.

If death, in the case of the male protagonist, figures the lack of
desire, it also serves as proof of the work – or worklessness – of
desire in his female partner. The infernal absence of desire is little
different here from its consuming presence; like death, it has an
inexhaustible circularity, and though the man and the woman are
not at first sexual objects for one another, they become bound
together by the same desperate necessity, for which the only name
available is desire itself. Duras confirms as much by the complex
relations of similarity and difference that she elaborates throughout
her text with regard to the pounding black sea visible from the flat
(*MM*, 27) and the billowing white sheets on the bed (*MM*, 30) in
which the pair pursue their failed erotic encounter. For though the
couple cannot agree whether the sea is black or white (*MM*, 46),
the ocean nonetheless, as for the woman and her lover in *L'Homme
atlantique*, symbolises the possibility of love and fusion for which
they both yearn. After all, bodily fluids are just as much a sign of
desperate lamentation as a token of sexual excitement (*MM*, 7).
And at the end, just before an apocalyptic dawn arrives to seal the
final separation between them (*MM*, 53), what the pair discover
together, as the culmination of the chaste, unconsummated union
that has been theirs, is the impenetrable night (*MM*, 53) into which
the man finally penetrates in spite of everything, and within which

the woman welcomes him at last, in an impossible, but ecstatic act of intercourse.

In *La Maladie de la mort* the malady of death names both sexual difference and the inescapable circularity of desire. By that token, in Duras, it necessarily also names the act of writing, and it comes as no surprise to learn how, as Yann Andréa recounts in *M.D.*, writing *La Maladie de la mort* put its own author's survival severely in the balance. In this and other ways, the desire the text enacts might best be termed an apocalyptic desire, one which accentuates to the point of intolerability the bodily differences that exist between male and female, but only in order to arrive at a more radically catastrophic, purer affirmation of the sublime relationship of non-relationship on which Duras here confers the implicit name of love. Nowhere perhaps, in the whole of the author's work, is the revelation of the simultaneous impossibility and necessity of that relation rendered so powerfully and with such disturbing violence. Destroyed here is any complacent attachment to the stabilities or fixities of sexual identity; writing *La Maladie de la mort*, for Duras, becomes the only authentic, radically affirmative manner of living out revelation, community, love, death, and desire.

Notes

1 IMAGES OF AUTHORSHIP

1 The list of texts by Duras that deal explicitly with her childhood is extensive. It includes: *Un barrage contre le Pacifique* (Paris, Gallimard, 1950), *L'Eden Cinéma* (Paris, Mercure de France, 1977), *L'Amant* (Paris, Minuit, 1984), and *L'Amant de la Chine du Nord* (Paris, Gallimard, 1991), as well as a number of the pieces included in *Outside* (Paris, Albin Michel, 1981) and *La Vie matérielle* (Paris, P.O.L., 1987); to these must be added at least two published collections of conversations, *Les Lieux de Marguerite Duras*, with Michelle Porte (Paris, Minuit, 1976), and *Marguerite Duras: la passione sospesa*, with Leopoldina Pallotta della Torre (Milan, La Tartaruga edizioni, 1989), together with numerous other interviews; relevant, too, are some of the short prose texts written during the 1970s, notably 'Mothers' (*Le Monde*, 10 February 1977), and the brief memoir, also known under the title 'Ma mère, une femme honnête', contained in: Marcel Bisiaux and Catherine Jajolet (eds), *A ma mère, 60 écrivains parlent de leur mère* (Paris, Pierre Horay, 1988), pp. 159–66.

2 Typical of the uncertainties surrounding the facts of Duras's life are the details concerning the death of the younger of her two brothers. In 'Ma mère, une femme honnête', for example, the author gives her own age and that of her two brothers in 1918 as 4, 7, and 9. This is borne out by the family photographs reproduced in *Les Lieux de Marguerite Duras*. In *L'Amant* (*A*, 71; 60), the younger brother, said to be two years older than the author (*A*, 130; 113), is reported to have died in December 1942. But later in the same text (*A*, 128; 111), and again in a press conference in Montreal in 1981 (*Marguerite Duras à Montréal* [Montréal, Editions Spirale, 1981], p. 19), she states he was 27 when this happened. This cannot of course be the case if he died in 1942; either the date of his death is incorrect or Duras has miscalculated his age. (In giving the figure of 27, Duras is in fact supplying the age of her Chinese lover at the time of their liaison [*A*, 62; 53; *ACN*, 91], as well as her own age when she was pregnant with her first son, stillborn in May 1942. Speaking on radio in 1984 during *Le Bon Plaisir de Marguerite Duras*, Duras admitted to Marianne Alphant that she often made the slip of saying 'brother' ['frère'] instead of 'son' ['fils'].) In

1984, during the television programme, *Apostrophes*, in a salutary warning to naive readers who might want to take her fiction as transparently autobiographical, Duras also made it clear that, contrary to what is stated in *Un barrage contre le Pacifique* and *L'Eden Cinéma*, her mother did not play the piano in a cinema: the pianist was 'une autre' (though, to confuse matters further, Duras rehabilitates the story later [*ACN*, 179–80]).

3 On the life and two marriages of Duras's mother, see 'Ma mère, une femme honnête', and *ACN*, 33, 158. In 'Mothers', Duras gives the date of her mother's departure to Indochina as between 1905 and 1910, when she was twenty-five. In *L'Amant de la Chine du Nord* (*ACN*, 119), the year given is 1905, while in the 1988 version of the play *Eden Cinéma* Duras writes that it was in 1902 (the 1977 text had said 1912!). Duras confirmed in an 1992 interview that her father already had two sons from an earlier marriage. See 'La Brune de la Dordogne', *Libération*, 27 February 1992.

4 *L'Empire français* (Paris, Gallimard, 1940). The book, dated April 1940, was published early in May, shortly before the defeat of France at the hands of the German army. One passage in particular, from the book's rapid survey of colonial Cambodia, seems to have been written – with grammatical errors to boot – with future readers of *Un barrage contre le Pacifique* in mind; Donnadieu and Roques write:

> La plaine des joncs, ainsi qu'une partie de la région côtière du Cambodge, sont [*sic*] encore impropres à la culture. Une large frange de palétuviers les borde et il est difficile de délimiter exactement la terre de la mer. Le sel marin, qui se trouve à quelques centimètres de la surface, brûle les jeunes plants de riz dès que leurs racines l'ont atteinte [*sic*]. Mais ces terres à peine délivrées de la mer sont d'année en année plus cultivables, et on peut s'attendre d'ici quelques centaines d'années qu'elles le soient tout à fait.

> (p. 108)

> (The rush plain, like part of the Cambodian coastal area, are still unfit for farming. A thick line of mangroves runs along the edge and it is difficult to tell where land ends and sea begins. The sea salt, which is a few centimetres below the surface, scorches the young rice shoots as soon as their roots reach that far down. But these lands have barely been reclaimed from the sea and, with each year that passes, are increasingly suitable for cultivation, and it may be expected that within a few hundred years they will be under cultivation entirely.)

5 *La Vie tranquille* (Paris, Gallimard, 1944). Queneau recalls his first encounter with Duras in: 'Un lecteur de Marguerite Duras', *Cahiers de la compagnie Renaud-Barrault*, 52, December 1965, 3–5.

6 *Les Impudents*, dedicated to the author's half-brother, Jacques, was eventually published by Plon; having been unobtainable for many years, it was reissued – virtually unchanged – by Gallimard in 1992. On the connection with the town of Duras, see *Marguerite Duras à Montréal*, 55–7, and 'La Brune de la Dordogne', *Libération*, 27 February 1992.

7 See Leopoldina Pallotta della Torre, *Marguerite Duras: la passione sospesa*, p. 16; and *ACN*, 33–4.

8 On the circumstances surrounding Antelme's rescue, see Dionys Mascolo, *Autour d'un effort de mémoire: sur une lettre de Robert Antelme* (Paris, Maurice Nadeau, 1987), and Marguerite Duras, *La Douleur* (Paris, P.O.L., 1985). Mitterrand comments on the events in 'Le Bureau de poste de la rue Dupin', interview by Marguerite Duras, *L'Autre Journal*, 26 February–4 March 1986, 31–40. Antelme's own account can be found in *L'Espèce humaine* (Paris, Gallimard, [1947] 1957). It is reviewed by Maurice Blanchot in *L'Entretien infini* (Paris, Gallimard, 1969), pp. 191–200, and also discussed in: Sarah Kofman, *Paroles suffoquées* (Paris, Galilée, 1987). Antelme left an indelible impression on all those who knew him. See for instance the description given by Claude Roy in: *Nous* (Paris, Gallimard, 1972), pp. 102–9; and the obituary by Edgar Morin in *Le Monde*, 2 November 1990.

9 See Dionys Mascolo, *Le Communisme: révolution et communication ou la dialectique des valeurs et besoins* (Paris, Gallimard, 1953). Duras gives conflicting versions of the date she left the PCF. In a 1959 interview she tells André Bourin – correctly – that she was expelled in 1950; but in 1964 Pierre Dumayet is given to believe it was in 1954; while in *Le Nouvel Observateur* in 1986 Duras states that, like many others, she left in 1956 at the time of the Soviet invasion of Hungary. The circumstances of her resignation and subsequent expulsion from the Party are recalled in *Le Camion* (*C*, 119–20); and by Alain Vircondelet in his otherwise superficially researched biography, *Duras* (Paris, François Bourin, 1991), pp. 167–71.

10 'C'est la Seine-et-Oise qui est coupable', *Le Monde*, 22 February 1963.

11 For a general account of the protest movement in France against the Algerian war, see Hervé Hamon and Patrick Rotman, *Les Porteurs de valise: la résistance française à la guerre d'Algérie* (Paris, Seuil, revised edition 1982). Mascolo recalls his own involvement in an interview with Aliette Armel in *Le Magazine littéraire*, 278, June 1990, 36–40. The three issues of *Le 14 Juillet* have recently been republished in facsimile (Paris, Lignes, 1990). The 'Manifeste des 121' is reprinted, with brief commentaries by Duras and Mascolo, in: *L'Autre Journal*, 9, November 1985, 67–70. Among the original signatories were: Robert Antelme, Simone de Beauvoir, Maurice Blanchot, André Breton, Michel Leiris, Maud Mannoni, Alain Resnais, Alain Robbe-Grillet, Nathalie Sarraute, Jean-Paul Sartre, Claude Simon, and many others.

12 See Maurice Blanchot, 'Mots de désordre', *Libération*, 28–29 January 1984; and 'Tracts, affiches, bulletin', *Gramma*, 3/4 (1976), 33–4 (p. 34). It is worth comparing here Blanchot's essay on *Détruire, dit-elle*, in: *L'Amitié* (Paris, Gallimard, 1971), pp. 132–6, as well as his evocation of Duras and May '68 in *La Communauté inavouable* (Paris, Minuit, 1983), pp. 52–6.

13 See Marguerite Duras, 'Sur le comité d'action étudiants-écrivains', *Les Lettres nouvelles*, June-July 1969, 144–50.

14 On Bataille and politics, see Francis Marmande, *Georges Bataille politique* (Lyon, Presses universitaires de Lyon, 1985); and Jean-Michel Besnier, *La Politique de l'impossible* (Paris, La Découverte, 1988).

15 René Clément's adaptation of *Un barrage contre le Pacifique*, starring Jo Van Fleet as the mother, and Silvana Mangano and Anthony Perkins as her two children, seems initially to have met with some approval from the author – if only for publicity reasons – at least according to an interview Duras gave to *L'Express*, 8 May 1958. See also her enthusiastic piece entitled 'La Littéralité des faits', *France-Observateur*, 8 May 1958. By 1959, as she explains to André Bourin in *Les Nouvelles littéraires*, 18 June 1959, she had come to the view – which she repeats in a note to *L'Eden Cinéma* in 1977 (*EC*, 157) – that the film version was a disaster, and that responsibility for the failure lay largely with producer and co-writer Irwin Shaw.

16 On the sales figures for *Un barrage contre le Pacifique*, see the interview in *L'Express*, 8 May 1958. (Vircondelet, in his biography [p. 182], suggests, however, that the book sold 5,000 copies within its first week!) The reference to Hemingway (and bad grammar!) is a persistent one among early critics hostile to Duras; but the author goes some way towards endorsing the jibe when in the last of the programmes in *Au-delà des pages* she tells Luce Perrot *Le Marin de Gibraltar* (1952) was written in enthusiastic homage to Hemingway's *Green Hills of Africa*. Blanchot wrote more favourably of *Le Square* in a review collected in *Le Livre à venir* (Paris, Gallimard, 1959), pp. 185–94; an extract was used in the programme notes for the stage version of *Le Square* in 1956, to which, it is reported, Samuel Beckett was a frequent visitor.

17 See Régis Debray, *Le Pouvoir intellectuel en France* (Paris, Ramsay, 1979).

18 Godard makes the point in a television discussion with Duras on the programme *Océaniques*, broadcast by FR3, 28 December 1987. Part of the text of the discussion is published in *Le Magazine littéraire*, 278, June 1990, 46–8.

19 See the interview with Luce Perrot by Dominique Borde in *Le Figaro*, 22 June 1988.

20 'L'Inconnue de la rue Catinat', *Le Nouvel Observateur*, 28 September 1984. Duras voices similar feelings in other interviews: see, for example, her conversation with Bernard Pivot on *Apostrophes*, 28 September 1984, or 'Duras tout entière', *Le Nouvel Observateur*, 14–20 November 1986. And in *Emily L.*, the figure who is Duras's authorial mouthpiece remarks that the emotion that gives rise to writing and against which it also protects is the same: fear (*EL*, 58; 40).

21 See Aliette Armel, *Marguerite Duras et l'autobiographie* (Paris, Le Castor Astral, 1990).

22 The remark to Dominique Noguez may be found in the booklet accompanying the *Œuvres cinématographiques: édition vidéographique critique* (Paris, Ministère des relations extérieures, 1984), p. 58. The statement regarding *L'Homme atlantique* appeared in *Le Monde*, 27 November 1981, and is reprinted in *Les Yeux verts*, nouvelle édition (Paris, Cahiers du cinéma, 1987), pp. 222–4.

23 See, for instance, 'Je ne suis pas la femme d'Hiroshima', *Les Nouvelles littéraires*, 18 June 1959 (in which she makes the remark about her mother); 'Entretien avec Marguerite Duras', *L'Express*, 30 June 1960;

and 'Le Bonheur n'est pas ce qui m'intéresse le plus', in: Pierre Dumayet, *Vu et entendu* (Paris, Stock, 1964), pp. 105–9.

24 'Entretien avec Marguerite Duras', *L'Express*, 30 June 1959.

25 'Les Hommes de 1963 ne sont pas assez féminins', *Paris-Théâtre*, 198 (1963), 32; and 'Un silence peuplé de phrases', *Synthèses*, 254–5, August-September 1967.

26 See 'Marguerite Duras cherche la liberté et la vérité dans le crime', *Combat*, 16–17 February 1963; 'L'Amour est un devenir constant comme la révolution', *Le Monde*, 7 March 1967; and 'La Séduction de la folie', *Le Monde [des livres]*, 29 March 1967.

27 'Entretien avec Marguerite Duras', *L'Express*, 30 June 1959.

28 'La Destruction la parole', *Les Cahiers du cinéma*, 217, November 1969, 45–57 (p. 45).

29 'La Destruction la parole', 51.

30 The remarks were first made during a television interview with Pierre Dumayet by Duras, entitled 'L'Arroseur arrosé', broadcast as part of the weekly documentary programme *Dim dam dom* in 1965. In the same interview Duras declared: 'je ne suis pas du tout féministe', adding, for Dumayet's benefit, with something of the ghost of an ironic smile, that after all, 'tout ce que nous [i.e. the two interlocutors] trouvons aux femmes, les vertus de la femme, ces vertus qui sont ancrées dans une sorte de silence fondamental, s'évanouiraient avec une émancipation totale' ('I'm not at all a feminist. All the things we find in women, you and I, all the female virtues, those virtues that are rooted in a kind of fundamental silence, would simply fade away with complete emancipation'). It is perhaps fair to say in Duras's defence that these words did not necessarily have the same connotations in 1965 as they do a quarter of a century later!

31 See Hélène Cixous and Catherine Clément, *La Jeune Née* (Paris, Union Générale d'Editions, 1975), pp. 158 and 175. For a discussion of Cixous and *écriture féminine*, see Helen Wilcox and others (eds), *The Body and the Text: Hélène Cixous, Reading and Teaching* (London, Harvester Wheatsheaf, 1990).

32 Luce Irigaray, *Speculum: de l'autre femme* (Paris, Minuit, 1974); Annie Leclerc, *Parole de femme* (Paris, Grasset, 1974); and Marguerite Duras and Xavière Gauthier, *Les Parleuses* (Paris, Minuit, 1974); Cixous's footnote can be found in 'Le Rire de la Méduse', *L'Arc*, 61, 1975, 39–54 (p. 42). For an illuminating account of some of the implications involved here, see Jane Gallop, *Thinking Through the Body* (New York, Columbia University Press, 1988).

33 It is impossible to indicate here the scope and range of the debate still going on within feminism around the question of essentialism. For a recent summary of some of the issues involved, see Diana Fuss, *Essentially Speaking* (London, Routledge, 1990). Duras has sometimes served as a straw target for attacks on so-called 'essentialism'; this is the case, notably, with Trista Selous's polemical study, *The Other Woman: Feminism and Femininity in the Work of Marguerite Duras* (London, Yale University Press, 1988). For an alternative perspective, see Sharon Willis, *Marguerite Duras: Writing on the Body* (Urbana and Chicago, University of Illinois Press, 1987).

34 'Marguerite Duras. Interview', in: Suzanne Horer and Jeanne Soquet, *La Création étouffée* (Paris, Pierre Horay, 1973) (pp. 178–9).

35 'An Interview with Marguerite Duras', *Signs: Journal of Women in Culture and Society*, 1, 2, Winter 1975, 423–34 (p. 423).

36 Horer and Soquet, *La Création étouffée*, p. 187.

37 The remark is made during *Le Bon Plaisir de Marguerite Duras*, France-Culture, 20 October 1984.

38 Germaine Brée records the first remark in an interview with Duras in *Contemporary Literature*, XIII, 4, 1972, 399–422 (pp. 416 and 417); the comment to Vircondelet appears in his *Marguerite Duras ou le temps de détruire* (Paris, Seghers, 1972), p. 175. Finally, the comment about children (prefiguring the 1985 film, *Les Enfants*, and *La Pluie d'été*, the 1990 novel based on it) can be found in *Marguerite Duras à Montréal*, p. 59.

39 'Entretien avec Marguerite Duras', *Jeune Cinéma*, 104, July-August 1977. A similar, but more emphatic recantation on the subject of *écriture féminine* may be found in 'The Thing', *Gai Pied*, 20, November 1980.

40 See *Marguerite Duras à Montréal*, pp. 33–4 and 68–70.

41 'Marguerite Duras explique sa position politique', *Le Quotidien de Paris*, 26 May 1977; and 'Un acte contre tout pouvoir', *Cinéma 77*, 223, July 1977.

42 See 'Voter Giscard, c'est voter contre Lech Walesa', *Les Nouvelles littéraires*, 7–14 May 1981; and 'Un pays du Nord', *Des femmes en mouvements: hebdo*, 3–10 July 1981.

43 'Sublime, forcément sublime Christine V.', *Libération*, 17 July 1985. Three months earlier, when *La Douleur* first came out, Duras explained that part of her fascination with Christine Villemin as a potential infanticide was due to her own sense of horror at having participated in torture during the Resistance, as she recounts in the story 'Albert des Capitales' (*D*, 135–62; 116–41). In the figure of Villemin, therefore, it was also – perhaps even principally – her own past that Duras was accusing, in the process turning herself and Villemin into a pair of apocalyptic witnesses, martyrs to a mythic crime. See 'Avril 45: nuit et Duras', *Libération*, 17 April 1985.

44 For this hostile reaction to the piece, see *L'Evénement du jeudi*, 25 July 1985; and the special issue of *Esprit*, 116, July 1986. See also David Amar and Pierre Yana, ' "Sublime, forcément sublime". A propos d'un article paru dans *Libération*', *Revue des sciences humaines*, 202, 1986–2, 153–76.

45 See 'La Perte de la vérité', *L'Autre Journal*, 8, October 1985; 'Le Froid comme en décembre', *L'Autre Journal*, 9, 23–29 April 1986; and 'Moi', *L'Autre Journal*, 10, 30 April–6 May 1986.

2 TRANSFERENTIAL LOVES

1 The texts I shall be dealing with in this chapter are as follows: *Les Impudents* (Paris, Plon, 1943); *La Vie tranquille* (Paris, Gallimard, 1944); *Un barrage contre le Pacifique* (Paris, Gallimard, 1950); *Le Marin de Gibraltar* (Paris, Gallimard, 1952); *Les Petits Chevaux de Tarquinia* (Paris, Gallimard, 1953); *Des journées entières dans les arbres, suivi de:*

...me *Dodin, Les Chantiers* (Paris, Gallimard, 1954); *Le*
...Gallimard: folio, [1955] 1990); *Moderato cantabile* (Paris,
...I shall also be making reference to the first version of
... dans le couloir', in: *L'Arc*, 20, October 1962, 70–6,
...sed version, *L'Homme assis dans le couloir* (Paris,

...unt of brother-sister incest in Duras is provided by
...Histoire d'un fantôme', *Revue des sciences humaines*,
...8. For a different, more metaphorical view of incest,
...sion, see Danielle Bajomée, *Duras ou la douleur*
...s universitaires, 1989). On the reciprocity between
...on, see Georges Bataille, *Œuvres complètes*, 12 vols
...1970–88), X (1987), 66–8. When Bataille's book
...eared in 1957, Dionys Mascolo reviewed it enthusi-
...*bservateur* (20 February 1958). Through Mascolo,
...ely close terms with Bataille, whom she had inter-
...December; the following month she also contrib-
...Bataille to the magazine *La Ciguë*. In April 1960,
...he offered Bataille her share of the windfall profits
that, as a bonus, the producers of *Hiroshima mon amour* offered Alain
Resnais and part of which he, in turn, wished to pass on to Duras. She
voices later, more critical thoughts on Bataille in: Leopoldina Pallotta
della Torre, *Marguerite Duras: la passione sospesa*, pp. 62–3.

3 In 1990 *Le Square* was revised by Duras before it was reprinted as a
folio paperback. The changes made to the 1955 text are for the most
part minor and affect only word order or the choice of individual words.
(For convenience, unless otherwise indicated, I refer to the paperback
reprint throughout this chapter.).

4 See Maurice Blanchot, *Le Livre à venir* (Paris Gallimard, 1959),
pp. 185–94. Interestingly, Blanchot in this piece anticipates much of
what he writes apropos of *La Maladie de la mort* in *La Communauté
inavouable* (Paris, Minuit, 1983), some twenty-five years later, prompt-
ing the view that Duras's 1982 text might itself best be read as a radical
revision of *Le Square*.

5 In 1955, *Le Square* ended as follows: 'Elle ne se retourna pas. Et
l'homme le prit comme un encouragement à aller à ce bal' ('She did
not turn round. And he took this as a sign of encouragement to go to
that dance', *Le Square*, 1955 version, 156; 104). The 1990 reprint omits
the second of these sentences. When Duras adapted the story for the
stage in 1965, the play also concluded, like the 1955 novel, with a
relatively optimistic exchange (*T1*, 135–6; 64).

6 See Dionys Mascolo, *Le Communisme. Révolution et communication
ou la dialectique des valeurs et des besoins*. There is a succinct summary
of Mascolo's sometimes rambling and tortuous book in Maurice
Blanchot, *L'Amitié* (Paris, Gallimard, 1971), pp. 109–14. For a more
polemical version of Mascolo's position, see his *Lettre polonaise sur
la misère intellectuelle en France* (Paris, Minuit, 1957). For a more
recent elaboration of some of the issues at stake, see Jean-Luc Nancy,
La Communauté désœuvrée (Paris, Christian Bourgois, 1990) and
Maurice Blanchot, *La Communauté inavouable*.

7 Mascolo, *Le Communisme*, p. 8.

8 Mascolo, *Le Communisme*, pp. 303–4. Mascolo's definition of need is somewhat at variance with the more usual definition inspired by Lacan. Lacan, following Hegel, contrasts need with desire. Needs are natural, biological, pre-linguistic deficiencies, like hunger, say, or lack of warmth; once alleviated by food or heat, the need is extinguished (albeit provisionally). Desire, however, is a lack in the cultural or symbolic register and is inseparable from the effects of language; desire, for Lacan, can in principle never be satisfied or expunged: the object it seeks is an object that has always already been lost and will therefore never be found. (On this, see Lacan, *Ecrits* [Paris, Seuil, 1966], pp. 414–15.) Mascolo, however, rejects the opposition of nature and culture; for him the two are irrevocably fused. In Mascolo's account, need is the radical, indeterminate origin of desire; unlike desire, he argues, need has no specific goal or object; need therefore precedes desire as the general ground on which particular desires are founded. As Mascolo explains in *Le Communisme*: 'C'est que le désir peut toujours être vu comme une hypothèse faite sur la nature du besoin qu'il est censé développer. Le besoin serait alors comme la substance du désir' ('Desire can always be seen as a hypothesis concerning the nature of the need it is meant to develop. Need, one could say, is the very substance of desire', pp. 47–8). Despite their divergences, Mascolo and Lacan share a common background in that both insist on the transcendental implications of human insufficiency, irrespective of whether lack is thematised primarily as desire or need. This joint intellectual context extends, too, to the work of numerous other writers, whom Lacan and Mascolo both knew well, including Bataille, Queneau, Kojève, and others. There is here an important and neglected chapter in French intellectual history which, if it were better documented, would clarify considerably the true measure of Lacan's alleged influence on Duras and the relationship between them.

9 *Moderato cantabile* is one of the most widely discussed of all Duras's texts. Among the more perceptive accounts of the novel, see, for instance, Bruce Bassoff, 'Death and Desire in Marguerite Duras's *Moderato cantabile*', *MLN*, 94 (1979), 720–30; David Coward, '*Moderato cantabile*' (London, Grant and Cutler, 1981); Marianne Hirsch, 'Gender, Reading, and Desire in '*Moderato cantabile*', *Twentieth-Century Literature*, 28, 1, Spring 1982, 69–85; and George Moskos, 'Women and Fictions in Marguerite Duras's *Moderato cantabile*', *Contemporary Literature*, XXV, 1, Spring 1984, 28–52. I have discussed the novel at greater length myself in 'Marguerite Duras: Sexual Difference and Tales of Apocalypse', *Modern Language Review*, 84, 3, July 1989, 601–14.

10 Georges Bataille, *Œuvres complètes*, X, 17.

11 The phrase – usually rendered in English as 'it's done' – occurs in many other texts, where it signifies the finality and intensity of desire: see *L'Après-midi de Monsieur Andesmas* (*AMA*, 39; 231); *Le Ravissement de Lol V. Stein* (*R*, 112, 149); *Le Vice-consul* (*VC*, 58–9, 142; 43, 112); *L'Amante anglaise* (*AA*, 142; 89); *Détruire dit-elle* (*DD*, 45; 26); *L'Amour* (*AM*, 106); *Nathalie Granger suivie de La Femme du Gange*

(*NG*, 77); *L'Eté 80* (*E*, 32, 95); *La Maladie de la mort* (*MM*, 53); *L'Amant* (*A*, 111; 96); *La Pluie d'été* (*PE*, 22); *L'Amant de la Chine du Nord* (*ACN*, 92); and *Yann Andréa Steiner* (*YA*, 133). And in *Emily L.*, for instance, the words serve to describe the apocalyptic enactment of writing itself: 'On commence. Et puis ça arrive, on écrit, on continue. Et puis voilà, c'est fait' ('You start. And then there you are, writing, so you go on. And then there it is. It's happened', *EL*, 58; 40).

12 Duras supplies some of the background to the story in an introductory piece published in *Les Cahiers du cinéma*, 312–13, June 1980, 32–3. Duras states that the story was initially written about 1958 and first published in English, anonymously, some ten years later; the 1962 printing of the story – which Duras omits to mention – is fragmentary in that it has omission marks and suspension points at crucial moments in the text (if one compares the 1980 text, these correspond to the main orgasmic moments of the narrative, where Duras's erotic language is at its most explicit). In other ways the 1962 text is more specific than the revised version; it names the woman in the story as the depressive, melancholy figure of Anne-Marie Stretter and describes the setting as overlooking the delta of the Ganges at Calcutta. (Fragments of material from this earlier text also survive in the closing sections of *Le Vice-consul* [*VC*, 197–8, 203–4; 157–8, 161–2].) A later, edited version of the text was staged by Duras as a dramatic reading for three voices (one male and two female) in January 1984 at the Théâtre du Rond-Point; extracts from this production are included in the radio broadcast, *Le Bon Plaisir de Marguerite Duras*, produced by Marianne Alphant for France-Culture in October 1984. On the questions of categorisation that the story raises, see Marcelle Marini, 'La Mort d'une érotique', *Cahiers Renaud-Barrault*, 106, September 1983, 37–57. The textual similarities between the story and *Moderato cantabile* are explored by Yvonne Guers-Villate in: 'De l'implicite à l'explicite: de *Moderato cantabile* à *L'Homme assis dans le couloir*', *French Review*, 58, 3, February 1985, 377–81.

13 See 'L'Homme assis dans le couloir', *Les Cahiers du cinéma*, 312–13, June 1980, 32–3. Duras writes: 'j'ai trouvé que les amants n'étaient pas isolés mais vus, sans doute par moi, et que cette vue était, devait être mentionnée, intégrée aux faits' ('I came up with the idea that the lovers were not alone but seen, and that this act of seeing was, or ought to be mentioned and integrated into the story', p. 33).

14 The literature on the relationship between fetishism, voyeurism, and aesthetic enjoyment is extensive, and has its beginnings in readings of Freud's 1927 paper on 'Fetishism'. The paper has been of considerable interest particularly to feminist film theorists who have used it, together with other work by Freud, to formulate more explicitly the relationship between gender and looking. For various contributions to the debate, see Christian Metz, *Le Signifiant imaginaire* (Paris, Union générale d'éditions, 1977); Laura Mulvey, *Visual and Other Pleasures* (London, Macmillan, 1989), pp. 14–38; and E. Ann Kaplan, *Women and Film* (London, Methuen, 1983), pp. 23–35. Unfortunately, the debate has sometimes been marred by a rather mechanical approach to the question of gender positioning, and has sometimes seemed to imply far too close

a match between biological sex and modes of vision. Duras constitutes a difficult case for any theory that is forced to claim that the gaze is in principle a male attribute; such a view fails to take account of the powerful affective investment in looking that is displayed not only in Duras's writing, but also in her work for the cinema. For Duras, vision is not an activity aimed at reification; on the contrary, as she writes in 1987, 'aimer c'est voir' ('to love is to see', *EL*, 139; 101).

15 On the colour green in Duras, see Madeleine Borgomano, *Duras: une lecture des fantasmes* (Bruxelles, Cistre, 1985), pp. 52–5. References to eyes are common in Duras's fiction. In *La Vie tranquille*, for instance, speaking of her brother Nicolas, the narrator writes that it is always his eyes she remembers when she recalls the fact that he is dead (*VT*, 137). Nicolas's eyes, though, turn violet in the bright sun (ibid.). The first character in Duras to be described as having a 'green and avid gaze' (*PC*, 20; 19) is Jean in *Les Petits Chevaux de Tarquinia*; but, more usually, green eyes are attributed to women, like the French actress in Duras's first film script, *Hiroshima mon amour* (*H*, 37; 26), Anne-Marie Stretter in *Le Vice-consul* (described as having water-green eyes [*VC*, 125; 97]), the mother in *L'Eden Cinéma* (*EC*, 14; 57) or *L'Amant de la Chine du Nord* (*ACN*, 113), and the female protagonist in *La Maladie de la mort* (*MM*, 25) and the figure of Theodora Kats in *Yann Andréa Steiner* (*YA*, 37). The phrase 'les yeux verts' was also the name given to the column Duras wrote for *Libération* during July, August, and September 1980, later published under the title *L'Eté 80*. Duras also begins her short memoir to her mother in the collection *A ma mère* with the words: 'Ma mère avait les yeux verts' ('My mother had green eyes', p. 159); green eyes tend to proliferate in the later texts, as, for instance, in *La Pluie d'été*, where the eyes of the hero Ernesto as well as those of his mother and sister are all given as green (*PE*, 26, 68). The same is true, also, of the French girl in *L'Amant de la Chine du Nord* (*ACN*, 24); she, however, inherits her green eyes from both her mother and father!

3 SCENES OF DESIRE

1 Marguerite Duras, *Le Ravissement de Lol V. Stein* (Paris, Gallimard, 1964). All translations from the novel are my own. Contrary to what Duras seems to imply in *Les Parleuses* (*P*, 161; 117), the novel was generally well received, despite a patronising and hostile review by *Le Monde*'s chief critic, Jacqueline Piatier; within three months of publication the book had achieved sales of more than 30,000 copies.

2 The texts by Duras I am referring to here are as follows: *L'Amour* (Paris, Gallimard, 1971); *Nathalie Granger suivie de La Femme du Gange* (Paris, Gallimard, 1973); *India Song* (Paris, Gallimard, 1973); *L'Amant* (Paris, Minuit, 1984); *L'Amant de la Chine du Nord* (Paris, Gallimard, 1991). An outline of the film treatment of *Le Ravissement de Lol V. Stein* was published under the title 'Le Cinéma de Lol V. Stein', in: *Art Press International*, 24, January 1979. The film itself was never made: Duras explains that the scenario as a whole was lost. She summarises its main points again in *La Vie matérielle* (*VM*, 32–4; 27–8).

In 'Duras tout entière . . .', in *Le Nouvel Observateur*, 14–20 November 1986, Duras declared that the character of Hélène Lagonelle from *L'Amant* (*A*, 89–94, 124–6; 76–80, 107–9) was 'obviously' Lol V. Stein. This identification of Lol with Duras's old Saigon schoolfriend is also made implicitly in *L'Amant de la Chine du Nord*.

3 Lacan's 'Hommage à Marguerite Duras, du ravissement de Lol V. Stein' first appeared in *Cahiers de la compagnie Renaud-Barrault*, 52 (December 1965), 7–15; it is reprinted in: François Barat and Joël Farges (eds), *Marguerite Duras* (Paris, Editions Albatros, [1975] revised edition 1979), pp. 131–7. (The essay is available in English in a translation by Peter Connor in: *Duras on Duras* [San Francisco, City Lights Books, 1987], pp. 122–9.) A revised version of Montrelay's original presentation of the novel is published in her book, *L'Ombre et le nom: sur la féminité* (Paris, Minuit, 1977), pp. 7–23. Other analysts who have written on Duras after Lacan include, amongst others, Daniel Sibony in *La Haine du désir* (Paris, Christian Bourgois, 1978), pp. 81–141; and Julia Kristeva in *Soleil noir: dépression et mélancolie* (Paris, Gallimard, 1987), pp. 227–65. Duras gives her own version of the meeting with Lacan in 'La Destruction la parole', *Les Cahiers du cinéma*, 217, November 1969, 45–57 (p. 56); she mentions it again in an interview by Catherine Francblin, in *Art Press International*, 24, January 1979, 4. I have discussed Lacan's often densely allusive text on Duras at greater length elsewhere. See Leslie Hill, 'Lacan with Duras', *Journal of the Institute of Romance Studies*, 1, 1992, 405–24.

4 On Lacan's reading of Poe's 'The Purloined Letter' and the different responses it has provoked, see John P. Muller and William J. Richardson (eds), *The Purloined Poe: Lacan, Derrida, and Psychoanalytic Reading* (Baltimore, The Johns Hopkins University Press, 1988). Lacan's account of *Hamlet* is contained in the still unpublished seminar series of 1958–9 on desire and interpretation. Extracts from the sessions are available in *Ornicar?*, 24 (1981), 7–31; 25 (1982), 13–36; and 26–7 (1983), 7–44.

5 Accounts of *Le Ravissement de Lol V. Stein* tend to fall into various distinct camps. Among those sympathetic to Lacan are: Philippe Boyer, *L'Ecarté(e)* (Paris, Seghers/Laffont, 1973), pp. 187–205; Christiane Rabant, 'La Bête chanteuse', *L'Arc*, 58, 1974, 15–20; Elisabeth Lyon, 'The Cinema of Lol V. Stein', in Constance Penley (ed.), *Feminism and Film Theory* (London, BFI and Routledge, 1988), pp. 244–71; Carol J. Murphy, *Alienation and Absence in the Novels of Marguerite Duras* (Lexington, French Forum, 1982), pp. 95–102; Michèle Druon, 'Mise en scène et catharsis de l'amour dans *Le Ravissement de Lol V. Stein*, de Marguerite Duras', *The French Review*, 58, 3, February 1985, 382–90; Sharon Willis, *Marguerite Duras: Writing on the Body* (Urbana and Chicago, University of Illinois Press, 1987), pp. 63–95; Karen Smythe, 'The Scene of Seeing: Perception and Perversion in *The Ravishing of Lol V. Stein*', *Genders*, 6, November 1989, 49–59; and Bernard Alberti and Marie-Thérèse Mathet, 'Le "Ravissement" de Lol V. Stein', *French Studies*, 44, 4, October 1990, 416–23. Among readers of the novel critical of Lacan, Marcelle Marini, in *Territoires du féminin: avec Marguerite Duras* (Paris, Minuit, 1977) adopts a view closer to Luce

Irigaray; in *Gynesis: Configurations of Woman and Modernity* (New York, Cornell University Press, 1985), pp. 172–7, Alice Jardine draws attention to the gender politics implicit in Lacan's reading; while Martha Noel Evans, in *Masks of Tradition: Women and the Politics of Writing in Twentieth-Century France* (Ithaca, Cornell University Press, 1987) pp. 123–56, argues, contra Lacan, that Duras's male narrator 'in confronting Lol's architecture of prevarication, [. . .] comes face to face with radical otherness' (p. 137). Trista Selous, in *The Other Woman: Feminism and Femininity in the Work of Marguerite Duras*, condemns both Lacan and Duras for their supposed essentialism and anti-feminism. A more rigorous study of *Le Ravissement de Lol V. Stein* which demonstrates some of the shortcomings of Lacan's analysis on textual rather than ideological grounds is provided by Marie-Claire Ropars-Wuilleumier in *Ecraniques: le film du texte* (Lille, Presses universitaires de Lille, 1990), pp. 57–83; and Susan Rubin Suleiman, in *Subversive Intent: Gender, Politics, and the Avant-Garde* (Cambridge, Mass., Harvard University Press, 1990), pp. 88–118, examines how Lacan's essay and Duras's novel might each be read as a commentary on the other. It is impossible here to enter into any detail regarding the debate about the relationship between Lacanian theory and feminism. The key texts by Lacan are available in English translation in: *Feminine Sexuality: Jacques Lacan and the 'Ecole freudienne'*, ed. Juliet Mitchell and Jacqueline Rose (London, Macmillan, 1982). Much useful background material and discussion may be found in: Marcelle Marini, *Jacques Lacan* (Paris, Pierre Belfond, 1986), and Teresa Brennan (ed.), *Between Feminism and Psychoanalysis* (London, Routledge, 1989). For a reliable assessment of the issues at stake, see Elizabeth Grosz, *Jacques Lacan: A Feminist Introduction* (London, Routledge, 1990).

6 There is a similar disregard of potentially troubling narrative indeterminacies in Michèle Montrelay's chapter on the novel in *L'Ombre et le nom*. At the end of her analysis, Montrelay claims to have been taking fiction at its word (p. 23). Oddly, this seems to mean ignoring the fact that *Le Ravissement de Lol V. Stein* is a fiction and treating the characters as real, separate entities who, as in the case of Lol, may be diagnosed as suffering from this or that form of madness.

7 I am quoting here from the following two essays: Susan D. Cohen, 'From Omniscience to Ignorance: Voice and Narration in the Work of Marguerite Duras', in Sanford Scribner Ames (ed.), *Remains to be Seen: Essays on Marguerite Duras* (New York, Peter Lang, 1988), pp. 51–77 (p. 66); and Martha Noel Evans, *Masks of Tradition*, pp. 141 and 154. (Elsewhere, in 'Phantasm and Narration in Marguerite Duras' *The Ravishing of Lol V. Stein*', in: Joseph Reppen and Maurice Charney [eds], *The Psychoanalytic Study of Literature* [Hillsdale, NJ, The Analytic Press, 1985], pp. 255–77, Susan Cohen makes a similar confusion between voice and vision, and proceeds to efface the tension between them, in claiming of Jacques Hold that 'contrary to first impressions, the eyes through which everything is seen and the voice expressing that vision are always only his' [p. 269].) It is worth adding that, though it is clearly impossible to separate Jacques Hold's 'male' voice from the author's 'female' voice, this does not mean that Duras does not on

occasion treat her part-time narrator with noticeable irony. The point is brought out clearly by Michael Sheringham in his 'Knowledge and Repetition in *Le Ravissement de Lol V. Stein*', *Romance Studies*, 2, Summer 1983, 124–40; and by Susan Rubin Suleiman in her discussion of the novel in *Subversive Intent*, pp. 88–118.

8 There is, of course, an important debate still continuing in feminist criticism as to the importance of signatures in relation to the gendered production of texts. Different views of the issue are set out in Nancy K. Miller, *Subject to Change: Reading Feminist Writing* (New York, Columbia University Press, 1988), and Peggy Kamuf, *Signature Pieces* (London and Ithaca, Cornell University Press, 1988). It goes without saying that the name Duras, specifically invented as it was by Marguerite Donnadieu as an author's pseudonym, is an integral part of the texts that it heads; and indeed, as I have suggested, it functions in relation to the writing now associated with the signature of 'Duras' in a number of important ways. But precisely because the signature is part of the text that it underwrites, it cannot exercise proprietorial control over the text; even less can it guarantee, whether by reference to gender or not, the truth or authenticity of what is explicitly written as fiction.

9 Carol J. Murphy comments, for instance, in the course of a surprisingly confused reading of *L'Amour* in *Alienation and Absence in the Novels of Marguerite Duras*, that 'The anonymous characters are actually remains or "fragments" of other Durasian characters, and they act out a ballet on the beach of S. Thala, in effect remembering and reliving the triangular dance of desire in *Le Ravissement de Lol V. Stein*, in which Lol's ravishing consists both of her exclusion or absence from the dance of Anne-Marie Stretter and Michael Richardson and of her necessary presence during this seduction' (pp. 137–8). The effect of this diagnosis is to immobilise Lol in a pathological or voyeuristic triangular scenario rather different from the one explored in Duras's novel; it also seems to conflict with Lacan's suggestion that Lol, though she is in the middle of the scene as a third-party presence, is far from being an excluded middle (*MD*, 136; 128).

10 On the primal scene and its relationship to fantasy, see Jean Laplanche and J.-B. Pontalis, *Fantasme originaire, fantasmes des origines, origines du fantasme* (Paris, Hachette, 1985). The role of such scenes in Duras's work as a whole is a topic covered, albeit somewhat superficially, by Madeleine Borgomano in *Duras: une lecture des fantasmes* (Bruxelles, Cistre, 1985), pp. 113–90.

4 CROSSING GENRES

1 Texts referred to in this chapter are as follows: 'La Musica', in: *Théâtre I* (Paris, Gallimard, 1965); *Le Vice-consul* (Paris, Gallimard, 1966); *Détruire, dit-elle* (Paris, Minuit, 1969); *India Song* (Paris, Gallimard, 1973); *Le Camion* (Paris, Minuit, 1977); *Le Navire Night et autres textes* (Paris, Mercure de France, 1979); *La Musica deuxième* (Paris, Gallimard, 1985). I shall also be referring in detail to the following films: *Nuit noire, Calcutta* (1964); *La Musica* (1966); *Détruire, dit-elle* (1969); *India Song* (1974); *Son nom de Venise dans Calcutta désert*

(1976); *Le Camion* (1977); and *Le Navire Night* (1979). With regard to these films, it is worth pointing out that there are often significant differences between the texts actually used in the films and the versions given in published scripts or other texts. However, for convenience, when discussing Duras's films I have made reference, wherever possible, to the relevant passages in the published texts, even when these are not necessarily a wholly accurate record of what is actually said in a specific film (or where or by whom). In the case of both *India Song* and *Son nom de Venise dans Calcutta désert*, a meticulous shot-by-shot description, established by Marie-Claire Ropars-Wuilleumier, is published in *L'Avant-scène Cinéma*, 225, April 1979; when referring to these two films I shall use the shot numbers allocated by Ropars-Wuilleumier in her synopsis. For an overview of Duras's work for the cinema, see Youssef Ishaghpour, *D'une image à l'autre* (Paris, Denoël-Gonthier, 1982), pp. 225–98; and Madeleine Borgomano, *L'Ecriture filmique de Marguerite Duras* (Paris, Editions Albatros, 1985). For a complete filmography of Duras's work for the cinema, established by Jérôme Beaujour, see *Marguerite Duras*, Paris and Milan, Cinémathèque française and Nuove Edizioni Gabriele Mazzotta, 1992, pp. 37–61.

2 On *La Musica* and *La Musica deuxième*, see Marie-Pierre Fernandes, *Travailler avec Duras: La Musica deuxième* (Paris, Gallimard, 1986). The closing phrase about prohibition, Fernandes reports (p. 66), was eventually excised by Duras from the revised text.

3 See '*India Song* and Marguerite Duras', *Sight and Sound*, 45, 1, Winter 1975–6, 32–5.

4 See Maurice Blanchot, *L'Amitié* (Paris, Gallimard, 1971), p. 132. On the relationship between book and film in Duras in general, see Marie-Claire Ropars-Wuilleumier, *Ecraniques: le film du texte*.

5 In 1963, at an earlier stage, Duras described *Le Vice-consul de France à Calcutta* (as it then was) to a magazine as follows:

C'est un livre très compliqué qui se développe parallèlement sur deux plans: une femme qui habite Neuilly, invente une histoire à partir d'un petit hôtel particulier qui est vide la plupart du temps. Cette femme, dont le rôle n'est que d'être narratrice, apprend que cette villa appartient à un monsieur qui s'appelle Hohenhole, vice-consul de France à Calcutta. Cette histoire est concomitante à une autre. Elles n'ont que ceci en commun: elles se passent dans la même ville, au même moment. C'est l'histoire de la femme qui a vendu son enfant. Il y a longtemps. Elle a abouti à Calcutta. Elle est folle. J'ai connu personnellement cette femme. J'avais dix ans. Elle me faisait très peur.

(It's a very complicated book that develops on two parallel levels: a woman living in Neuilly invents a story on the basis of a small town house which is empty most of the time. This woman, whose only role is as the narrator, discovers this villa belongs to someone called Hohenhole, who is the French Vice-Consul in Calcutta. This story co-exists with another. All they have in common is that they are happening in the same town, at the same time. The other is the story of the woman who sold her child. It was a long time ago. She ends up in Calcutta, mad. I knew this woman personally. I was ten years old and she scared me a lot.)

See 'L'Auteur de *Hiroshima mon amour* vous parle', *Réalités*, 206, March 1963, 91–5. At some point, this woman narrator gave way to a male story-teller and the location of the story switched from Neuilly to Trouville, and, finally, in the completed novel, to Calcutta itself.

6 This and other information relating to *Nuit noire, Calcutta* is derived from an interview with Marin Karmitz by the author, 18 April 1991.

7 There has been much critical writing on Duras devoted to *Le Vice-consul* and *India Song*. On *Le Vice-consul*, see for instance Marcelle Marini, *Territoires du féminin: avec Marguerite Duras*; Mieke Bal, *Narratologie: essais sur la signification narrative dans quatre romans modernes* (Paris, Editions Klincksieck, 1977); and Micheline Besnard-Coursodon, 'Significations du métarécit dans *Le Vice-consul* de Marguerite Duras', *French Forum*, 3, 1, January 1978, 72–83. Useful accounts of *India Song* may be found in the following: Nicole Lise Bernheim, *Marguerite Duras tourne un film* (Paris, Editions Albatros, 1974); René Prédal, 'Marguerite Duras: un livre, un film: *India Song*', *Annales de la Faculté des lettres et sciences humaines de Nice*, 29, 1977, 279–90; Dominique Noguez, 'Les India Songs de Marguerite Duras', *Cahiers du vingtième siècle*, 9, 1978, 31–48; Marie-Claire Ropars-Wuilleumier, *Le Texte divisé, essai sur l'écriture filmique* (Paris, Presses Universitaires de France, 1981); Elisabeth Lyon, 'The Cinema of Lol V. Stein', in: Constance Penley (ed.), *Feminism and Film Theory* (London, BFI and Routledge, 1988), pp. 244–71; Sylvia Williams, 'Marguerite Duras's *India Song* – *texte théâtre film*', *Australian Journal of French Studies*, 23, 3, September–December 1986, 277–89.

8 On the story of the exchange of the child, see Madeleine Borgomano, 'L'Histoire de la mendiante indienne: une cellule génératrice de l'œuvre de Marguerite Duras', *Poétique*, 48, November 1981, 479–94. On the autobiographical aspects of the story, see Aliette Armel, *Marguerite Duras et l'autobiographie*, pp. 21–3; the figure of the beggar woman is of course also recalled in *L'Amant* (*A*, 103–4, 106–8; 89–90, 91–3).

9 See Marie-Claire Ropars-Wuilleumier, *Le Texte divisé*, pp. 131–61. On the relationship beween image and text in general, see Michel Chion, *La Voix au cinéma* (Paris, Editions de l'Etoile, 1982), and *Le Son au cinéma* (Paris, Editions de l'Etoile, 1985).

10 For an illuminating discussion of the use of mirrors in *India Song*, see Marie-Claire Ropars-Wuilleumier, *Le Texte divisé*, pp. 163–99.

11 *Baxter, Véra Baxter* is a story of a sexual contract, by which Jean Baxter, Véra's husband, hires Michel Cayre (Gérard Depardieu) to have an affair with his wife (Claudine Gabay), and thus allow him greater freedom with his mistress. Cayre, however, falls in love with Véra; and the major part of the film is taken up with Véra recounting her side of the story to an unnamed stranger. When making the film, Duras changed the role of the stranger, originally intended as a man, into a part for a woman (Delphine Seyrig). Duras subsequently regretted the change because it dramatically altered the implicit sexual relationship that develops between Véra and the stranger. The failure

of the film in Duras's view was an occasion for her to voice her dissent from the women's movement (which, she claimed, had misled her into substituting a woman for a man). See 'Un acte contre tout pouvoir', *Cinéma 77*, 223, July 1977, 48–58. In 1980 Duras published a rectified version of the script under the title *Véra Baxter, ou les plages de l'Atlantique*.

5 THE LIMITS OF FICTION

1 The texts by Duras I shall be referring to in this chapter are as follows: *Hiroshima mon amour* (Paris, Gallimard, 1960); *Une aussi longue absence* (Paris, Gallimard, 1961); *Abahn Sabana David* (Paris, Gallimard, 1970); *Le Navire Night suivi d'autres textes* (Paris, Mercure de France, 1979); 'Les Yeux verts', *Cahiers du cinéma*, 312–13, June 1980; *L'Eté 80* (Paris, Minuit, 1980); *L'Amant* (Paris, Minuit, 1984); and *La Douleur* (Paris, P.O.L., 1985).

2 See, for instance, Yann Andréa, *M.D.* (Paris, Minuit, 1983). The book, written by Duras's gay live-in companion of the 1980s and 1990s, is an account of Duras's admission to hospital in 1982 for alcoholism. The M.D. emblem appears on a number of more recent texts and is used as a personal trademark by Duras at the beginning of each of the 1988 television interviews for *Au-delà des pages*.

3 See 'L'Inconnue de la rue Catinat', *Le Nouvel Observateur*, 28 September 1984.

4 Duras writes of her admiration for *The Night of the Hunter* in 'Les Yeux verts' (*YV*, 60–2); but Duras's summary of the plot is somewhat misleading. She confuses, for instance, the death of the mother with that of the father in the story and suggests that both are murdered: in Laughton's film the true father, Ben Harper (Peter Graves), is captured by the police and executed for murder; during his time in jail he meets Harry Powell (Robert Mitchum), who has been arrested for stealing a car; Powell marries Harper's widow, Willa (Shelley Winters), but, once she realises his only interest is in the stolen money Ben had given to the two Harper children, John and Pearl, Powell stabs her to death and dumps her body in the river. At the end, contrary to what Duras recalls, only John, not both children, rushes up to Powell, his stepfather, and offers him the money as he is held down by a State Trooper. Forgiveness triumphs, but what is more thrilling, in Duras's eyes, is the collapse of moral dualism as John rushes to help Powell rather than see him condemned. It is not difficult to imagine the reasons why Duras might wish to view (and thus misremember) the film as a displaced version of her own family plot.

5 One section of *La Douleur* (corresponding to material now found in *D*, 67–73, 81; 56–62, 68) exists in two earlier versions; the first was published, anonymously, in *Sorcières*, 1, January 1976, 43–4; it then appeared for a second time, with numerous minor changes, under Duras's name, in *Outside* (*O*, 288–92). A second fragment, also published anonymously, appeared in *Sorcières*, 2, March 1976, 53–4 (corresponding to material now found in *D*, 30–1, 43–4, 45–7; 22–3, 34–5, 36–7). There are numerous major and minor changes between this

version and the final 1985 text. Duras comments on her revisions in: 'Avril 1945: nuit et Duras', *Libération*, 17 April 1985; and: Marie-Pierre Fernandes, *Travailler avec Duras: La Musica Deuxième* (Paris, Gallimard, 1986), p. 157.

6 On the notion of testimony in the context of post-war writing in France, see Margaret Atack, *Literature and the French Resistance* (Manchester, Manchester University Press, 1989).

7 Robert Antelme, *L'Espèce humaine* (Paris, Gallimard, [1947] 1957), p. 229.

8 Robert Antelme, *L'Espèce humaine*, p. 9; the preceding quotation is taken from Maurice Blanchot, *L'Entretien infini* (Paris, Gallimard, 1969), p. 192.

9 Dionys Mascolo, *Autour d'un effort de mémoire: sur une lettre de Robert Antelme* (Paris, Maurice Nadeau, 1987), p. 14.

10 A similar view of Judaism is presented by Blanchot in *L'Entretien infini*, pp. 180–90. The objection is sometimes made that the position adopted by both Duras and Blanchot essentialises Judaism in rather dubious manner and to that extent proposes merely a mirror-image reversal of anti-Semitism. Blanchot's response to this, which appears in a lengthy note (p. 190), is to argue that any account of Judaism that reduces it to a purely historical phenomenon amounts in effect – if not in intent – to an attempt to empty Judaism of any cultural specificity and thus collude in its historical destruction.

11 There are in all six different works by Duras all with the title *Aurélia Steiner*. In my discussion I follow the author in distinguishing the three main texts (which appear in the volume *Le Navire Night suivi d'autres textes*) according to the city that is named at the end: 'Aurélia Melbourne', 'Aurélia Vancouver', and 'Aurélia Paris' (*N*, 15). The first two of these exist also as films (though the texts spoken by Duras in the films are not strictly identical with the published versions); the third exists in a revised stage version, which is contained in *La Douleur* (*D*, 198–208; 173–83).

12 See Elie Wiesel, *La Nuit* (Paris, Minuit, 1958), pp. 99–105. The plot of 'Aurélia Paris' is said to be based on the real childhood experiences of the actor Sami Frey.

6 WRITING SEXUAL RELATIONS

1 The works by Duras I am referring to in this chapter are as follows: *Agatha* (Paris, Minuit, 1981); *L'Homme atlantique* (Paris, Minuit, 1982); *La Maladie de la mort* (Paris, Minuit, 1982); *Savannah Bay* (Paris, Minuit [1982] 1983); *Les Yeux bleus cheveux noirs* (Paris, Minuit, 1986); and *La Pute de la côte normande* (Paris, Minuit, 1986). The film, *Agatha et les lectures illimitées*, based on the earlier stage play, was released in 1981, closely followed by the film version of *L'Homme atlantique*. In this chapter all translations from *La Maladie de la mort* are my own.

2 *La Maladie de la mort*, together with *Les Yeux bleus cheveux noirs*, is one of the most fiercely debated of recent texts by Duras. See, for instance, Marcelle Marini, 'La Mort d'une érotique', *Cahiers de la compagnie Renaud-Barrault*, 106, September 1983, 37–57; Maurice

Blanchot, *La Communauté inavouable* (Paris, Minuit, 1983), pp. 51–93; Sharon Willis, 'Staging Sexual Difference: Reading, Recitation, and Repetition in Duras's *Malady of Death*', in: Enoch Brater (ed.), *Feminine Focus: The New Women Playwrights* (New York, Oxford University Press, 1989), pp. 109–25; and George Moskos, 'Odd Coupling: Duras Reflects (on) Balzac', *Contemporary Literature*, 32, 4, Winter 1991, 520–33.

3 There are no doubt echoes here, for some readers, of Lacan's dictum, as glossed at length in *Le Séminaire, Livre XX: Encore* (Paris, Seuil, 1975), to the effect that sexual relations do not exist (as Lacan puts it: 'il n'y a pas de rapport sexuel'). In Lacan's account of love there is, however, an almost Jansenist-like austerity and pessimism far removed from the apocalyptic tone adopted by Duras.

4 Yann Andréa is a major participant in much of Duras's work during the early 1980s. In addition to his involvement in *Agatha et les lectures illimitées*, Andréa also appears on the image track of *L'Homme atlantique* and reads, together with Duras, the off-screen dialogue making up the soundtrack for *Dialogue de Rome* (1982); he is a powerful, if unnamed presence in a number of later fictional texts, too, including notably *La Maladie de la mort*, *Les Yeux bleus cheveux noirs* (which Duras dedicates to him), and *Emily L*. Duras recounts how her relationship with Andréa came about in *Yann Andréa Steiner*; she seems to have begun introducing him in public as her accredited companion during her 1981 visit to Montreal (as the volume *Duras à Montréal* records). However, this was not the first time that Duras incorporated one of her current companions or former lovers into her work. Dionys Mascolo, Duras's partner of the 1940s and 1950s, has an acting role in *Jaune le soleil*, *Nathalie Granger* and *La Femme du Gange*, and reads one of the narrative voices in *India Song* and *Son nom de Venise dans Calcutta désert*. *L'Homme assis dans le couloir*, Duras revealed in 1980, also originated as a homage to a particular lover, according to a principle she first voiced in an interview with Jeanne Moreau in 1960: 'Ce que je peux offrir à un homme,' Duras told her, 'le mieux que je puisse lui offrir c'est ce que j'ai écrit à partir de lui' ('The best thing I can give a man is what I have written on the basis of knowing him'). See 'La Comédienne et la romancière', *Afrique-Action*, 17 October 1960.

5 The importance of the maternal body as an image of ambivalence is a central and recurrent one throughout the whole of Duras's work, as she herself admits, for instance, in *L'Amant* (*A*, 34–5; 28–9). This has tempted some critics, like Julia Kristeva, in her *Soleil noir: dépression et mélancolie* (pp. 229–65), to ground the whole of their interpretation of Duras on the question of the difficulty of separating from the mother. However, Kristeva's case, persuasive though it may seem, is not aided by gaffes like her analysis of the opening pages of *Le Ravissement de Lol V. Stein*, in which she misconstrues the arrival of Anne-Marie Stretter as referring to Lol's mother!

6 Duras first adapted the story for the stage in collaboration with James Lord in 1962, before rewriting it, on her own, for the 1981 revival. The text of the new version is given in Duras's *Théâtre II* (Paris, Gallimard,

1984), and she describes her revisions in 'Le Château de Weatherend (*La Bête dans la jungle*)', *L'Arc*, 89, October 1983, 100–2. James's tantalisingly apocalyptic story already displays something of the same asymmetry in the relation between the sexes as *La Maladie de la mort*; interestingly, in *Epistemology of the Closet* (Berkeley, University of California Press, 1990), Eve Kosofsky Sedgwick takes the story in this respect to be paradigmatic of what she describes as homosexual panic in a number of early twentieth-century texts. In reworking in *La Maladie de la mort* the situation explored in James's story, Duras would seem to be committing herself to a rearticulation of the relationship between homosexuality and heterosexuality which seriously challenges the separation between them and thus the whole notion of sexual identity founded on object choice.

7 For a helpful description of Duras's involvement in the theatre, see Arnaud Rykner, *Théâtres du nouveau roman: Sarraute, Pinget, Duras* (Paris, Corti, 1988).

8 On Duras's reading of Musil, see *E*, 35–6, and 'Une des plus grandes lectures que j'ai jamais faites', *La Quinzaine littéraire*, 16–31 January, 1982. The incestuous relationship between Ulrich and his sister Agatha constitutes one of the main centres of interest in the unfinished third section of Musil's novel. At one point, for instance, the pair are on holiday together, staying in a hotel by the sea, where they rediscover the pleasures of naturism, as though they were children again; they eventually decide, however, to stay in their hotel bedroom. 'Alors,' Duras will have read in Philippe Jaccottet's standard French translation, 'pour les corps, le miracle se produisit. Soudain Ulrich fut en Agathe ou Agathe en lui' ('Then, for their bodies, the miracle happened. Suddenly Ulrich was inside Agatha and Agatha inside him'). See Robert Musil, *L'Homme sans qualités*, translated by Philippe Jaccottet, 2 vols (Paris, Seuil/Points, 1956), II, 834.

9 *La Communauté inavouable*, pp. 52–4. Duras's own reaction to Blanchot's reading of *La Maladie de la mort* was a surprisingly hostile and defensive one, and also extended to Peter Handke's German-language film version of the text. See Marguerite Duras, 'Dans les jardins d'Israël il ne faisait jamais nuit', *Les Cahiers du cinéma*, 374, July–August 1985.

Works by Duras

1 NOVELS AND OTHER PROSE

Les Impudents, Paris (Plon, 1943) Gallimard: folio, 1992
La Vie tranquille, Paris, Gallimard: folio, 1944
Un barrage contre le Pacifique, Paris, Gallimard: folio, 1950
Le Marin de Gibraltar, Paris, Gallimard: folio, 1952
Les Petits Chevaux de Tarquinia, Paris, Gallimard: folio, 1953
*Des journées entières dans les arbres, suivi de: Le Boa; Madame Dodin;
    Les Chantiers*, Paris, Gallimard, 1954
Le Square, Paris, Gallimard: folio, 1955, revised 1990
Moderato cantabile, Paris, Minuit: double, 1958
Dix heures et demie du soir en été, Paris, Gallimard: folio, 1960
L'Après-midi de Monsieur Andesmas, Paris, Gallimard, 1962
Le Ravissement de Lol V. Stein, Paris, Gallimard: folio, 1964
Le Vice-consul, Paris, Gallimard, 1966
L'Amante anglaise, Paris, Gallimard, 1967
Détruire, dit-elle, Paris, Minuit, 1969
Abahn, Sabana, David, Paris, Gallimard, 1970
L'Amour, Paris, Gallimard, 1971
Ah! Ernesto, with illustrations by Bernard Bonhomme, Boissy Saint-Léger,
    François Ruy-Vidal and Harlin-Quist, 1971
L'Homme assis dans le couloir, revised version, Paris, Minuit, 1980
L'Eté 80, Paris, Minuit, 1980
Outside, papiers d'un jour, Paris, Albin Michel, 1981 (reissued with same
    pagination by P.O.L., 1984)
L'Homme atlantique, Paris, Minuit, 1982
La Maladie de la mort, Paris, Minuit, 1982
L'Amant, Paris, Minuit, 1984
La Douleur, Paris, P.O.L., 1985
Les Yeux bleus cheveux noirs, Paris, Minuit, 1986
La Pute de la côte normande, Paris, Minuit, 1986
La Vie matérielle, conversations with Jérôme Beaujour, Paris, P.O.L.,
    1987
Emily L., Paris, Minuit, 1987
La Pluie d'été, Paris, P.O.L., 1990
L'Amant de la Chine du Nord, Paris, Gallimard, 1991

Yann Andréa Steiner, Paris, P.O.L., 1992

2 PLAYS

Les Viaducs de la Seine-et-Oise, Paris, Gallimard, 1960
Théâtre I: Les Eaux et forêts [1965]; Le Square [1965]; La Musica [1965],
Paris, Gallimard, 1965
L'Amante anglaise, Paris, Cahiers du Théâtre National Populaire, 1968
(also in: *L'Avant-scène du théâtre*, 422, 15 March 1969, 8–24; reissued
in a modified version and with a new preface as: *Le Théâtre de l'amante
anglaise* [Paris, Gallimard: L'Imaginaire, 1991])
*Théâtre II: Suzanna Andler [1968]; Des Journées entières dans les arbres
[1965]; Yes, peut-être [1968]; Le Shaga [1968]; Un homme est venu me
voir [1968]*, Paris, Gallimard, 1968
India Song, Paris, Gallimard, 1973
L'Eden Cinéma, Paris, Mercure de France: folio, 1977
Agatha, Paris, Minuit, 1981
Savannah Bay, new revised edition, Paris, Minuit, (1982) 1983
*Théâtre III: La Bête dans la jungle; Les Papiers d'Aspern; La Danse de
mort*, including Duras's French version of James Lord's stage adaptation
of the story, 'The Beast in the Jungle' by Henry James (1962, revised
1981); her French version, done in collaboration with Robert Antelme,
of Michael Redgrave's stage adaptation of 'The Aspern Papers' by Henry
James (1961); and a French adaptation of 'Dödsdansen' by August
Strindberg (1970), Paris, Gallimard, 1984
La Musica deuxième, Paris, Gallimard, 1985
La Mouette de Tchékhov, adapted by Marguerite Duras, Paris, Gallimard,
1985
Eden cinéma, nouvelle version scénique, Paris, Actes Sud-Papiers, 1988

3 FILM SCRIPTS

Hiroshima mon amour, Paris, Gallimard: folio, 1960 (this is Duras's initial
shooting script; for a synopsis of the completed film, see 'Hiroshima
mon amour', *L'Avant-scène du cinéma*, 61–2, July–September 1966, 1–26
and 59–65)
Une aussi longue absence (with Gérard Jarlot), Paris, Gallimard, 1961
Nathalie Granger, suivie de: La Femme du Gange, Paris, Gallimard, 1973
Le Camion, suivi de: Entretien avec Michelle Porte, Paris, Minuit, 1977
*Le Navire Night, suivi de: Césarée; Les Mains négatives; Aurélia Steiner;
Aurélia Steiner; Aurélia Steiner*, Paris, Mercure de France: folio, 1979
Véra Baxter ou les plages de l'Atlantique, Paris, Editions Albatros, 1980

4 UNPUBLISHED FILM SCRIPTS

Sans merveille (with Gérard Jarlot), directed by Michel Mitrani, 1964
Nuit noire, Calcutta, directed by Marin Karmitz, 1964
Les Rideaux blancs, directed by Georges Franju, 1965
La Voleuse, directed by Jean Chapot, 1966

5 FILMS

La Musica (with Paul Seban), 1966
Détruire, dit-elle, 1969
Jaune le soleil, 1971
Nathalie Granger, 1972
La Femme du Gange, 1972
India Song, 1974
Des journées entières dans les arbres, 1976
Son nom de Venise dans Calcutta désert, 1976
Baxter, Véra Baxter, 1976
Le Camion, 1977
Le Navire Night, 1979
Césarée, 1979
Les Mains négatives, 1979
Aurélia Steiner, dit Aurélia Melbourne, 1979
Aurélia Steiner, dit Aurélia Vancouver, 1979
Agatha et les lectures illimitées, 1981
L'Homme atlantique, 1981
Dialogue de Rome, 1982
Les Enfants (with Jean Mascolo and Jean-Marc Turine), 1985

6 INTERVIEWS, JOURNALISM, UNCOLLECTED PROSE

This is not an exhaustive bibliography, but lists, in chronological order of publication, all Duras's journalism, interviews, and occasional writings that it has been possible to trace, together with her more important radio broadcasts and television appearances. The abbreviations used are listed at the front of this book.

'Le Boa', *Les Temps modernes*, 3, 25, October 1947, 613–22 (*J*, 97–115).
'Madame Dodin', *Les Temps modernes*, 7, 79, May 1952, 1952–81 (*J*, 117–84).
'Interview avec Marguerite Duras', interview by Adrien Jans, *Le Soir*, 17 October 1953.
'Rencontre avec Marguerite Duras', interview by Clarisse Francillon, *La Gazette de Lausanne*, 19 February 1956.
'Une pièce involontaire', *L'Express*, 14 September 1956.
'*Le Square*: un roman de Marguerite Duras était conçu comme une pièce', interview by Henri Marc, *Franc-Tireur*, 14 September 1956.
'J'ai écrit une pièce de théâtre sans le savoir', interview by Yvonne Donon, *L'Information*, 15 September 1956.
'Propos dans un "Square" au Studio des Champs-Elysées', *Libération*, 17 September 1956.
'Rendez-vous dans un Square avec Marguerite Duras', interview by Claude Sarraute, *Le Monde*, 18 September 1956.
'Du théâtre malgré moi', interview by André Calas, *Demain*, 20 September 1956.
'Les Fleurs de l'Algérien', *France-Observateur*, 28 February 1957 (*O*, 17–18).
'Paris-Canaille', *France-Observateur*, 14 March 1957 (*O*, 40–1).

'La Bourrée à Paris', *France-Observateur*, 11 April 1957 (*O*, 57–9).

'Les Travailleurs contre le gouvernement', news report in collaboration with Jacques-Francis Rolland, *France-Observateur*, 18 April 1957.

'Elève Dufresne pourrait faire mieux', *France-Observateur*, 9 May 1957, (*O*, 19–23).

'Horreur à Choisy-le-Roi', *France-Observateur*, 6 June 1957 (*O*, 119–22).

'Le Sang bleu de la Villette', *France-Observateur*, 20 June 1957 (*O*, 47–53).

'La France à l'italienne, *France-Observateur*, 27 June 1957.

'L'Internationale Tintin', *France-Observateur*, 4 July 1957.

'Le Dimanche des héros', *France-Observateur*, 11 July 1957.

'Le Jeune Funambule', *France-Observateur*, 15 August 1957 (*YV*, 69).

'Les Marais du duc de Morny', *France-Observateur*, 22 August 1957 (*O*, 54–6).

'Le Mot lilas presque haut comme il est large . . .', *France-Observateur*, 17 October 1957 (*O*, 24–6).

'Un roman sur cent voit le jour', *France-Observateur*, 7 November 1957 (*O*, 60–5).

'Les Enfants du spoutnik ne sont pas dans la lune', *France-Observateur*, 21 November 1957 (*O*, 66–9).

'Bataille, Feydeau et Dieu', *France-Observateur*, 12 December 1957 (*O*, 27–33).

'Alors, on ne guillotine plus?', *France-Observateur*, 19 December 1957 (*O*, 37–9).

'Drieu La Rochelle et notre temps', debate with Emmanuel Berl, Brice Parain, Jacques Chardonne, and Bernard Frank, organised by Marguerite Duras, *France-Observateur*, 2 January 1958.

'Dialogue avec une carmélite', *France-Observateur*, 16 January 1958 (*O*, 162–70).

'Le Séquestré de Venise: Sartre', *France-Observateur*, 16 January 1958 (*O*, 187–9).

'Quand il y en a pour deux, il n'y en a pas pour trois', *France-Observateur*, 23 January 1958 (*O*, 70–3).

'Djuna Barnes: *L'Arbre de la nuit*', *France-Observateur*, 23 January 1958.

'A propos de Georges Bataille', *La Ciguë*, 1, January 1958 (*O*, 34–6).

'Ces Messieurs de la Société des autobus', *France-Observateur*, 6 February 1958 (*O*, 74–6).

'Un train de mille cadavres qui nous arrive du Pakistan', *France-Observateur*, 6 February 1958 (*O*, 195–7).

'La Reine des Nègres vous parle des blancs', interview with Sarah Maldoror by Marguerite Duras (on Genet's *Les Nègres*), *France-Observateur*, 20 February 1958.

'Des Samourai d'un type nouveau', *France-Observateur*, 27 February 1958.

'Racisme à Paris', *France-Observateur*, 6 March 1958 (*O*, 77–8).

'Confucius et l'humanisme chinois', *France-Observateur*, 13 March 1958.

'Le Bénéfice de l'enfance . . .', *France-Observateur*, 20 March 1958.

' "Poubelle" et "la Planche" vont mourir', *France-Observateur*, 27 March 1958 (*O*, 114–18).

'Notre pauvre Group Captain Townsend', *France-Observateur*, 10 April 1958.

'Circulez!', *France-Observateur*, 2 May 1958 (*O*, 79–80).

'L'Exposition Joe Downing', *France-Observateur*, 8 May 1958.

'La Littéralité des faits', *France-Observateur*, 8 May 1958.

'Le *Barrage* est mon histoire', interview with Marguerite Duras, *L'Express*, 8 May 1958.

' "Elle nous abandonna pour les mathématiques" ', *La Nef*, 17, May 1958, 74–6.

'Pierre A . . . , sept ans et cinq mois', *France-Observateur*, 26 June 1958 (*O*, 81–5).

'Assassins de Budapest', *Le 14 Juillet*, 1, 14 July 1958 (*O*, 88–91; also in: *Le 14 Juillet*, facsimile reprint, edited by Daniel Dobbels, Francis Marmande, and Michel Surya, Paris, Lignes, 1990).

'Pourquoi *14 Juillet*', *France-Observateur*, 24 July 1958 (*O*, 86–7).

'Travailler pour le cinéma', *France-Observateur*, 31 July 1958.

'Paris, six d'août', *France-Observateur*, 7 August 1958 (*O*, 92–5).

'Deschamps, Simone', *France-Observateur*, 16 October 1958 (*O*, 122–5).

'Peinture de Jean-Marie Queneau', *France-Observateur*, 16 October 1958.

'La Reine Bardot', *France-Observateur*, 23 October 1958 (*O*, 246–9).

'Détruite, Sélinonte', *L'Arc*, 4, October 1958, 63–5.

'*Le Repos du Guerrier*', *France-Observateur*, 27 November 1958.

'Uneuravek', interview with Raymond Queneau by Marguerite Duras, *L'Express*, 22 January 1959.

'Le Comique universel de *Trois Chapeaux claque* [by Miguel Mihura]', *L'Avant-scène*, 191, 15 February 1959, 8.

'Resnais travaille comme un romancier', *Les Lettres nouvelles*, 20 May 1959, 36–8.

'Réponses à l'enquête auprès d'intellectuels français', with a contribution by Marguerite Duras, *Le 14 Juillet*, 3, 18 June 1959 (republished in: *Le 14 Juillet*, facsimile reprint, Paris, Lignes, 1990).

'Non, je ne suis pas la femme d'Hiroshima', interview by André Bourin, *Les Nouvelles littéraires*, 18 June 1959 (republished in: *Les Nouvelles littéraires*, 5 January 1976).

'Les Impressions de Marguerite Duras', interview by Michel Delahaye, *Cinéma 59*, 38, July 1959, 14–15.

'Conversation with Marguerite Duras', interview by Richard Roud, *Sight and Sound*, 29, 1, Winter 1959–60, 16–17.

'Marguerite Duras, Alain Resnais et Peter Brook', interview by Claude-Marie Trémois, *Radio Cinéma TV*, 533, 3 April 1960.

'Entretien avec Marguerite Duras', interview by Madeleine Chapsal, *L'Express*, 30 June 1960 (also in: Madeleine Chapsal, *Quinze écrivains: entretiens*, Paris, Juillard, 1963, pp. 55–64).

'La Comédienne et la romancière', interview with Jeanne Moreau by Marguerite Duras, *Afrique-Action*, 17 October 1960.

'C'est l'ennui qui m'a poussée à écrire', interview by Catherine Valogne, *La Tribune de Lausanne*, 23 October 1960.

'L'Ecrivain d'aujourd'hui qui a le mieux compris l'amour', interview by Marlyse Schaeffer, *Elle*, 28 April 1961.

'Le Silence de millions d'hommes m'oppresse', interview by Nicole Zand, *Libération*, 10 May 1961.

'Une seule et même chose', response to a questionnaire on 'Les écrivains et le cinéma', *Réforme*, 23 July 1961.

'Tendre et douce Nadine d'Orange', interview by Marguerite Duras, *France-Observateur*, 12 October 1961 (*YV*, 50–4; and *O*, 106–13).

'Les Deux Ghettos', *France-Observateur*, 9 November 1961 (*O*, 150–61).

'Marguerite Duras', interview by Denise Bourdet, *La Revue de Paris*, 11, November 1961 (also in: Denise Bourdet, *Brèves rencontres*, Paris, Grasset, 1963, pp. 65–71).

'Le Mot "objectivité" me fait fuir', interview by Thérèse de Saint-Phalle, *Le Monde*, 20 January 1962.

'Entretien avec un "voyou" sans repentir', *France-Observateur*, 26 April 1962 (*O*, 126–38).

'Propos d'un "voyou" sans repentir', *France-Observateur*, 10 May 1962 (*O*, 138–49).

'Seine-et-Oise, ma patrie', *France-Observateur*, 17 May 1962 (*O*, 99–103).

'L'Homme assis dans le couloir', first version, *L'Arc*, 20, October 1962, 70–6.

'Marguerite Duras cherche la liberté et la vérité dans le crime', interview by J.-C. Kerbourc'h, *Combat*, 16–17 February 1963.

'Marguerite Duras, le vertige et l'absurde', interview by Claude Cezan, *Les Nouvelles littéraires*, 21 February 1963.

'C'est la Seine-et-Oise qui est coupable . . .', interview by Nicole Zand, *Le Monde*, 22 February 1963.

'Un mélo qui devrait faire rire', interview by Jacqueline Autrusseau, *Les Lettres françaises*, 21–7 February 1963.

'François Billetdoux, Agnès Capri, et Marguerite Duras font le portrait de Katharina Renn', with a contribution by Marguerite Duras, *Arts*, 6–12 March 1963.

'L'Auteur de *Hiroshima mon amour* vous parle', interview by Alain Hervé, *Réalités*, 206, March 1963, 91–5.

'Marguerite Duras: a leading French novelist-playwright expounds her point of view', interview by Harold Hobson, *Theatre Arts*, 47, 11, November 1963, 22–4.

'Les Hommes de 1963 ne sont pas assez féminins', interview by Pierre Hahn, *Paris-Théâtre*, 198 (1963), 32–7.

'Le Ravissement de Lol V. Stein', interview by Tristan Renaud, *Les Lettres françaises*, 30 April–6 May 1964.

'J'ai peur, j'ai très peur', *Les Nouvelles littéraires*, 13 August 1964.

'Une journée étouffante et cruelle', interview with Marguerite Duras, *La Gazette de Lausanne*, 19–20 September 1964.

'Une œuvre éclatante', *France-Observateur*, 5 November 1964 (*O*, 271–4).

'Marguerite Duras: "Le bonheur n'est pas ce qui m'intéresse le plus" ', interview by Pierre Dumayet, in: Pierre Dumayet, *Vu et entendu*, Paris, Stock, 1964, pp. 105–9.

Marguerite Duras parle, gramophone recording, in the series 'Français de notre temps: Hommes d'aujourd'hui', under the auspices of the Alliance française, produced by Hugues Desalle, 1964.

'Marguerite Duras part en guerre contre l'exotisme', interview by Claudine Jardin, *Le Figaro*, 13 January 1965.

'Sylvie et ses fantômes', *Le Nouvel Observateur*, 25 March 1965 (*O*, 240–5).

'Une interview de Marguerite Duras', by Jacques Vivien, *Paris-Normandie*, 2 April 1965.

'Les Recalés de l'écriture', interviews with Raymond Queneau, Jean Paul-han, Dominique Aury, and Jean-Claude Brisville by Marguerite Duras, *Le Nouvel Observateur*, 22 April 1965.

'Des enfants parlent des enfants', interview with Frédéric, Laurent, Didier, and Sabine by Marguerite Duras, with the assistance of Peter Brook [on Brook's *Lord of the Flies*], *Le Nouvel Observateur*, 3 June 1965.

'Marguerite Duras réalisateur: *La Musica*', interview by Lia Lacombe, *Les Lettres françaises*, 7 July 1965.

'Vivre seule', interview with Jeanne Moreau by Marguerite Duras, *Le Nouvel Observateur*, 29 September 1965.

'Marguerite Duras interroge Jeanne Moreau', television interview with Jeanne Moreau by Marguerite Duras, *Dim dam dom*, directed by Roger Pic, produced by Daisy de Galard, ORTF, 1965.

'J'ai ri en écrivant *Les Eaux et forêts*', interview by Claude Fléouter, *Le Monde*, 7 October 1965.

'Des tableaux pour rire', *Le Nouvel Observateur*, 3 November 1965 (*O*, 96–8).

'La confidence n'est jamais privée', interview by Charles Sylvestre, *L'Humanité-dimanche*, 21 November 1965.

'Marguerite Duras s'amuse', interview by Claude Cezan, *Les Nouvelles littéraires*, 2 December 1965.

'Le Vice-consul (extrait)', *Cahiers de la compagnie Renaud-Barrault*, 52, December 1965, 57–75.

'Pièce russe (extrait de la première partie)', *Cahiers de la compagnie Renaud-Barrault*, 52, December 1965, 76–90.

'L'Arroseur arrosé', television interview with Pierre Dumayet by Marguerite Duras, *Dim dam dom*, directed by Paul Seban, produced by Daisy de Galard, ORTF, 1965.

'Les Enfants et Noël', with commentary by Marguerite Duras, *Dim dam dom*, directed by Claude Otzenberger, produced by Daisy de Galard, ORTF, 1965.

'Quand Marguerite Duras joue de la Musica', interview by Sonia Lescaut, *Arts*, 26 January–1 February 1966.

'Madeleine Renaud a du génie', *Vogue*, April 1966 (*O*, 229–33).

'Je veux faire un anti-Hiroshima', interview by Pierre Maillard, *Paris-Normandie*, 3 June 1966.

'Marguerite Duras collabore à la mise en scène de *La Musica*', interview by René Quinson, *Combat*, 13 June 1966.

'Tordre le cou au social balzacien', interview by Jean Vuilleumier, *La Tribune de Genève*, 9–10 July 1966.

'Pourvu que ça marche!', interview by Anne Capelle, *Arts*, 27 July–2 August 1966.

'Gugusse, c'est moi! . . .', interview with Georges Michel by Marguerite Duras, *Le Nouvel Observateur*, 12 October 1966.

'Marguerite Duras chez les lions', television interview at Vincennes zoo by Marguerite Duras, *Dim dam dom*, directed by Paul Seban, produced by Daisy de Galard, ORTF, 1966.

'Melina la superbe', *Arts*, 1–7 February 1967.

'Interview de Melina Mercouri', television interview with Melina Mercouri by Marguerite Duras, *Dim dam dom*, directed by Paul Seban, produced by Daisy de Galard, ORTF, 4 February 1967.

'La Femme d'Evreux: notes pour Delphine Seyrig et Robert Hossein (extraits)', *Les Cahiers du cinéma*, 187, February 1967, 43.

'L'Amour est un devenir constant comme la révolution', interview by Yvonne Baby, *Le Monde*, 7 March 1967.

'La Séduction de la folie: *L'Amante anglaise* de Marguerite Duras', interview by Jacqueline Piatier, *Le Monde [des livres]*, 29 March 1967.

'Marguerite Duras: "Un silence peuplé de phrases" ', interview by Hubert Nyssen, *Synthèses*, 254–5, August-September 1967, 42–50 (republished in: Hubert Nyssen, *Les Voies de l'écriture*, Paris, Mercure de France, 1969, pp. 125–42).

'Marguerite Duras: oui . . . mais . . .', interview by Pierre Montaigne, *Le Figaro*, 9–10 September 1967.

'Entretien de Marguerite Duras avec Jean Schuster' (15 December 1966), *Archibras*, 2, October 1967 (republished in: Alain Vircondelet, *Marguerite Duras ou le temps de détruire*, Paris, Seghers, 1972, pp. 171–84).

'Interview avec Marguerite Duras', interview by Jean-Michel Fossey, *The Paris Magazine*, 1, October 1967, 18–21.

'Les Hardes de Salonique', *Le Nouvel Observateur*, 8 November 1967.

'Marguerite Duras se met en scène', interview by Claude Cezan, *Les Nouvelles littéraires*, 28 December 1967.

'Duras à la Petite Roquette', television interview with a female prison governor by Marguerite Duras, *Dim dam dom*, directed by Jean-Noël Roy, produced by Daisy de Galard, ORTF, 1967.

'La Vie des mots', interview by Claude Sarraute, *Le Monde*, 6 January 1968.

'Dix questions à Marguerite Duras', interview by Katia Klein, *Aux écoutes*, 10–16 January 1968.

'Les Lycéens ont la parole', with Marguerite Duras, *Dim dam dom*, directed by Pierre Zaidline, produced by Daisy de Galard, ORTF, 1968.

Preface, Jean-Marie Dallet, *Les Antipodes*, Paris, Editions du Seuil, 1968, pp. 7–8.

'Deux pièces de Marguerite Duras au Théâtre Gramont', interview by Emile Copfermann, *Les Lettres françaises*, 3 September 1968.

'Marguerite Duras: Irreligious Salvationist', interview by Langley Lee, *The Guardian*, 7 September 1968.

'*L'Amante anglaise* ou la chimie de la folie', interview by Claude Sarraute, *Le Monde*, 20 December 1968.

'Je cherche qui est cette femme', *L'Avant-scène du théâtre*, 422, 15 March 1969, 6–7.

'*Détruire, dit-elle*, lu par Pierre Dumayet, commenté par Marguerite Duras', *Le Monde [des livres]*, 5 April 1969.

'Sur le Comité d'action écrivains-étudiants (septembre 1968)', *Les Lettres nouvelles*, June-July 1969, 144–50 (first published anonymously; then, with slight modifications, in: *YV*, 39–42).

'La Destruction la parole', interview by Jean Narboni and Jacques Rivette, *Les Cahiers du cinéma*, 217, November 1969, 45–57 (English version available, in a translation by Helen Lane Cumberford, in: *Destroy, She Said* [New York, Grove Press, 1970], pp. 91–133).

'La Folie me donne de l'espoir', interview by Yvonne Baby, *Le Monde*, 17 December 1969.

'Delphine Seyrig, inconnue célèbre', *Vogue*, 1969 (*O*, 203–8, and in: *Libération*, 17 October 1990).

'Préface', in: Barbara Molinard, *Viens*, Paris, Mercure de France, 1969, pp. 7–11.

'Interview with Marguerite Duras', by Bettina L. Knapp, *The French Review*, 44, 4, March 1971, 653–59.

'Asking for the Impossible', interview by Nina Sutton, *The Guardian*, 13 July 1971.

'Marguerite Duras s'entretient avec Bacon', interview with Francis Bacon by Marguerite Duras, *La Quinzaine littéraire*, 129, 16–30 November 1971 (*O*, 265–70).

'Le Tombeau de l'impossible', *La Quinzaine littéraire*, 130, 1–15 December 1971.

'Duras l'étrangère', interview by François-Marie Banier, *L'Express*, 24 January 1972.

'Entretien libre avec Marguerite Duras', interview by Alain Vircondelet, in: Alain Vircondelet, *Marguerite Duras ou le temps de détruire*, pp. 162–70.

'Marguerite Duras en toute liberté', interview by Fernand Dufour, *Cinéma 72*, 165, April 1972, 48–51.

'An Interview with Marguerite Duras', by Germaine Brée, *Contemporary Literature*, 13, 4, 1972, 399–422.

'Book of the Film', *New Statesman*, 5 January 1973 (republished in the original French as: 'Book and Film', *YV*, 63–5).

'Marguerite Duras: deux films', interview by Benoît Jacquot, *Art Press*, September-October 1973.

'Marguerite Duras. Interview', in: Suzanne Horer and Jeanne Socquet, *La Création étouffée*, Paris, Pierre Horay, 1973, pp. 172–87 (a short extract, in a translation by Virginia Hules, is reproduced in: Elaine Marks and Isabelle de Courtivron [eds], *New French Feminisms*, Brighton, Harvester, 1981, pp. 111–13).

Les Parleuses, conversations with Xavière Gauthier, Paris, Minuit, 1974

'Ce que parler ne veut pas dire . . .', interview by Jean-Louis Ezine, *Les Nouvelles littéraires*, 15–21 April 1974.

'Marguerite Duras tourne *India Song: texte, théâtre, film*', interview by Colette Godard, *Le Monde*, 28–29 July 1974.

'Marguerite Duras: interview', by Nicole-Lise Bernheim, in: Nicole-Lise Bernheim, *Marguerite Duras tourne un film*, Paris, Albatros, 1974, pp. 100–28.

'Parce que le silence est féminin', interview by Pierre Bregstein, *Cinématographe*, 13, May-June 1975, 22–4.

'Comment, pourquoi *India Song*', *Le Monde*, 5 June 1975.

'Marguerite Duras et *India Song*', interview by Ritta Mariancic, *Construire*, 30, 23 July 1975.

'*India Song*, a Chant of Love and Death', interview by Jan Dawson, *Film Comment*, 11, 6, November-December 1975, 52–5.

'An Interview with Marguerite Duras', by Susan Husserl-Kapit, *Signs: Journal of Women in Culture and Society*, 1, 2, Winter 1975, 423–34.

'*India Song* and Marguerite Duras', interview by Carlos Clarens, translated by Tom Milne, *Sight and Sound*, 45, 1, Winter 1975–6, 32–5.

'Notes sur *India Song*', in: François Barat and Joël Farges (eds), *Marguerite Duras*, Paris, Albatros, (1975) revised edition 1979, pp. 14–22.

'*India Song* (découpage)', ibid., pp. 23–71.

'Notes pour le théâtre sur le décor', ibid., pp. 72–3.

'Note pour rien', ibid., p. 74.

'Dépossédée', conversation with Xavière Gauthier, ibid., pp. 75–91.

'Son nom de Venise dans Calcutta désert', interview by Pierre and François Barat, ibid., pp. 93–7.

'Baxter, Véra Baxter', ibid., pp. 103–5.

'La Soupe aux poireaux', *Sorcières*, 1, January 1976, 36 (*O*, 275–6).

'Les Enfants maigres et jaunes', *Sorcières*, 1, January 1976, 37–8 (also in: *Cahiers de la compagnie Renaud-Barrault*, 96, October 1977, 5–8; and *O*, 277–9).

'Pas mort en déportation', *Sorcières*, 1, January 1976, 43–4 (first published anonymously; then, with minor revisions, in *O*, 288–92, and, in a revised version and with deletions restored, in *D*, 67–73, 81).

'Seyrig-Hiss', *Sorcières*, 2, March 1976, 32 (*O*, 201–2).

'Pas mort en déportation (deuxième fragment)', *Sorcières*, 2, March 1976, 53–4 (first published anonymously; then, in a revised version and with deletions restored, in *D*, 30–1, 43–4, 45–7).

'Au fond de la mer', *Sorcières*, 2, March 1976, 61 (*O*, 257–8).

'D'*India Song* à *Véra Baxter*, Marguerite Duras et les vertus de l'ellipse', interview by Pierre Montaigne, *Le Figaro*, 28 April 1976.

'Marguerite Duras tourne *Des journées entières dans les arbres*', interview by Alain Remond, *Télérama*, 1–4 May 1976.

'Le Cinéma ouvert', *Le Quotidien de Paris*, 3 June 1976.

'Ça me touche là où je crie', interview with Marguerite Duras by Absis, *Libération*, 15 June 1976 (also in: *Sorcières*, 4, 1976, 59).

'*Son nom de Venise dans Calcutta désert*: entretien avec Marguerite Duras', interview by Claire Clouzot and Absis, *Ecran*, 49, 15 July 1976, 62–3.

'Rencontre des Cahiers Renaud-Barrault', special issue on 'Ecriture romanesque, écriture dramatique', with contributions from Marguerite Duras and others, *Cahiers de la compagnie Renaud-Barrault*, 91, September 1976, 3–26.

'L'Horreur d'un pareil amour', *Sorcières*, 4, 1976, 31–2 (first published anonymously; then in *O*, 280–2).

'Postface', Erica Lennard, *Les Femmes, les sœurs*, Paris, Editions des femmes, 1976.

Les Lieux de Marguerite Duras, television interviews by Michelle Porte, Institut National de l'Audiovisuel, 1976, broadcast by TF1, 3 and 17 May 1976 (the text of the interviews published in: Marguerite Duras and Michelle Porte, *Les Lieux de Marguerite Duras*, Paris, Minuit, 1977).

'Je ne me laisserai pas récupérer', interview by Anne de Gasperi, *Les Nouvelles littéraires*, 25 November–1 December 1976.

'Renaud-Duras: une profonde connivence', interview by Anne de Gasperi, *Le Quotidien de Paris*, 9 February 1977.

'Mothers', *Le Monde*, 10 February 1977 (republished in: François Barat and Joël Farges [eds.], *Marguerite Duras*, revised edition 1979, pp. 99–101).

'Le Feu d'artifice de Marguerite Duras', interview by Jack Gousseland, *Le Point*, 230, 14 February 1977.

'Irrésistible et jalouse, Madeleine', interview by Anne de Gasperi, *Les Nouvelles littéraires*, 17 February 1977.

'Son nom Marguerite Duras . . .', interview by René Bernard, *Elle*, 28 February 1977.

'Le Désir est bradé, saccagé. On libère le corps et on le massacre, dit Marguerite Duras', interview by Michèle Manceaux, *Marie-Claire*, 297, May 1977.

'Marguerite Duras explique sa vision politique', interview by Anne de Gasperi, *Le Quotidien de Paris*, 26 May 1977.

'Je hais la narration au cinéma', interview by Anne de Gasperi, *Le Quotidien de Paris*, 8 June 1977.

'La Voie du gai désespoir', interview by Claire Devarrieux, *Le Monde*, 16 June 1977 (republished in: François Barat and Joël Farges [eds], *Marguerite Duras*, revised edition 1979, pp. 111–17, and *O*, 171–9).

'Un acte contre tout pouvoir', interview by Jacques Grant and Jacques Frenais, *Cinéma 77*, 223, July 1977, 48–58 (republished in François Barat and Joël Farges [eds], *Marguerite Duras*, revised edition 1979, pp. 119–30).

'Entretien avec Marguerite Duras', interview by René Prédal, *Jeune Cinéma*, 104, July–August 1977, 16–21.

'Citations de Marguerite Duras', transcribed by Simone Benmussa, *Cahiers de la compagnie Renaud-Barrault*, 96, October 1977, 5–10, 23–4, 31, 56–7, 69, 81.

'Marguerite Duras', interview by Jean-Claude Bonnet and Jacques Fieschi, *Cinématographe*, 32, November 1977, 25–8.

'Entretien avec Michelle Porte', interview by Michelle Porte, in: Marguerite Duras, *Le Camion*, Paris, Minuit, 1977, pp. 85–136.

Adoracion, by Eduardo Chillida, translated by Marguerite Duras, Paris, 1977.

'Le Savoir de l'horreur: *L'Etabli* de Robert Linhart', *Libération*, 23 March 1978 (*O*, 183–6).

'Le Navire "Night" ', first version, *Minuit*, 29, May 1978, 2–14.

'L'Etat sauvage du désir', interview by Anne de Gasperi, *Le Quotidien de Paris*, 27 June 1978.

'La Nuit sur le navire de Marguerite Duras', interview by Pierre Montaigne, *Le Figaro*, 2 August 1978.

'Cette grande animale de couleur noire', *Le Matin de Paris*, 9 November 1978 (*O*, 180–2).

'Interview', by Catherine Francblin, *Art Press International*, 24, January 1979.

'Le Cinéma de Lol V. Stein', *Art Press International*, 24, January 1979.

'En effeuillant la marguerite', interview by Patrick Duval, *Libération*, 22 March 1979.

'*Le Navire Night* ou l'embarcation du désir', interview by Anne de Gasperi, *Les Nouvelles littéraires*, 22–29 March 1979.

'Théodora', *Les Nouvelles littéraires*, 26 July–2 August 1979 (*O*, 293–5).

'Interview de Marguerite Duras', radio interview by Jacques Duchateau, Jacques Floran, and Michel Chapuis, *Le Pont des Arts*, France-Culture, 26 January 1980.

'Les Yeux verts', *Les Cahiers du cinéma*, special number by Marguerite Duras, 312–13, June 1980 (reissued, with additional texts, as *Les Yeux verts*, nouvelle édition, Paris, Cahiers du cinéma, 1987).

'Les Yeux verts: l'été 1', *Libération*, 16 July 1980.

'Les Yeux verts: l'été 2', *Libération*, 23 July 1980.

'Les Yeux verts: l'été 3', *Libération*, 30 July 1980.

'Les Yeux verts: l'été 4', *Libération*, 6 August 1980.

'Les Yeux verts: l'été 5', *Libération*, 13 August 1980.

'Les Yeux verts: l'été 6', *Libération*, 20 August 1980.

'Les Yeux verts: l'été 7', *Libération*, 27 August 1980.

'Les Yeux verts: l'été 8', *Libération*, 3 September 1980.

'Les Yeux verts: l'été 9', *Libération*, 10 September 1980.

'Les Yeux verts: l'été 10', *Libération*, 17 September, 4–5 (the whole series republished in *E*).

'Présentation', in Jean-Pierre Ceton, *Rauque la ville*, Paris, Minuit, 1980, pp. 7–9 (*O*, 263–4).

'Entretiens avec Marguerite Duras', radio interviews by Jean-Pierre Ceton, *Les Nuits magnétiques*, France-Culture, 27–31 October 1980.

'The Thing', interview by Rolland Thélu, *Gai Pied*, 20, November 1980.

'L'Homme tremblant', interview with Elia Kazan by Marguerite Duras, *Les Cahiers du cinéma*, 318, December 1980, 5–13 (*Les Yeux verts*, nouvelle édition, 192–221).

'Les Ténèbres de Aki Kuroda', in: Aki Kuroda, *Ténèbres*, Galerie Adrien Maeght, Paris, 1980 (*O*, 259–61).

'Je vais faire un film avec Godard', interview by Anne de Gasperi, *Le Quotidien de Paris*, 3 February 1981.

'Le Rêve heureux du crime', *O*, 283–7.

'Conférence de presse du 8 avril 1981', in: Suzanne Lamy and André Roy (eds.), *Marguerite Duras à Montréal*, Montreal, Editions Spirale, 1981, pp. 15–28.

'Rencontre du 10 avril 1981', ibid., pp. 29–41.

'Interview du 11 avril 1981', by Françoise Faucher, ibid., pp. 43–53.

'Interview du 12 avril à Montréal et du 18 juin 1981 à Paris', interviews by Suzanne Lamy, ibid., pp. 55–71.

'Interview du 12 avril', interview by Danièle Blain, ibid., pp. 73–77.

'Voter Giscard, c'est voter contre Lech Walesa', interview by Jane Hervé, *Les Nouvelles littéraires*, 7–14 May 1981.

'*Agatha* est le premier film que j'écris sur le bonheur', *Les Cahiers du cinéma*, 323–4, May 1981, 64–5.

Duras filme, interviews with Marguerite Duras with extracts from *Agatha et les lectures illimitées*, directed by Jérôme Beaujour and Jean Mascolo, Paris, Médiane films, 1981.

'Un Pays du Nord', *Des femmes en mouvements: hebdo*, 48, 3–10 July 1981.

'Le Noir atlantique', *Des femmes en mouvements: hebdo*, 57, 11–18 September 1981.

'*Agatha, ou les lectures illimitées*', *Des femmes en mouvements: hebdo*, 57, 11–18 September 1981.

'Je n'ai rien à justifier', *Le Quotidien de Paris*, 8 October 1981.

'L'Homme atlantique', *Le Monde*, 27 November 1981 (*Les Yeux verts*, nouvelle édition, pp. 222–4).

'Les Rendez-vous manqués: après 1936 et 1956, 1981?', petition organised by Michel Foucault and signed by Marguerite Duras and nine others, *Libération*, 15 December 1981.

La Jeune Fille et l'enfant, audio tape, read by Marguerite Duras, adapted from *L'Eté 80* by Yann Andréa, Editions des femmes, 1981.

'Une des plus grandes lectures que j'ai jamais faites' (on Robert Musil), *La Quinzaine littéraire*, 16–31 January 1982.

'Sur le pont du Nord un bal y est donné', interview with Jacques Rivette by Marguerite Duras, *Le Monde*, 25 March 1982.

'C'est fou c'que j'peux t'aimer', interview by Yann Andréa, *Libération*, 4 January 1983.

'Entretien avec Marguerite Duras', interview by Jacqueline Aubenas, *Alternatives théâtrales*, 14, March 1983, 10–15.

'Je suis muette devant le théâtre que j'écris', interview by Gilles Costaz, *Le Matin*, 3 June 1983.

'Il n'y a sans doute rien de plus difficile que de décrire un amour', interview by Gilles Costaz, *Le Matin*, 29 September 1983.

'Au Théâtre du Rond-Point Marguerite Duras met en scène sa dernière pièce, *Savannah Bay*, écrite pour Madeleine Renaud et Bulle Ogier', interview by Armelle Heliot, *Le Quotidien de Paris*, 30 September, 1983.

'Entretien entre Marguerite Duras et Roberto Plate pour le décor de *Savannah Bay*', *Cahiers de la compagnie Renaud-Barrault*, 106, September 1983, 7–12.

'Pour Juliette, pour le cinéma', *Libération*, 18 October 1983 (*Les Yeux verts*, nouvelle édition, pp. 224–7).

'Le Château de Weatherend (*La Bête dans la jungle*)', *L'Arc*, 89, October 1983, 100–2.

Savannah Bay, c'est toi, directed by Michelle Porte, Institut National de l'Audiovisuel, 1983, broadcast by Antenne 2, 2 April 1984.

'La Classe de la violence', interview by Dominique Noguez, in: Marguerite Duras, *Œuvres cinématographiques: édition vidéographique critique*, Paris, Ministère des relations extérieures, 1984, pp. 11–20.

'La Couleur des mots', interview by Dominique Noguez, ibid., pp. 21–31.

'Le Cimetière anglais', interview by Dominique Noguez, ibid., pp. 33–41.

'La Dame des Yvelines', interview by Dominique Noguez, ibid., pp. 43–52.

'La Caverne noire, suivi de Work and words', interview by Dominique Noguez, ibid., pp. 53–63.

'Carte blanche à une 1ʳᵉ A', television discussion with the participation of Marguerite Duras, directed by Valérie Mannel, produced by Jean-Pierre Janiaud, Antenne 2, 3 September 1984.

'Duras à l'état sauvage', interview by Marianne Alphant, *Libération*, 4 September 1984.

'Ce qui arrive tous les jours n'arrive qu'une seule fois', interview by Gilles Costaz, *Le Matin*, 28 September 1984.

'L'Inconnue de la rue Catinat', interview by Hervé Le Masson, *Le Nouvel Observateur*, 28 September 1984.

Television interview by Bernard Pivot, produced by Jean-Luc Léridon, *Apostrophes*, Antenne 2, 28 September 1984 (available on video as *Apostrophes: Bernard Pivot rencontre Marguerite Duras*, Paris, Seuil, 1990).

'*Quelque part ailleurs en étant là*': *Le Bon Plaisir de Marguerite Duras*, produced by Marianne Alphant, with Jean Daniel and Denis Roche, and Gérard Desarthe, Nicole Hiss, and Catherine Sellers, with extracts from the sound archives of the Institut National de l'Audiovisuel, France-Culture, 20 October 1984.

'Ils n'ont pas trouvé de raisons de me le refuser', interview by Marianne Alphant, *Libération*, 13 November 1984.

'Pascale', letter from Marguerite Duras, *Libération*, 30 November 1984.

'Comment ne pas être effrayée par cette masse fabuleuse de lecteurs?', interview by Pierre Assouline, *Lire*, January 1985.

'La Droite la mort', *Le Monde*, 17–18 March 1985.

'A Vintage Year for Duras', including an interview by Mary Blume, *The International Herald Tribune*, 22 March 1985.

'Pourquoi écrivez-vous?', response to a questionnaire by Marguerite Duras, *Libération*, hors-série, March 1985.

'Musica Duras, Acte II', interview by Gilles Costaz, *Le Matin de Paris*, 25 March 1985.

'L'Homme nu de la Bastille', *L'Autre Journal*, 4 (monthly), April 1985.

'Avril 45: nuit et Duras', interview by Marianne Alphant, *Libération*, 17 April 1985.

'La Chair des mots', *Autrement*, 70, May 1985, 210.

'Usine', conversation between Marguerite Duras and Leslie Kaplan (January 1982), in: *L'Autre Journal*, 5 (monthly), May 1985 (also published in: Leslie Kaplan, *L'Excès-l'usine*, Paris, P.O.L., 2nd edition 1987, pp. 109–19).

'Les Journalistes, dit-on . . .', letter from Marguerite Duras, Jean Mascolo and Jean-Marc Turine, *Libération*, 12 June 1985.

'Les Amants', *Le Nouvel Observateur*, 14–20 June 1985.

'Sublime, forcément sublime Christine V.', *Libération*, 17 July 1985.

'Réponses de Marguerite Duras', *Libération*, 23 July 1985.

'Dans les jardins d'Israël il ne faisait jamais nuit', interview by Pascal Bonitzer, Charles Tesson, and Serge Toubiana, *Les Cahiers du cinéma*, 374, July–August 1985, 5–12 (*Les Yeux verts*, nouvelle édition, pp. 229–48).

'Le Scandale de la vérité', *Les Cahiers du cinéma*, 374, July-August 1985, 13.

'Elle a sorti la France de ses gonds' (on the death of Simone Signoret), *Le Quotidien de Paris*, 1 October 1985.

'La Perte de la vérité', *L'Autre Journal*, 8 (monthly), October 1985.

'La Lecture dans le train', *L'Autre Journal*, 9 (monthly), November 1985

'Ecrit pour tous les temps, tous les carêmes' (on the 'Déclaration des 121'), *L'Autre Journal*, 9 (monthly), November 1985.

'Marguerite Duras', *The South Bank Show*, with an interview with Marguerite Duras, produced by Hilary Chadwick, London Weekend Television, 17 November 1985.

'La Princesse Palatine à Versailles. Portrait d'une famille royale', *L'Autre Journal*, 10 (monthly), December 1985.

'Lectures: *Manhattan Blues*', *L'Autre Journal*, 10 (monthly), December 1985.

'Lectures: *Hôpital Silence*', *L'Autre Journal*, 10 (monthly), December 1985.

'L'Insomnie creuse l'intelligence', interview by Michèle Manceaux (20 November 1983), in: Michèle Manceaux, *Eloge de l'insomnie*, Paris, Hachette, 1985, pp. 31–44.

'Recevez chers amis, nos salutations mystiques et polyflores', feature on the overflow of Baby Doc Duvalier compiled by Marguerite Duras with a text by René Depestre, *L'Autre Journal*, 1 (weekly), 26 February–4 March 1986.

'Le Bureau de poste de la rue Dupin', interview with François Mitterrand by Marguerite Duras, *L'Autre Journal*, 1 (weekly), 26 February–4 March 1986.

'Le Dernier Pays avant la mer', interview with François Mitterrand by Marguerite Duras, *L'Autre Journal*, 2 (weekly), 5–11 March 1986.

'Le Ciel et la terre', interview with François Mitterrand by Marguerite Duras, *L'Autre Journal*, 3 (weekly), 12–18 March 1986.

'L'Innocence infernale de Roger Knobelspiess', interview with Thierry Levy by Marguerite Duras, *L'Autre Journal*, 3 (weekly), 12–18 March 1986.

'Africa, Africa', interview with François Mitterrand by Marguerite Duras, *L'Autre Journal*, 4 (weekly), 19–25 March 1986.

'Lettre à Amnesty International. Lettre au président Pham Van Dong à propos de Nguyên Sy Tê', *L'Autre Journal*, 5 (weekly), 26 March–2 April 1986.

'Parler des otages ou ne pas parler des otages', interview with Joëlle Kauffmann by Marguerite Duras, *L'Autre Journal*, 5 (weekly), 26 March–2 April 1986.

'Les Chiens de l'Histoire', *L'Autre Journal*, 6 (weekly), 3–8 April 1986.

'Le Prix Ritz-Paris-Hemingway 1986 à Marguerite Duras', with a brief statement by the author, *Le Monde*, 19 April 1986.

'Le Froid comme en décembre', *L'Autre Journal*, 9 (weekly), 23–29 April 1986.

'Moi', *L'Autre Journal*, 10 (weekly), 30 April–6 May 1986.

'La Nouvelle Angoulême', interview with François Mitterrand by Marguerite Duras, *L'Autre Journal*, 11 (weekly), 7–13 May 1986.

'Jean-Marie Tjibaou, kanak', interview with Jean-Marie Tjibaou by Marguerite Duras, *L'Autre Journal*, 13 (weekly), 22–28 May 1986.

'Tchernobyl, la mort géniale', interview by Gilles Costaz, *Le Matin*, 4 June 1986.

'L'Amant magnifique', interview with Aline Issermann by Marguerite Duras, *L'Autre Journal*, 16 (weekly), 11–17 June 1986.

'La Pute de la côte normande', *Libération*, 14 November 1986 (republished as *PCN*).

'La Littérature est illégale ou elle n'est pas', interview by Gilles Costaz, *Le Matin*, 14 November 1986.

'Duras tout entière . . .', interview by Pierre Bénichou and Hervé Le Masson, *Le Nouvel Observateur*, 14–20 November 1986.

'Marguerite Duras par Anne Sinclair', interview by Anne Sinclair, *Elle*, 8 December 1986.

Travailler avec Duras: La Musica deuxième, edited by Marie-Pierre Fernandes, containing numerous interviews and conversations with Duras, Paris, Gallimard, 1986.

'Au peigne fin: Marguerite Duras', interview by André Rollin, *Lire*, 136, January 1987.

'Duras, de gauche complètement', spoof interview by Michel Bergain (offering Duras the position of Minister of Culture in a new socialist administration), *Globe*, 13, January 1987.

'Le Livre, un plaisir partagé', questionnaire by Pierrette Rosset and Françoise Ducout, with responses from Marguerite Duras and others, *Elle*, 23 March 1987.

'Ceux qui veulent continuer à nous lire, de gauche à droite', with a contribution by Marguerite Duras, *Le Matin*, 13–14 June 1987.

'A tort et à travers *Le Matin*', interview by Gilles Costaz, Sophie Fontanel, and J.-P. Iommi-Amunategui, *Le Matin*, 23 June 1987.

Radio interview by Pierre Assouline and others, *Inter-lire*, France-Inter, 5 July 1987.

'La Lecture: un bonheur sans mélange', questionnaire by Pierrette Rosset, with responses from Marguerite Duras and others, *Elle*, 31 August 1987.

'L'Exacte Exactitude de Denis Belloc', interview with Denis Belloc by Marguerite Duras, *Libération*, 19–20 September 1987.

'Remarques générales sur "*Les Juifs*" de *Jaune le soleil* (1971) et note de tournage sur *Jaune le soleil*', *Les Cahiers du cinéma*, 400, October 1987, 20–1.

'Comme une messe de mariage', interview by Didier Eribon, *Le Nouvel Observateur*, 16–22 October 1987.

'*Emily L.* ou le procès de l'homme', interview by Françoise Ducout and Pierrette Rosset, *Elle*, 9 November 1987.

'Entretien avec Marguerite Duras', radio interview with Marguerite Duras by Alain Veinstein, *Les Nuits magnétiques*, France-Culture, 25 November 1987.

'Pour Duras, le plus beau c'est Hulot' (on Jacques Tati), interview by Pierre Léon and Brigitte Ollier, *Libération*, 27 November 1987.

'L'Internationalisme de l'idée française' (declaring her support for Mitterrand's campaign for re-election), *Globe*, 23, December 1987.

'Duras-Godard', television interview with Jean-Luc Godard, *Océaniques*, produced by J.D. Verhaeghe, FR3, 28 December 1987 (text published in part in: *Le Magazine littéraire*, 278, June 1990, 46–8).

'Qu'est-ce que c'est que ce jeu-là? Démoniaque et divin', interview with Michel Platini by Marguerite Duras, *Libération*, 14 December 1987.

'Duras-Platini: le stade de l'ange', interview with Michel Platini by Marguerite Duras, *Libération*, 15 December 1987.

'Duras dans les régions claires de l'écriture', interview by Colette Fellous, *Le Journal littéraire*, 2, December 1987–January 1988.

'La letteratura è femmina', interview by Paolo Tortonese, *Corriere della sera*, 24 January 1988.

'Marguerite Duras', in: Marcel Bisiaux and Catherine Jajolet (eds), *A ma mère, 60 écrivains parlent de leur mère*, Paris, Pierre Horay, 1988, pp. 159–66 (also published as: 'Ma mère, une femme honnête' in *Elle*, 18 April 1988).

'Parler, dit-elle', interview by Jean-Claude Raspiengeas, *Télérama*, 22 June 1988.

Au-delà des pages, interviews with Marguerite Duras by Luce Perrot (February–March 1988), produced by Guy Lopez, TF1, 26 June–17 July 1988.

'Intervista a Marguerite Duras' (June 1987), interview by Flavia Celotto, *Micromégas*, 15, 41–2, June–August 1988, 55–60.

'La Cigarette dans le couple: un ménage à trois', questionnaire by Christine Bravo and Patricia Gandin, with responses from Marguerite Duras and others, *Elle*, 11 July 1988.

'Duras est sexy!', interview by Pierre Bergé, *Globe*, 30, July–August 1988.

'Interview avec Marguerite Duras et Yann Andréa' (2 June 1982), in: Liliane Papin, *L'Autre Scène: le théâtre de Marguerite Duras*, Saratoga, Ca., Anma Libri, 1988, pp. 153–62.

'Le Bruit et le silence', preface to *Yves Saint-Laurent et la photographie de mode*, Paris, Albin Michel, 1988, pp. 9–15 (also in *Elle*, 31 October 1988).

'Interview with Marguerite Duras', translated by Heidi Gilpin, in: Alice A. Jardine and Anne M. Menke, 'Exploding the Issue: "French" "Women" "Writers" and "The Canon"?', *Yale French Studies*, 75, 1988, 229–58 (238–40) (republished, in an uncut version, in a translation by Katherine Ann Jensen, in: Alice A. Jardine and Anne M. Menke, *Shifting Scenes. Interviews on Women, Writing and Politics in Post-68 France*, New York, Columbia University Press, 1991, pp. 71–8).

'Le Coupeur d'eau', interview by Michel Marcus, *Autrement*, 104, February 1989, 16–21.

'J'ai toujours désespérément filmé . . .', interview by Colette Mazabrard, *Les Cahiers du cinéma*, 426, December 1989, 62–5.

Marguerite Duras: la passione sospesa, interviews by Leopoldina Pallotta della Torre, Milan, La Tartaruga edizioni, 1989.

'La Vie Duras', interview by Marianne Alphant, *Libération*, 11 January 1990.

'Duras parle du nouveau Duras', interview by Pierrette Rosset, *Elle*, 15 January 1990.

'Duras: un mondo di paure', interview by Ulderico Munzi, *Corriere della sera*, 25 January 1990.

'Duras 89–90', interview by Jean-Marcel Bouguereau, *L'Evénement du jeudi*, 1–7 February 1990.

Television interview by Patrice Poivre d'Arvor, *Ex-libris*, TF1, 15 February 1990.

'Des années entières dans les livres', interview by Renaud Monfourny, *Les Inrockuptibles*, 21, February–March 1990.

'Du jour au lendemain', radio interview by Alain Veinstein, France-Culture, 16 March 1990.

'Marguerite retrouvée', interview by Frédérique Lebelley, *Le Nouvel Observateur*, 24–30 May 1990.

'J'ai vécu le réel comme un mythe', interview by Aliette Armel, *Le Magazine littéraire*, 278, June 1990, 18–24.

'L'Année 90: les 12 photos émotion', with captions by Marguerite Duras, *France-Soir*, 29 December 1990.

'La Francia si sente in prima linea e treme', article by Ulderico Munzi with quotations from Marguerite Duras, *Corriere della sera*, 14 January 1991.

'La Lanterne magique de Marguerite Duras', interview by Gilbert Guez, *Le Figaro*, 7 February 1991.

'Duras dans le parc à amants', interview by Marianne Alphant, *Libération*, 13 June 1991.

'Vous faites une différence entre mes livres et mes films?', interview by Jean-Michel Frodon and Danièle Heymann, *Le Monde*, 13 June 1991.

'Je suis pour les femmes de plus en plus', interview by Jean-Claude Lamy, *France-Soir*, 20 June 1991.

Radio interview by Patricia Martin and Gérard Courchelle, *Inter 13/14*, France Inter, 29 June 1991.

Television interview by Bernard Rapp, *Caractères*, Antenne 2, 5 July 1991.

Radio interviews by Jean-Christophe Marty, *Discothèques privées*, France-Musique, 5–9 August 1991.

'Mes amours, c'est à moi', interview with Pierre Assouline, *Lire*, 193, October 1991.

Television interview with Marguerite Duras, *Cinéma de poche*, La Sept, broadcast FR3, 1 February 1992.

'La Brune de la Dordogne', interview by Marianne Alphant, *Libération*, 27 February 1992.

'Vive Cresson et la lutte des classes!', interview by Jean-Louis Ezine, *Le Nouvel Observateur*, 2–8 April 1992.

'Les Nostalgies de l'amante Duras', interview by Jean-Louis Ezine, *Le Nouvel Observateur*, 24 June–1 July 1992.

'Le Jeune Serge avec son feutre noir', *Les Cahiers du cinéma*, 458, July–August 1992, 26.

'Appelez moi Marguerite Duras de Trouville', interview by Roland Godefroy, *Ouest-France*, 3 August 1992.

'Trouville, le 10 septembre 1992', *Marguerite Duras*, Paris and Milan, Cinémathèque française and Nuove edizioni Gabriele Mazzotta, 1992, back cover.

'Trouville, le 2 octobre 1992', ibid., pp. 13–14.

7 WORKS IN ENGLISH TRANSLATION

L'Amante anglaise, translated by Barbara Bray, London, Hamish Hamilton, 1968.

Blue Eyes, Black Hair, translated by Barbara Bray, London, Collins: Flamingo paperback, 1988.

Destroy, She Said, translated by Barbara Bray, New York, Grove Press, 1970.

La Douleur (also published as: *The War: A Memoir*), translated by Barbara Bray, London, Collins: Flamingo paperback, 1986.

The Eden Cinema, translated by Barbara Bray, in: *Eden Cinéma*, version scénique, Paris, Actes Sud-Papiers, 1988.

Emily L., translated by Barbara Bray, London, Collins: Flamingo paperback, 1989.

Green Eyes, translated by Carol Barko, New York, Columbia University Press, 1990.

Hiroshima Mon Amour and Une aussi longue absence, translated by Richard Seaver and Barbara Wright, London, Calder & Boyars, 1966.

India Song, translated by Barbara Bray, New York, Grove Press, 1976.

The Little Horses of Tarquinia, translated by Peter DuBerg, London, John Calder, 1960.

The Lover, translated by Barbara Bray, London, Collins: Flamingo paperback, 1985.

The Malady of Death, translated by Barbara Bray, New York, Grove Press, 1986.

'The Seated Man in the Passage', translated by Mary Lydon, *Contemporary Literature*, 24, 1983, 268–75.

Moderato cantabile, translated by Richard Seaver, London, John Calder, 1966.

Outside: Selected Writings, translated by Arthur Goldhammer, London, Collins: Flamingo paperback, 1987.

'The Places of Marguerite Duras', with Michelle Porte, translated by Edith Cohen, *Enclitic*, 7, 1, 1984, 54–61 and 7, 2, 1984, 55–62.

Practicalities, translated by Barbara Bray, London, Collins: Flamingo paperback, 1990.

The Ravishing of Lol Stein, translated by Richard Seaver, New York, Grove Press, 1966.

The Sailor from Gibraltar, translated by Barbara Bray, London, Calder & Boyars, 1966.

Summer Rain, translated by Barbara Bray, London, HarperCollins, 1992.

The Sea-Wall, translated by Herma Briffault, London, Faber & Faber, 1986.

Suzanna Andler, La Musica, L'Amante anglaise, translated by Barbara Bray, London, John Calder, 1975.

Three Novels (including: *The Square*, translated by Sonia Pitt-Rivers and Irina Morduch [1959]; and *Ten-Thirty on a Summer Night* [1962] and *The Afternoon of Monsieur Andesmas* [1964], translated by Anne Borchardt), London, John Calder, 1977.

Three Plays: The Square; Days in the Trees; The Viaducts of Seine-et-Oise, translated by Barbara Bray and Sonia Orwell, London, Calder & Boyars, 1967.

The Vice-Consul, translated by Eileen Ellenbogen, London (Hamish Hamilton, 1968), Collins: Flamingo paperback 1990.

Whole Days in the Trees and Other Stories, translated by Anita Barrows, London, John Calder, 1984.

Woman to Woman, conversations with Xavière Gauthier, translated by Katharine A. Jensen, Lincoln, University of Nebraska Press, 1987.

Index